Mathematics *versus* the National Curriculum

Mathematics *versus* the National Curriculum

Edited by
Paul Dowling and Richard Noss

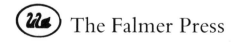 The Falmer Press

(A member of the Taylor & Francis Group)
London ● New York ● Philadelphia

UK The Falmer Press, Rankine Road, Basingstoke, Hampshire, RG24 0PR

USA The Falmer Press, Taylor & Francis Inc., 1900 Frost Road, Suite 101, Bristol, PA 19007

First published in 1990

Library of Congress Cataloging-in-Publication Data
Mathematics versus the national curriculum/edited by
    Paul Dowling and Richard Noss.
        p.   cm.
    Includes index.
    ISBN 1-85000-891-4
            1-85000-892-2 (pbk.)
    1. Mathematics – Study and teaching – Great Britain.
    2. Education – Great Britain – Curricula.
    I. Dowling, Paul.   II. Noss, Richard.
    QA14.G7M34 1990
    510'.71'041 – dc20

Jacket design by Caroline Archer

Typeset in 11/13 points Bembo
by Graphicraft Typesetters Ltd., Hong Kong

Printed in Great Britain by Burgess Science Press, Basingstoke on paper which has a specified pH value on final paper manufacture of not less than 7.5 and is therefore 'acid free'.

Contents

The Authors   vii

Abbreviations   viii

Foreword: Mathematics in the National Curriculum:
The Empty Set?   1
Richard Noss and Paul Dowling

Theme 1:   A Critique of Fundamentals   11

1. The National Curriculum and Mathematics:
   A Case of Divide and Rule?   13
   Richard Noss

2. The Shogun's and Other Curriculum Voices   33
   Paul Dowling

Theme 2:   Assessing Assessment   65

3. The Fundamental Assumptions of National Assessment   67
   Harvey Goldstein

4. Hierarchies in Mathematics: A Critique of the CSMS
   Study   77
   Declan O'Reilly

5. Ratio in the National Curriculum   98
   Dietmar Küchemann

Theme 3:   Lost Opportunities   113

6. Neglected Voices: Pupils' Mathematics and the National
   Curriculum   115
   Celia Hoyles

Contents

7. Testing Investigations   137
    Alison Wolf

8. The Changing Role of Algebra in School Mathematics: 154
    The Potential of Computer-based Environments
    Rosamund Sutherland

9. Creating Aternative Realities: Computers, Modelling and   176
    Curriculum Change
    Harvey Mellar

Theme 4:   From Notional to National: problems of   193
implementation

10. From Notional to National Curriculum: The Search for a   195
    Mechanism
    Andrew Brown

11. Training Teachers in Crisis: A Case Study of a Part-time   216
    Postgraduate Certificate in Education
    Pat Drake

Afterword: Multiplying by Zero   235
Paul Dowling and Richard Noss

Index   241

The Authors

All the contributors to this volume work in the Department of Mathematics, Statistics and Computing at the Institute of Education, University of London. As part of the preparation for the compilation of this volume, each contribution was presented at a departmental seminar and subjected to criticism. All the authors would like to acknowledge the helpful comments they have received from all the others. The editors wish to thank David Pimm for his helpful comments on the manuscript.

Acknowledgement
Extracts from *Mathematics in the National Curriculum* and *Mathematics for Ages 5 to 16* are reproduced with the permission of the Controller of Her Majesty's Stationery Office.

Abbreviations

The following is a list of abbreviations used in the text.

AI	Artificial Intelligence
APU	Assessment of Performance Unit
AT	Attainment Target
BEd	Bachelor of Education
CATE	Council for the Accreditation of Teacher Education
CDT	Craft, Design and Technology
CSE	Certificate in Secondary Education (replaced by GCSE as from summer 1988)
CSMS	Concepts in Secondary Mathematics and Science (research programme based at Chelsea College, University of London)
DES	Department of Education and Science
ERA	Education Reform Act
ESC	Education Support Grant
ESRC	Economic and Social Research Council
GAIM	Graded Assessments in Mathematics (curriculum development project based at King's College, University of London)
GCE	General Certificate in Education (Ordinary-level replaced by GCSE as from summer 1988, Advanced-level retained at 18+)
GCSE	General Certificate in Secondary Education (replaced General Certificate of Education (GCE) Ordinary Levels (O-level) and Certificate of Secondary Education (CSE) as from summer 1988)
HATS	Hertfordshire Action on Teacher Supply

HMI	Her Majesty's Inspectorate/Her Majesty's Inspector (employed by the DES)
ILEA	Inner London Education Authority (dissolved as from March 1st 1990)
INSET	In-service Education for Teachers
IT	Information Technology
LEA	Local Education Authority
LEAG	London and East Anglia Group (GCSE regional examining group)
LEATGS	Local Education Authority Training Grants Scheme
LMS	Local Management of Schools (localized management resulting from the ERA)
MSC	Department of Mathematics, Statistics and Computing, Institute of Education, University of London or Manpower Services Commission (now the Training Agency)
NC	National Curriculum
NCC	National Curriculum Council
NCTM	National Council of Teachers of Mathematics (USA)
NEA	Northern Examining Association (GCSE regional examining group)
NFER	National Foundation for Educational Research
OU	Open University
PC	Personal Computer or Profile Component
PGCE	Postgraduate Certificate in Education
SAT	Standard Assessment Task
SEAC	Schools Examination and Assessment Council
SEG	Southern Examining Group (GCSE regional examining group)
SMILE	Secondary Mathematics Individual Learning Experience (mathematics curriculum scheme originally based in ILEA and organized on an individualized learning approach)
SMP	School Mathematics Project (curriculum development project based at Southampton University; materials published by Cambridge University Press)
TASC	Teaching as a Career (unit set up by the DES)
TGAT	Task Group on Assessment and Testing
TVEI	Technical and Vocational Education Initiative (Originally under the direction of the Manpower Services Commission (MSC).

Foreword: Mathematics in the National Curriculum: The Empty Set?

Richard Noss and Paul Dowling

The current government is a government of privatisation. In all things, it seems, it argues that the market should hold sway, that government intervention be pared to a minimum, and that competition should determine what is produced and consumed. And yet we have a national curriculum: schools are no longer (relatively) free to determine what is taught — even how it is taught. They are to be policed by a massive system of centralized assessment, certainly more bureaucratic than the most extreme bureaucracy of any nationalized industry which the government has so readily condemned over the past decade. The government of privatisation has carried through a massive programme of nationalization.

This volume is an attempt to examine this phenomenon by taking as its central (if not exclusive) focus the case of mathematics. It is our belief that Mathematics in the National Curriculum — as the National Curriculum Council document for mathematics is called — is nothing but a misnomer. There *is* no mathematics in the National Curriculum. We argue that the National Curriculum has effectively emptied the mathematics curriculum of mathematics: hence the title of this foreword — and of this volume.

We should start by clarifying that the National Curriculum itself — the lists of statements of attainments, the detailed Standard Assessment Tasks (which at the time of writing still have to emerge), and the statutory and non-statutory guidelines are only the tip of the educational iceberg. Inevitably, many of the contributions focus on just these issues, but we reiterate: that is not what the book is about.

While the title might suggest that it is of primary interest to teachers of mathematics, our intention is to aim the book at a wider educational audience. The pace with which legislation has been prepared has denied any possibility of serious consideration — let alone public discussion — of the form, content and implications of the Education Reform Act and its attendant infrastructures. There have, of course, been some exceptions, and these contributions have emanated in the main from a general curricular or sociological perspective: inevitably, some of this debate has raised specific issues of curriculum content and assessment. Our intention is to stand this approach on its head: we address a wide range of general educational issues raised by the National Curriculum, from the perspective of mathematics education. In one sense therefore, we do not need to justify this perspective: the National Curriculum will, of course, be mediated through individual subject disciplines,[1] and it seems reasonable to take as a focus one such discipline. Nevertheless, the specific role of mathematics within schooling, and the more general nature of mathematics within the educational culture, may make it a particularly advantageous vantage point from which to scan the broader educational horizons of the Act, the National Curriculum and its assessment procedures.

Certain of the mathematics educators who agreed to participate on the National Curriculum Mathematics Working Party defended their decision by suggesting that at least they could ensure that the very best of current practice was reflected in the construction of the Attainment Targets. We suggest that the contributions to this volume indicate that they were misguided. As we shall argue in the Afterword, the real damage which may be perpetrated by the imposition of a National Curriculum which is constructed on the basis of subjects defined in terms of assessment objectives, is the reinforcing of teachers' allegiances to limited bodies of content which will become enshrined as ritual. Since the 'National' Curriculum is to be enforced only in state schools, its effect may well be the reduction of public schooling to fragmentation and destructive competition, and the privatization of creativity through its restriction to the independent sector. Because we understand the National Curriculum as a general assault on education, and because we see great value in real cross-curricular approaches (on which we elaborate in the afterword), we assert that this collection is directly relevant to teachers and educationalists of *all* subject specialisms.

It is difficult now to reconstruct our thinking in deciding to put this volume together. In part, it was born out of a sense of dissatisfaction and disappointment at the almost complete failure of the mathematics education community to maintain even the degree of criticism of the National Curriculum that it had aspired to at its inception. But this does not sufficiently explain how the fundamentally oppositional stance of the book arose: we are, however, certain that there was and is no 'departmental view' which has been explicitly formulated, no 'party line' to which all of us adhere. On the contrary, within our department there is a wide diversity of research and teaching interests which goes far beyond mathematics education, and a range of theoretical stances in general as well as positions on the National Curriculum in particular. We hope that this diversity has strengthened the book: yet we feel that it might be helpful to outline a little of the history and interests of the department, if only to explain to ourselves how it was that the oppositional perspectives of this volume arose as a basically non-contentious issue for refinement and elaboration within the department.

We should begin by stating that all but one of the contributors to this book have been classroom teachers. Of course, this does not in any sense invest their contributions with the widsom of the class-room, or even guarantee that such wisdom as exists in the classroom has any privileged role in making sense of the National Curriculum. But we might claim that our collective classroom experience does at least make us sensitive to the sheer bureaucracy of the innovation and, as Brown points out in his contribution, perhaps wary of seeing it as an innovation whose main problematic lies merely in its implementa-tion. At the same time, all of us are involved in pre-service or teacher education, and some of this work has itself incorporated a research dimension (see, for example, Drake's contribution). Similarly, classroom-based experience, either at first or second hand, has in-formed various projects involving curriculum development (e.g. Küchemann, Hoyles, Noss, Sutherland).

The Department of Mathematics, Statistics and Computing is relatively young, having been formed out of an administratively-motivated merger some six or seven years ago. Yet despite its admi-nistrative origins, it works — and nowhere more effectively than in its research endeavours. For some years, there has been considerable effort in the investigation of computational media for mathematics and, in particular, in the creation and investigation of Logo environ-ments (Hoyles, Noss, Sutherland). This work has ranged over a number of areas, many of them investigating the micro-level of chil-dren's activities from a basically psychological perspective. But it rapidly became clear that no real understanding of the computer's role could be gained without taking account of the cultural and social questions which the computer throws into relief: and so the work has variously taken into account questions of gender and learning style, cultural issues, and, most recently, an attempt to build in teacher practices and school settings into the equation. From a less overtly mathematical perspective, this research endeavour has been complemented by the addition of a strand on computer-based education and artificial intelligence (Mellar), and this has, in turn, focused our collective attention on broader epistemological and pedagogical issues which are nicely catalysed by the introduction of the computer into the educational arena.

Equally, the work of Goldstein in assessment techniques and Wolf in the application of mathematics to the workplace has to a large extent encouraged us to attend to issues which have broadened our perspectives beyond either the mathematical or the psychological. After all, the critique of the notion of psychological or epistemological hierarchies (Goldstein) or the analysis of the traditional notion of transfer (Wolf) challenges two of the most widespread and influential assumptions of mathematics education (see the chapter by O'Reilly for a detailed critique of the first of these assumptions); these challenges once again lift our sights beyond the psychological paradigm to the neglected social and political dimensions of mathematics education.

Over the last two years, the work of the department has also been given a more explicit sociological focus by staff whose main interests and training lie in the field of sociology (Brown, Dowling). Whenever one is forced to look at old questions from new perspectives, there is at least a good chance of enrichment: certainly the language and discourse of current sociological literature has offered many workers within the department new axes along which to analyse and re-analyse their work, and shifted the boundaries around and among their findings. Perhaps more importantly, it has problematised many categories which have tended to be taken for granted in our own research and in our reading of the mathematics education literature in general.

Almost by accident, therefore, we find ourselves in an atmosphere of criticism of established orthodoxies in the field, formed from a rich and diverse programme of research in a variety of areas. We are at present trying to draw some of these threads together, and this book is one way in which we hope to codify and elaborate our thoughts (our research effort in this direction is ongoing: see, for example, Noss *et al.*, 1990).

Our rationale for this book, however, aims beyond merely clarifying our own thoughts. We are uncompromising in our wish to provide alternative views of the National Curriculum which teachers and other educators may find helpful in their practice. That is not to say that we provide an alternative perspective, or that we are able to map detailed practical suggestions for classroom practice. We are sufficiently realistic to know that neither of these perspectives is feasible even if it were desirable: on the contrary, one major thrust of our criticism is precisely that even those 'progressive' aspects of the National Curriculum which might be gleaned by tearing them out of their context, are unlikely to offer much precisely because they are prescribed by governmental edict.

We postpone serious consideration of alternative responses to the National Curriculum until the Afterword. Here we do two things; first we present an overview of the book in order to try to situate it both theoretically and historically: second we provide an outline of what we intend an alternative to provide — we think of the alternative itself being comprised of the subsequent chapters and the Afterword.

The book is arranged in four themes. While we have no intention of either summarising the contributions in detail, we turn our intention to our thematic presentation of the chapters; in doing so we hope to clarify our overall intentions for the book. Theme 1 we have entitled *A critique of fundamentals*. Misconceptions concerning the National Curriculum abound: perhaps none is more pervasive than the separation of the specifically *curricular* elements (in the form of statements of attainment) and its assessment (in the form of SATs and teacher-assessments). The two contributions in this introductory theme point out that this separation effectively turns the intention of the National Curriculum on its head: that the primary motivation is in fact, the assessment of schools, teachers and pupils — and that a corollary of such assessment is that a common currency is conjured into being in the form of attainment targets and their attendant paraphernalia. Noss critically examines the origins of the proposals and offers a theoretical framework for understanding their rationale; Dowling, in addition to providing a direct criticism of the texts of the National Curriculum, allows these texts to 'speak for themselves' so as to emphasise their inherent irony. The two papers in this theme attempt to provide a setting for the subsequent chapters of the book, by positioning the National Curriculum as part of the overall plans of the government for state education.

The second theme, *Assessing assessment* looks in greater detail at the basis for the crucial assessment components of the National Curriculum. Goldstein examines the underlying logic of the national assessment procedures, and illustrates the absence of any coherent theoretical framework. O'Reilly looks at the historically influential report of the Concepts in Secondary Mathematics and Science study

(CSMS) which laid much of the foundations for the hierarchies of attainment which underpin the National Curriculum. He argues that there are major theoretical and methodological shortcomings of this work which have been imported uncritically into the framework of national assessment procedures. Finally, Küchemann takes a specific example of a mathematical topic — ratio, and presents a convincing case that the ordering of the attainments statements is arbitrary and likely to result in a fragmented curriculum lacking in any coherent pedagogical structure.

In *Lost opportunities* (Theme 3), the four authors present aspects of the National Curriculum on terms approaching those set out by its instigators, and investigate whether there is any sense in which the structures are likely to bring about any educational benefits (not to mention 'improvement in standards') which the accompanying educational veneer is suggesting will accrue. Hoyles' paper takes a broad look at the positivist model of mathematical learning which, in her view underpins the National Curriculum, and argues that the crucial positioning of the pupil and his/her social world has been effectively ignored within it. Wolf takes up the argument on the level of curriculum content to examine the contradictions between the demands of GCSE mathematics (for investigation) and the widespread advocacy of 'practical applications'. She argues that these contradictions bedevil the National Curriculum throughout, and is further evidence of the contradictory perspectives contained within it.

The two remaining contributions remain on the level of curriculum content, both pointing to the failure of the mathematics National Curriculum to take account of the potential offered by the computer. Sutherland suggests that the computer affords the possibility of solving some of the outstanding psychological difficulties children have with algebra, but argues that the National Curriculum has effectively ignored its potential. Finally, Mellar considers the computer's role from a broader (extra-mathematical) perspective and suggests that the Curriculum in its present form by-passes the possibilities it could bring to the learning process.

In the final theme, *From notional to national: problems of implementation*, the two authors focus on the problems of transforming the proposals into curricular reality. Brown argues that the plans for the implementation of the National Curriculum have ignored the specificities of contexts and treated curriculum change as a technical problem and thereby facilitate a potential pathologising of teachers. Brown draws on data derived from a study of the contextualizing of curriculum change in two groups of primary schools within a Local Education Authority. Finally, considering the implications of the ERA for teacher supply, Drake takes as her starting point, a pre-service course which was part of a general governmental initiative to increase the supply of mathematics teachers, pointing to the ways in which the course was influenced by the ambient space in which it operated.

In summary, the book attempts to outline a basis for fundamental theoretical and practical objections to the National Curriculum, its inherent curricular shortcomings, and provide a framework for understanding what role teachers have been assigned in its development. What the contributions do not do — at least not in a coherent way — is outline a programme for action. What should teachers and mathematics educators do?

In part this is hardly surprising. This is a volume of papers which, in the main, addresses specific issues within the ERA/NC framework. As we said earlier, it simply does not make sense to try to outline alternatives to each decontextualized component. Indeed, we argue that it is foolhardy. There is an entire educational industry currently at work in trying to design 'child-friendly' SATs, develop 'teacher-proof' assessment procedures as well as tinkering with the coverage and order of particular topics within the 296 mathematical statements of attainment. Within and outside the boundaries of mathematics, in-service courses abound in every LEA (as well as within our own institution) claiming to offer implementation mechanisms for this or that specific group of pupils. While these are, in the main, laudable attempts to help teachers survive in the short term, they offer no long-term solutions. Indeed, we suggest that there are no solutions within the framework of the National Curriculum, and while it is possible to see how corners may be smoothed out in terms of implementation, the national imposition of the curriculum and its assessment ensures that very little can actually be done to salvage educational benefits from within.

On the other hand, there is much that can be done — provided that we start from the proposition that the National Curriculum itself is only the mechanism by which the underlying rationale of the Education Reform Act can be implemented: the ERA is designed to privatise education (and of course, mathematics education) by introducing the mechanisms of the market into individual (state) schools. So much is clear. What then would comprise an alternative for teachers and educators?

We cannot maintain the position that opposition will force the government to relent — the Act and its attendant curricula are in place. And to suggest a straightforward slogan of 'opposition to the national curriculum' is neither practical nor theoretically tenable — impractical because it is simply too late, and untenable because its undoubted impotence would certainly encourage a lapse into theoretical (and practical) apathy.

Let us begin by saying that we do not see our role as engendering optimism. In the first place there is little to be optimistic about. In the second, it seems strange that there are so many teacher-educators scratching in the dust of the attainment targets for optimistic signs as if it were here that the salvation of the (state) education system might lie. All around us there are teacher-shortages (of course mathematics is particularly hard-hit), plummeting morale, low salaries and status, and crumbling school buildings. Yet somehow the National Curriculum is thought to provide some salvation. In fact the reverse is true: it is our view that the imposition of the National Curriculum provides the government with a fig-leaf for the educational shortcomings of many schools: shortcomings which are far from being about the sequencing of statements of attainment, or the comparability of levels across attainment targets, and much more to do with the calculated running down of state education.

In fact, it would be wrong to suggest that the government has succeeded in some kind of conspiracy to fool teachers into believing that the details of attainment targets are a surer way to improve schooling than doubling their salaries. There has been a generalized collapse of the teaching unions' opposition to the decline in educational provision, and an extreme readiness on the part of many educationalists to embrace this or that aspect of the Education Reform Act as potentially progressive. But there has also been a feeling of impotence which the NC proposals have paradoxically offset: at least the NC proposals *appear to be about what is taught in the classroom.* The paradox is that in reality the terrain which appears to offer teachers some room for manoeuvre is nothing less than a programme aimed at deskilling the teaching profession and removing what little autonomy remains.

Let us state our alternative. It is to oppose the National Curriculum as part of the ERA, to maintain a critical stance towards its underlying framework and its implementation. In practice, it means attempting to raise these issues as problematic at every in-service course, in staff rooms and at parents' evenings. This is, of course, not likely to bring about change overnight. But it is clear that the speed with which the proposals have become legal reality has in large part been due to the readiness on the part of educators precisely to suspend their powers of criticism in favour of an attempt to avoid further demoralisation of the teaching profession and to 'roll up our sleeves and get on with it' (Margaret Brown, 1989).

There are encouraging signs that the proposals for assessment may never become a reality, at least not in its present form. Teachers are beginning to see the Act in its true light: the ostrich-like attitude that 'business as usual' can be maintained behind the classroom doors is giving way to a genuine and understandable concern that the inevitable fetishisation of assessments will destroy the better parts of mathematics education in the UK. It is only a matter of time before parents begin to see the effects that the de facto privatisation of schools will have on most (but not all) children. We are not arrogant or foolhardy enough to suggest that teachers or parents hang on the words and thoughts of a few academics. Nonetheless, it is time to turn the tide; to criticize the Act's fundamentals, not to ease its passage: to point to the irrelevance of the National Curriculum rather than tinker with its implementation. The government has marginalised academic educationalists in pursuit of its goals: we see no reason to aid them in this process by ignoring the inevitable logic of its proposals.

Notes

1   This fragmentation of the curriculum into subject divisions is a central issue which we return to in our Afterword.

References

BROWN, M., 1989, 'Make the Best of It', *Times Educational Supplement*, 29. April.

DOWLING, P.C., 1990, 'Mathematics in the marketplace: The National Curriculum and numerical control', Teaching London Kids, 26.

NOSS, R. *et al.* (Eds), 1990, *Political Dimensions of Mathematics Education: action and critique (Proceedings of the First International Conference)*, London: Institute of Education, University of London.

Theme 1
A critique of fundamentals

1 The National Curriculum and Mathematics: A Case of Divide and Rule?

Richard Noss

Incredible as it would have seemed only a decade ago, the mathematics curriculum of state schools, enshrined in 296 statements of attainment, is now part of the law of the land. They are statutory requirements, and it is presumably only a matter of time before the first legal case to determine what penalties might be imposed on teachers and schools who display criminal intent (or negligence) by failing to implement them.[1]

In the final form of the statutory orders, the National Curriculum for mathematics has been stripped down to its bare essentials. As I shall argue below, this is no accident, but examination of the statements of attainment themselves provides little or no insight into the real rationale behind their introduction.[2] Given the lack of any serious public (or even academic) debate about the underlying intentions of the National Mathematics Curriculum, and the complete absence of any explicit theoretical pronouncements from those responsible for its introduction, the choice of sources is limited and somewhat arbitrary. In fact, successive documents emanating from the DES under the banner of the National Curriculum have included less and less educational justification, and thus I have chosen as starting points for the discussion, two early documents in the series (DES, 1988a; NCC, 1988). Most, if not all, of the important proposals referred to in these documents have now become legal reality: I shall, however, continue to refer to them as proposals.

Although I focus my discussion around mathematics, I intend to use the case of mathematics as an exemplar for a more general perspective of the National Curriculum, and reciprocally, to employ a framework derived from general considerations in order to make sense of the proposals as they apply to mathematics. I shall argue that although the underlying purpose of the proposals and the testing procedures which accompany them are profoundly and intentionally anti-educational, they are permeated by contradictions which derive from the origins of the proposals; and that by exploiting these contradictions it may be possible for teachers to use some of the proposals for educational purposes — effectively to subvert the implicit and explicit intentions of those responsible for their introduction.

The Working Party Report

I begin by looking at the Working Party Report for Mathematics (DES, 1988a; I refer to this document as Maths 5–16) which was published in August 1988 (the exact dates of the various publications are important given the breathtaking speed at which the government has dictated the pace of events). It is my contention that the document exemplifies the contradictions inherent in its development, and I begin by focusing on some of the anomalies and contradictory perspectives contained within it.

Mathematics 5–16 was the response of a working party appointed in July 1987 by the Secretary of State for Education and Science to advise on the setting of attainment targets, the construction of programmes of study, and the arrangements for testing procedures. It takes as its framework for curricular testing, the report of the Task Group on Assessment and Testing (TGAT: DES, 1988b) which reported early in 1988: 'We believe that this model is a good one: it is flexible enough to allow all pupils . . . to progress through the levels at their own rate, while at the same time setting clear age-related targets' (Maths 5–16, para 1.4). The authors of the report strike a rather optimistic note as to its potential: 'The significance of explicit, progressive curriculum objectives for mathematics extending through the period of compulsory schooling should not be underestimated: it has great potential to raise standards of pupil attainment at all ages and at all levels of ability' (DES, 1988a, § 1.5).

The underlying assumptions behind these assertions are i) that a centrally imposed system of curriculum and assessment will bring about the increase in 'standards' which the authors desire; and ii) that the TGAT proposals are valid and workable as a means of delivering it. It is my belief that neither of these assumptions are valid although it is not my intention to argue this case in detail here. Instead, as far as the first of these issues is concerned, I want to take up a more general question altogether; to ask whether the expressed intention of 'raising standards' really lies at the heart of the proposals, and to discuss what actually constitutes the rationale of the National Curriculum and its attendant testing procedures. The second issue — concerning the feasibility of the TGAT model — is elaborated in some detail in Noss, Goldstein and Hoyles (1989), and will not be discussed here.[3]

We can gain some insight into the report's underlying assumptions by looking at its view of the nature and purpose of mathematical learning. One of its more flowery descriptions of the purposes of mathematical instruction reads as follows:

> Mathematics ... should also be a source of delight and wonder, offering pupils intellectual excitement, for example, in the discovery of relationships, the pursuit of rigour and the achievement of elegant solutions. Pupils should also appreciate the essential creativity of mathematics: it is a live subject which is continuously evolving as technology and the needs of society evolve. (DES, 1988a; § 2.2)

Quite how these objectives are to be realized by the proposals to split the mathematics curriculum up into the disjoint areas of number, algebra, geometry etc. and renaming them as 'profile components' is not clarified in the document (it is revealing that many mathematics educators in the USA are currently trying to dismantle these same divisions which disappeared from the UK scene as much as three decades ago). More fundamentally, it is perhaps questionable whether a subject which is 'essentially creative' and 'continuously evolving' can be appreciated within a system of rigourous and centralized testing from the age of 7, the imposition of programmes of study from the age of 5 and the fragmentation of its constituent elements.

There is a coherent, if implicit, view of mathematical activity which underpins the report which is reiterated throughout; namely that 'The power and pervasiveness of mathematics accounts for its pre-eminent position, alongside English, in the school curriculum' (*ibid*, § 2.1). We examine below the purpose of mathematical instruction in some detail; here it is appropriate merely to ask whether this constitutes an explanation at all. After all, for many decades Latin held a similar position in the school curriculum, not, one can safely assume, because of its power and pervasiveness.

This question of the utility of the subject is an important one, for it underlies many of the detailed proposals of the report. Indeed, in stark contradiction to the rhetoric of mathematics as a source of delight and intellectual excitement, the authors assert that 'We have taken it as axiomatic that the mathematics which pupils learn at school should support the mathematics which they actually need to use in later life, particularly at work'. (*ibid*, § 3.15).[4] This utilitarian view of mathematical activity has important consequences. In the first place, the authors of the report note that while 'arithmetic is used almost universally, other areas of mathematics such as algebra, geometry and trigonometry are used in more specific contexts' (*ibid*, § 19). And it is this 'finding' which dictates the heavily arithmetic quality of the content in the attainment targets which follow.

But there is a more fundamental corollary of the report's utilitarian perspective which is expressed in the view that: 'All pupils should be taught how to apply their mathematics to practical as well as to theoretical problems' (*ibid*, § 3.23) and that 'Learning to use mathematical knowledge and skills must therefore be a vital part of mathematics education at school' (*ibid*, § 3.22). It is not clear what is the theoretical justification for this view. The idea that mathematics consists of decontextualized abstractions which somehow float above reality and can (with appropriate help) be brought down to earth and 'applied' does, of course, have a long history. But it seems to be without foundation in practice; or at least, it is currently a view which is under serious challenge from a variety of sources. For example, Lave (1988) has vividly illustrated how arithmetical activity enters into everyday discourse as part of an organic process in which people construct solutions to problems in the course of action; their solutions are structured by their activity '... dissolving problems ... making them disappear into solution within ongoing activity rather than "being solved"'. (p. 120).

In case this line of discussion be thought too far from the point, I outline just one corollary of the report's implicit theoretical framework. The working party suggest the introduction of three 'profile components'; number/algebra, shape/space and a third which it calls 'practical applications of mathematics' — 'to reflect the fact that it is concerned explicitly with putting mathematics into practice in a wide variety of contexts. When confronted with a task pupils need to select and use whatever mathematics is appropriate and draw from a range of techniques to implement it' (DES, 1988a, § 4.7). Here is the essential metaphor — mathematics is a set of tools; its application is in the solution of problems and the mechanism is in the selection of the appropriate tool. The metaphor becomes clearer as the component is outlined in more detail; having selected the appropriate mathematics, pupils should 'apply it sensibly and efficiently, try alternative strategies if needed, check on progress at appropriate stages and analyse the final results to ensure that the initial requirements have been met' (*ibid*, § 4.12).

Reading this description, it is not difficult to believe that its author had in mind a clear shop-floor image; a problem posed, some maths needed, a result obtained with maximum speed and efficiency. This is at odds with the way that — as Lave points out — mathematics actually enters peoples' lives; and it is somewhat different from the needs that people have to interpret and make sense of increasingly mathematized sources of information (it is interesting to note that the report restricts the interpretative status of mathematical learning to the workplace (*ibid*, § 3.18)). There is a tension here between mathematics as a way of making sense of the world, a way of thinking which offers a medium to express generality and pattern, and helps people to understand and perhaps change their environment; or a set of tools which can be applied to the solution of (industrial or economic) problems. One omission from the report provides further evidence that it is the latter view which dominates: in contrast to the Science profile components (and an increasingly influential strand of mathematical education thinking and practice), exploration and investigation are omitted from the profile components entirely — mathematical 'skills' are clearly defined as a means of solving other people's problems.

Because the authors of the report did not (and could not) resolve this tension, they were unable to map out the apparently rigorous (and largely arbitrary) levels which the other two profile components received. And largely because of that, profile component three was dropped altogether some six months after the publication of the Working Party report. We discuss this in more detail below.

A further, perhaps more concrete, corollary of the report's underlying theoretical position is the way in which it deals with the relationship between the setting of attainment targets and the outline of programmes of study. One may be forgiven for thinking that, if mathematics is the source of beauty which the authors claim, a primary task would be to develop the curricular outlines to be followed in schools on pedagogical principles, and then to develop the attainment objectives which grow from them. Not so. On the contrary, the report makes a virtue of its assessment driven approach:

> We approached the formulation of programmes of study after we had done the greater part of our work on attainment targets. This was logical since, following our terms of refer-

ence, the attainment targets represent curriculum objectives, while programmes of study are to describe the means of achieving those objectives.... In other words, we found that the clear specification of the targets at several levels of attainment had in effect defined content, skills and processes. (DES, 1988a, § 4.14)

Fortunately, the authors of the report in the following paragraph save me the trouble of indicating how this view follows from their implicit view of mathematical activity:

We suggest that our experience very largely reflects the nature of mathematics. Mathematics is the most abstract of subjects. Attainment targets in mathematics have to be very tightly defined to avoid ambiguity, and the degree of precision required gives a very clear indication of the 'content, skills and processes' associated with the targets. (DES, 1988a, § 4.15).

There are a number of fundamental objections which could be voiced in opposition to this view; I cite only one, namely the assumption that mathematical concepts can indeed be formed into a rigid hierarchy on either epistemological or psychological grounds. This issue is discussed in some detail elsewhere (see Noss, Goldstein and Hoyles, 1989), but it is worth remarking that even if such an invariant sequence could be given some meaning, it is still far from evident how it could be used as a basis for effective mathematical learning. On the contrary, there are ample grounds for assuming that the reverse is true; that the transposition of such hierarchical assumptions into pedagogical practice results in a distortion of both mathematical content and mathematical understandings.

I now want to return to the more general perception of mathematics as a set of (rigidly defined) skills and concepts which can be applied in practical settings. Some insight into just what kind of problems the report envisages as 'practical' in the school context is provided by the authors' inclusion of 'examples of practical mathematics'. I include it in full:

7.22 This problem is appropriate across the age range 7 to 16.

If British Airways runs flights between each of 8 major airports in Europe, how many routes is that? What happens for a different number of airports?

[Two 'lines of solution' are then provided]

7.33 The mathematics of the above example is exactly the same type (sic) as that needed in a variety of other contexts.

For example:

a) The offices of 15 cabinet ministers are linked by direct telephone lines. How many lines are needed?

b) If 30 people at a party shake hands with each other, how many handshakes will there be?

This use of the same mathematical content in widely different situations illustrates the power and beauty of mathematics. (DES, 1988a, § 7.23; my emphasis)

I am aware that it is bad taste to tell a joke and then proceed to explain it. But there two issues emerging from these examples which are worth underlining. Firstly, it should be clear that the view of mathematics, as 'content' which can be 'used' corresponds closely to the implicit utilitarian framework employed throughout the report. Secondly, I want to point to the extreme artificiality, not only of the examples a) and b) but of the original problem itself: just what is the role of the inclusion of British Airways in the problem? It can hardly be that this is a 'real problem' of the kind which people need to solve in their future work. And it is far from clear how the embedding of the 'content' in the setting of linking cabinet ministers' telephones is supposed, in some way, to expose the power and beauty of mathematics in making sense of situations that are real for pupils. This question of artificiality is, of course, not a new problem for mathematics education, and the authors of the report are not alone in their view that problem-solving is essentially concerned with the solution of artificial mini-stories full of spurious contextual clutter but devoid of meaning. The point here is that the explicit reinforcement of this view, and the theoretical framework which underpins it, stands in stark contrast to the expressed intentions of the report and its antecedents (see, for example, Cockcroft, 1982); namely, to somehow improve the repertoire of mathematical competences which pupils can later employ in their adult employment. My purpose in the rest of this paper is to attempt an explanation of this contradiction.

The 'Consultation Report'

In December 1988, the National Curriculum Council produced its 'Consultation Report' (NCC, 1988) which formed the basis of what became law in March 1989. Given that the report contained substantially the same proposals without the educational rhetoric of its predecessor, there is no need for further detailed analysis from the perspective of this paper. As I noted earlier, one major change between August and December was in the deletion of Profile Component 3 as a separate entity — despite nearly 80 per cent of respondents opposing the idea of combining the practical applications with the attainment targets. Moreover in so far as some aspects of PC3 are included under the remaining attainment targets, one set of elements has been dropped altogether — that is, those dealing with 'motivation', 'perseverance', and 'independence of thought'. I shall return to a discussion of the rationale for this decision in the following section.

There was, however, one addition to the Consultation Report which occasioned considerable interest and press coverage: namely the reintroduction of the explicit teaching of long multiplication and division. The report is explicit: 'Multiplying ... and dividing a 3-digit number by a 2-digit number, in both cases without a calculator (Attainment Target 3 — 'Number' — level 5). I find it interesting that, almost uniquely in the attainment targets, it was not thought necessary to provide an example of these activities — apparently they are self-evident and unproblematic to all.

It seems to me that this small change, apparently introduced thanks to the direct intervention of the Secretary of State for Education, is significant both in terms of what it represents, and in terms of illustrating the underlying rationale of the national curriculum itself. For the reintroduction of anachronistic algorithms — long made obsolete by the advent of the calculator and, in any case, largely irrelevant in terms of application in work and elsewhere — runs directly counter to the utilitarian perspective espoused by the working party and its government sponsors. And if this is so, we need to look elsewhere to explain its reintroduction into pupils' mathematical learning. My hope is that by focusing on this example, I may be able to make some more general observations concerning the contradictory assertions enshrined within the National Curriculum documents, and outline an alternative view of the rationale behind them.

A Framework for Understanding the National Curriculum

In essence I propose that the government is not serious about the curricular content of its own proposals. There are many indications of this ranging from the undue haste with which the documents were produced, the extreme arbitrariness of the profile components, and the numerous anomalies within the attainment targets themselves. Much the same observation has been made by other writers in a context more general than mathematics. Chitty for example, views the national curriculum as possibly nothing more than a

> fig-leaf for the divisive features of the educational policy of the New Right ... as justification for a massive programme of national testing at seven, eleven, fourteen and sixteen which will, in turn, result in differentiation, selection and streaming at both the primary and secondary levels.' (Chitty, 1988: 45–6).

I want to argue that this relative lack of governmental concern for the National Curriculum itself is a corollary of a more general phenomenon: namely that schooling performs primarily a social rather than a training function for its pupils. I argue that the changes in educational orthodoxy have not been arbitrary; they are not solely the result of the whim of a reactionary government. To understand the process it is necessary to look beneath the surface of both liberal and reactionary rhetoric, to the underlying economic and social changes which have occurred and the impact of these on the priorities of the educational system. The priorities for government have always been how rather than what pupils learn:

> ... it is the FORM of the educational encounter — the social relations of education — that accounts for both its capacity to reproduce capitalist relations of production and its inability to promote domination and healthy personal development. The actual CONTENT of the curriculum has little role to play in this process. (Gintis and Bowles, 1988: 28).

I do not propose to dwell on the theoretical or empirical basis for this assertion; there is a considerable body of work concerned with analysing the ways in which education transmits the rules of socially acceptable behaviour (see for example, Bowles and Gintis, 1976) and more recently, in analysing schools as sites of contradiction and struggle (Giroux, 1983; Cole, 1988). Schools in short, socialise future genera-tions of young people into the appropriate niches they are destined to fill as adults. But they do not do so unhindered — there is no necessary direct correspondence between the social relations of pro-duction and the social relations of education. It is precisely the failure of this correspondence that has brought about the intense pressure to bring about change into schools, to narrow the space between the needs of the system and the needs of pupils. It is within this space that teachers and pupils may find room to manoeuvre.

My general argument is that the trend which the national curricu-lum and the Education Reform Act exemplify, is a reassertion of the priorities of the system over the schooling of young people. Of course this rationale remains implicit in the National Curriculum documents, and in much of the discussion surrounding them. Indeed the contra-dictory assertions and theoretical bases underpinning the proposals are themselves a reflection of the tension between the educational and political rationales behind them (this distinction has been referred to as 'professional' versus 'bureaucratic', Chitty, 1988). It is exemplified by the modifications imposed on the first report with their strongly 'Back to Basics' flavour.

The complexity of the situation is illustrated by the following anecdote recently reported in the press:

> The Maths working group members originally planned to give 50 per cent of the marks to the third component and only changed their minds when told that it would be politically unacceptable. One of its strongest supporters was Dr Ray Peacock, research co-ordinator for Phillips (UK) and the in-dustrial representative on the group.... Dr Peacock said that it was essential to test co-operation and discussion because this was how young people would use their maths at work. (*Guar-dian* 30.11.88, 'Maths plans revised to emphasise basic skills')

The irony of this short anecdote is obvious. Educational opinion on the working group apparently favoured the retention of Profile Com-ponent 3 in some form (mainly, it seems, for the educationally beneficial effects of cooperative learning and discussion). A selected spokesperson for industry is 'one of its strongest supporters' (as this is how he perceives the needs of industry). And yet the component is entirely deleted from the proposals, by, it seems, direct governmental intervention. Although I do not wish to invest this anecdote with undue significance, it illustrates nicely the limitation of the view that PC3's demise is based on a perception of the utility of mathematics in work. Even where there is an expressed need on the part of industry for educationally positive curricular change, the priorities lie elsewhere — in the logic of the assessment process itself, and more generally in the political and social realm rather than the directly economic. As the authors of the first report found, the development of hierarchies of attainment in the area of cooperation and discussion proved impossible; yet it is in the need to grade and compare children, teachers and schools that the priorities of the National Curriculum lie. What cannot be assessed cannot be taught.

Viewed in this light, it is useful to consider the following characterisation of the 'back to basics' ideal:

> So-called 'back to basics', while having little rationale in terms of either pedagogical or technological reason, may be understood in part as a response to the failure of correspondence between schools and capitalist production brought about by the dynamics of the accumulation process confronting the inertia of the educational structures. (Gintis and Bowles, 1988: 20)

I have argued in some detail elsewhere a mechanism for understanding how the economic and social changes in British and other Western economies might provide a framework for explaining changes in the orthodoxies of mathematical education (see Noss, 1989). I should point out that the social function of mathematical learning has, at other times, been far more explicit than it is now. As Howson Keitel and Kilpatrick (1981) point out, there has been a view stretching back to the mid-nineteenth century that arithmetic could foster 'the habit of promptitude ... exactness and order' and that mathematics instils the 'acquisition of necessary truths' (p. 24). In fact, the National Curriculum Working Party contains echoes of this position — and at the risk of tearing one sentence out of context, I quote here: '[The programmes of study] ... seek to draw out each child's full potential through the development of sound work habits, self-discipline and industry together with good personal qualities' (DES, 1988a, § 8.4).

In terms of mathematical learning, there is no perceived rationale — and neither has there ever been — for educating the mass of children to seek pattern and structure within their social and economic surroundings, or to gain a critical awareness that will allow them to interpret their increasingly mathematized reality. To put it crudely, long division has not been imposed because anybody thinks it is useful; it has been imposed because it is acts as an efficient and workable mechanism of social control. It may not help on the production line, and it certainly will not be of assistance in the dole queue: but it might just help the pupil to know his or her place. Divide and rule indeed.[5]

It might be argued, and indeed the National Curriculum documents do so, that the advent of new technologies has changed the situation in some fundamental way. I think it has, but in a direction 180 degrees opposite to that which is claimed. The accepted wisdom is exemplified in the Maths 5–16 document:

New technology is a powerful tool which opens up new areas of mathematics and changes the way in which society **makes use** of mathematics in the factory, office and home. (DES, 1988a, § 1.8, emphasis is original)

To what extent does this correspond to reality? In fact, I want to argue that new technology has actually made the utilitarian view of mathematics less, not more, tenable. I suggest on the contrary that one of the key motivational factors driving the introduction of new technology is precisely the desire on the part of employers to decrease the amount of skill and training necessary on the part of their employees. This argument is essentially that put by Braverman (1974) who argues that the central impetus of twentieth century capitalism has been the 'deskilling' of the labour process (Carlson, 1988 argues that there is a corollary for the teaching profession which he refers to as the 'proletarianization of teachers'). The central argument is that the rapid changes in technology have created an impressive array of new jobs to act essentially as minders for machines — and that the system itself has actually required (and used the machines) to gain ever more control of the labour process at the expense of craft knowledge and employee control.

To be sure, there have been a small — in fact tiny — number of people whose role has been to create the technology. This tiny fraction in fact comprises the ones for whom mathematics and its applications have become ever more crucial. There has, in fact, been an increasing polarization between this small layer and the rest — between the few hundreds who design the computerized checkout systems and the hundreds of thousands — perhaps millions — who use them in the supermarkets. While it may be true that 'society' has, in some averaging process, required greater and greater degrees of mathematical sophistication, such an aggregation blurs the essential reality of the situation: namely that while there has been a massive increase in what we might call, borrowing Marx's terminology, 'dead mathematical labour' encapsulated in technology, the result for living labour has been a decrease in skill — including mathematical skill — required for its operation and entry into the production process (see Dowling, 1989 for further discussion on the distinction between living and dead mathematical labour).

Ignoring the actual role of technology can lead to some ironic consequences. Consider, for example, this sentence from a recent Equal Opportunities Commission poster, 'Maths and Good jobs — add up to success' which stresses how new technology has transformed the need for mathematics: 'Maths is more important now than it has ever been before — it's a skill we all use in our day-to-day lives, often without even thinking about it'.[6]

In fact, as I have argued, the introduction of new technology has created a need for particular kinds of pedagogic practices — and in particular, for particular kinds of socialization within schools; but this has not been in response to a direct need for increased skills. On the contrary, it has resulted in a need to deskill the curriculum (and teachers) alongside the deskilling of the labour process. In so far as these demands have been channelled through the content of the curriculum, the rationale has been to effect a change in the expectations of pupils, their aspirations and their attitudes.

The Response of Mathematics Educators

There are few grounds for the authors of the first report being disappointed with the consultation report: it merely carries through the logic of the first report. Yet there continue to be many in the educational community in general — and within mathematics education in particular — who are welcoming with or without qualification the report and its implications for schools.

The response of mathematics educators has been, in general, to accept the rhetoric of government, and to retreat behind a naive optimism. In fact, the nature of this retreat is worth charting, if only for the speed at which it has taken place. Of course the seeds had been sown by the Cockcroft committee's (1982) uncritical acceptance of the utilitarian perspective, and its advocacy of a 'foundation list' for all but the highest attainers; when the TGAT group, under the chair of Paul Black reported in 1987 (DES, 1988b), the response of many (mathematics) educators was one of relief that there would be teacher assessments and a softening of the absolute relationship between age and attainment targets which the original terms of reference had specified. They thus failed to appreciate that, as Broadfoot (1988) effectively argues, the incorporation of teacher assessments into a rigourous and centralized national testing structure 'may provide one of the most effective forms of surveillance ever devised in education' (p. 13).

One position which has found favour — particularly with some members of the working party — has been to construct a veneer of educational respectability around the whole enterprise, while remaining silent (publicly at least) about its counter-educational rationale. For example, teachers are entreated to see national assessment as 'beautiful', a tremendous opportunity for teachers to diagnose the difficulties of their pupils (Burkhardt, 1988). Others have emphasised the need for what is essentially an uncritical defence of the TGAT proposals and advise teachers to 'roll up our sleeves and make the best of it' (Brown, 1989).

There are two common themes underlying the naive optimists' position. The first is to find a way — however simplistic — of arguing against what they rightly perceive as the far worse proposals of the Radical Right. In this scenario, the acceptance of the TGAT structures and the incorporation of crumbs of 'progressive' educational thinking into the final orders, represents a victory over the 'theorists' of the Centre for Policy Studies who are urging much more draconian measures. One can understand and even sympathize with this perspective, but I think it is fundamentally misconceived for one reason — it views the struggle for a democratic educational system as if it was a struggle between individuals: between the 'enlightened' views of the mathematics education 'establishment' on the one hand, and the reactionary voices of the Hillgate group on the other.

I do not want to underestimate the importance of challenging the Right's attack, but I argue that the naive optimists do not offer a way to achieve it: worse, by hiding the realities from those who have most to lose, it hands over the educational initiative to the Right. The argument simply leaves out the crucial elements: the pupils, teachers and parents who will constitute the victims of the government's plans. In the absence of a clear alternative lead from educationalists (or from 'left' politicians), the arguments of the popular press and the Right have remained largely unchallenged. I shall have more to say about this in the final section.

The second theme underpinning the naive optimism of some

commentators is an apparently deliberate (or perhaps simply naive) attempt to blur the public and private functions of the assessments proposed at 7, 11 and 14 (see for example, Brown, 1988). They thus choose to ignore the central function of the assessment process; to grade, select and differentiate children, provide league tables of schools and destroy whatever existed of a comprehensive system of education (see Noss, 1989, and Goldstein, this volume, for further discussion of this issue).

A rather extreme variant of this position has recently emerged from an unexpected quarter of the Educational establishment. This position argues that the assessments are not assessments of children at all. In this view, the assessments are not concerned with grading or measuring children's abilities, they are there to improve and develop the curricular opportunities of children:

> The School Examinations and Assessment Council contract is NOT concerned with 'mental measurement' but with curriculum implementation.... The development of SATs (Standard Assessment Tasks) will be an important contribution to the gauging of achievement, but I do not think we should describe this as 'mental measurement' which has unfortunate connotations with the kind of IQ testing that provided neither accountability nor helpful guidance for teachers. Better to describe it as 'curriculum assessment'. (Lawton, *Times Educational Supplement*, 6.1.89).

In fact, Lawton himself (1988) has eloquently indicated the true state of affairs in describing the National Curriculum as 'educationally unacceptable' just a few months earlier (before his appointment as Chairman (sic) of the Consortium for Assessment and Testing in Schools): '... the Baker proposals for a national curriculum represent not a radical step forward but a retreat away from the ideals of comprehensive education ...' (p. 19).

An Alternative Approach

I think there is an alternative position, and moreover one which does not start from the premise that it is desirable to accommodate educational principles to governmental policy. It starts from a recognition that the content of the curriculum is, as far as the government is concerned, of very low priority compared to the political objectives of 'privatization, differentiation and selection' (Maw 1988: 63). As far as mathematics is concerned, this position views the proposals as a powerful means of restricting teachers' room for manoeuvre but, as I have argued above, one which is fraught with internal contradictions; and it is these contradictions which teachers can exploit to the advantage of the children they teach.

Faced with the apparently unstoppable juggernaut of the government's educational plans, it is easy to slip into a self-justifying optimism, or a passive acceptance of the reforms' underlying framework in favour of attempting to ameliorate the finer details. While I see no justification for the former, I do understand the temptations offered by the latter. There are a number of academics, for example, who have decided that there is no realistic alternative to working towards a more humane assessment system, or towards a more constructive curriculum. I think they are mistaken. My position is not merely in favour of grand revolutionary gestures, and against any reformist participation: it is simply a recognition of the fact that the National Curriculum is not about the enhancement of curricular content or the improvement of assessment procedures, and not about disagreements over the kinds of strategies which will improve children's (mathematical) learning: it is about a centrally imposed and nationally validated system of grading children, schools and teachers. To pretend that somehow this rationale can be subverted by tampering with the details of its implementation is short-sighted.

In fact, I think there is a worse danger. In order to justify tampering with the details of implementation of the National Curriculum, it is necessary to remain silent about its fundamentals. And so, inevitably, there is a de facto tendency towards a legitimation of the entire enterprise. To be sure, this generally takes the form of focusing on the (relatively harmless) lists of Attainment Targets and ignoring the (relatively harmful) questions of the Standardised Assessment Tasks. But it is my contention that this is at best fundamentally misguided and at worst dishonest. There is a substantial current of teacher-opinion which is opposed to the National Curriculum, and I suggest that this is likely to grow as the contradictions embedded within the structures emerge: and I propose that it is the duty of academics to encourage serious debate which is conducted not in the pseudo-educational terms of government departments or political speeches, but on the basis of informed academic discourse.

If teachers see clearly what they are up against, there is some chance that they will divert (or perhaps subvert) some of the National

Curriculum's worst effects. Already there are signs that attitudes within the profession are changing. One example has been the shift from one of deflection ('I teach most of this anyway, and I won't let it bother me') to outrage ('how can I possibly cope with all this emphasis on targets and testing?'). This is a significant change, since it marks the untenability of continued attempts by the educational establishment to downplay the testing element in favour of debates about the finer points of the individual statements of attainment. Indeed, whereas it was commonplace only a year ago to encounter teachers who saw the National Curriculum as essentially about which topics would be taught to whom, emphasis is now squarely on the testing procedures which, as I have argued, form the backbone of the whole enterprise.

This shift has been facilitated by the sometimes farcical changes between different versions of the statements of attainment themselves. So, for example, we had the example (in Maths 5–16) of Number Target 3, level 7 which stated baldly: 'Nothing new at this level'. We can only assume that the obvious implications for the meaning(less-ness) of the preceding and subsequent levels did not escape the DES, since in the final statutes (DES, 1989), this statement has been replaced by 'Use the knowledge, skills and understanding attained at lower levels in a wider range of contexts' (no example given). It is not clear whether 'applying' skills was thought to be equivalent to 'nothing new', if it is the case that *all* previously acquired knowledge and skills in the Attainment Target has to be 'applied' to qualify for the new level 7 (surely this would apply to *every* level?), or how this particular statement is thought to be equivalent to its corresponding levels in other Attainment Targets. Either way it is difficult to escape the conclusion that the bureaucratic hand of government was at work when this particular statement of attainment was redrafted.

I offer the preceding example merely as an illustration of the vacuum that the targets and the programmes of study represent. My claim in this paper is broadly that even within the confines of the National Curriculum and centralized assessment, there is room for teachers to teach and for children to learn; that content — precisely because it is such a low priority for those involved in the imposition of the National Curriculum — can be raised to a high priority by teachers. In arguing this case, I am aware that I run counter to some mathematical educational orthodoxies which seem in the recent past to have implicitly or explicitly advocated a policy of what amounts to disguising mathematical content in games, puzzles and investigations; rightly emphasising the importance of mathematical processes but wrongly, in my view, neglecting the need to help pupils to come into explicit contact with mathematical ideas. In contrast, I am advocating the potential of mathematical thought as a socially powerful set of ideas, in the sense proposed Mellin-Olsen (1987) who presents a convincing case for the role of 'thinking-tools' for critical consciousness, and for the 'functionality of knowledge as a means for a democratic education' (p. 206). If he is right, perhaps there is, after all, something that teachers can salvage from the National Curriculum.

Acknowledgements

I would like to thank Paul Dowling, Harvey Goldstein and Celia Hoyles, for their helpful comments on earlier drafts of this paper.

Notes

1 Teachers in private schools are exempt from this law. It is interesting to reflect on precedents for cases where the application of a law has been explicitly applied to only a subset of an otherwise well-defined population.
2 The recently published non-statutory requirements provide interesting reading: this document will be discussed elsewhere.
3 Noss *et al.* argue that the TGAT model blurs the necessary distinction between *public* and *private* assessment, and question the validity of the hierarchical model on which it is based.
4 The report goes on to document some of the expressions of opinion which the committee received in consultation with employers; it did not, apparently, think it important to consult any employees on the matter.
5 It should be clear that there is no need to invoke a conspiracy as an explanatory device. Neither is mathematics unique in performing as a mechanism of social control. All that is required is that it can fulfill this role: that it can do so is related to various factors, such as its historically privileged position in the curriculum, its universally respected (and feared) role as a litmus test for 'intelligence', and its suitability as a filter for social advancement (Walkerdine 1989).
6 In fact, the National Curriculum working party's view of gender and race is explictly racist and sexist. They adopt a race/gender 'blind' approach (paras 10.17,10.22) which conveniently ignores the underlying prejudices built into the system, in favour of bland statements about the necessity for equal treatment. Perhaps more sinister is its explicit linkage to the needs of the workplace and the flavour of xenophobia in the following: '. . . priority must be given to ensuring that they have the knowledge, understanding and skills which they will need for *adult life and employment in Britain in the twenty-first century*' (para 1.20, emphasis in original).

References

BOWLES, S. and GINTIS, H., 1976, *Schooling in Capitalist America*, London: Routledge and Kegan Paul.

BRAVERMAN, H., 1974, *Labor and Monopoly Capitalism: The Degradation of Work in the Twentieth Century*, New York: Monthly Review Press

BROADFOOT, P., 1988, 'The national assessment framework and records of achievement' in TORRANCE, H. (Ed.) *National Assessment and Testing: A Research Response*, British Educational Research Association.

BROWN, M., 1988, 'Professor Black has not led Mr Baker astray', *Times Educational Supplement*, 29. April.

BROWN, M., 1989, 'Make the best of it', *Times Educational Supplement*, 27. January.

BURKHARDT, H., 1988, 'National testing: Liability or asset?', *Mathematics Teaching*, **122**, pp. 33–35.

CARLSON, D., 1988, 'Beyond the reproductive theory of teaching' in COLE, M. (Ed.) *Bowles and Gintis Revisited*, Lewes: Falmer Press, pp. 158–173.

CHITTY, C., 1988, 'Two models of a National Curriculum: Origins and interpretation' in LAWTON, D. and CHITTY, C. (Eds) *The National Curriculum*, Bedford Way Paper 33; London: Institute of Education, University of London, pp. 34–48.

COCKCROFT, W.H. *et al.*, 1982, *Mathematics Counts*, London: HMSO.

COLE, M. (Ed.), 1988, *Bowles and Gintis Revisited*, Lewes: Falmer Press.

DES AND WELSH OFFICE, 1988a, *Mathematics for ages 5–16*, London: HMSO.

DES AND WELSH OFFICE, 1988b, *Task Group on Assessment and Testing*, London: DES.

DES AND WELSH OFFICE, 1989, *Mathematics in the National Curriculum*, London: HMSO.

DOWLING, P.C., 1989, 'The contextualizing of mathematics: Towards a theoretical map' in *Collected Original Resources in Education*, **13**, 2.

GINTIS, H. and BOWLES, S., 1988, 'Contradiction and Reproduction in Educational Theory', in COLE, M. (Ed.) *Bowles and Gintis Revisited*. Lewes: Falmer Press.

GIROUX, H., 1983, *Theory and Resistance in Education*. London: Heinemann.

HOWSON, G., 1989, *Maths problem. Can more pupils reach higher standards?* Policy Study No. 102, Centre for Policy Studies. London: CPS.

HOWSON, G., KEITEL, C. and KILPATRICK, J., 1981, *Curriculum Development in Mathematics*, Cambridge: Cambridge University Press.

LAVE, J., 1988, *Cognition in Practice*, Cambridge: Cambridge University Press.

LAWTON, D., 1988, 'Ideologies of education' in LAWTON, D. and CHITTY, C. (Eds) *The National Curriculum*, Bedford Way Paper 33; London: Institute of Education, University of London, pp. 10–20.

LAWTON, D., 1989, 'Measure of doubt', *Times Educational Supplement*, 6. January.

MAW, J., 1988, 'National Curriculum policy: Coherence and progression?' in, LAWTON, D. and CHITTY, C. (Eds) *The National Curriculum*. Bedford Way Paper 33; London: Institute of Education, University of London, pp. 49–64.

MELLIN-OLSEN, S., 1987, *The Politics of Mathematics Education*, Dordrecht: Reidel.

NCC, 1988, *Consultation Report: Mathematics*, London: NCC.

NOSS, R., 1989, 'Just testing: a critical view of recent change in the UK mathematics curriculum' in CLEMENTS, K. and ELLERTON, N. (Eds) *School Mathematics: The Challenge to Change*, Geelong: Deakin University Press.

NOSS, R., GOLDSTEIN, H. and HOYLES, C., 1989, 'Graded assessment and learning hierarchies in mathematics', *British Education Research Journal*, Vol. **15**, 2, pp. 109–120.

WALKERDINE, V., 1989, *The Mastery of Reason*, London: Routledge.

2   The Shogun's and Other Curriculum Voices

Paul Dowling

In his inaugural lecture given at the Collège de France in 1970, Michel Foucault recounted an 'anecdote' concerning a Japanese Shogun. Since my purposes do not entirely coincide with those of Foucault, I make no apologies for presenting the story here ripped out of the context of its telling and, worse still, riven in two; such is the butchery of analysis.

> At the beginning of the seventeenth century, the Shogun heard tell that the Europeans' superiority in matters of navigation, commerce, politics, and military skill was due to their know-ledge of mathematics. He desired to get hold of so precious a knowledge. As he had been told of an English sailor who possessed the secret of these miraculous discourses, he summoned him to his palace and kept him there. Alone with him, he took lessons. He learned mathematics. He retained power, and lived to a great old age. It was not until the nineteenth century that there were Japanese mathematicians. (Foucault, 1981: 62)

That which renders this anecdote amusing is the irony of a perverse understanding of mathematics which is being presented to us: we know mathematics to be a powerful set of tools which derives its force through its application (to navigation, commerce, politics, military skill); the Shogun misconstrues the discipline as a talisman. Of course, the Shogun's status as a foreigner — perhaps especially an oriental — and a historical figure is hardly irrelevant.

> But the anecdote does not stop there: it has its European side too. The story has it that this English sailor, Will Adams, was

> an autodidact, a carpenter who had learnt geometry in the
> course of working in a shipyard. (*ibid*)

Irony piled higher and deeper: the ignorant Shogun didn't even get a
proper mathematician. Despite the fact that his instruction was appropriately abstracted from application, his teacher hadn't even been to
school (nowadays, he'd probably be called a 'licensed teacher').

My use of Foucault's anecdote (and I shall return to it later) is
intended to illustrate the highlighting of certain key principles which
seem currently to dominate public domain discourse in mathematics
education. These principles being that, firstly, mathematical knowledge gains its use-value primarily in its application: an adept mathematician is not, as such, better or more 'intelligent' than an incompe-
tent. Secondly, and the first principle notwithstanding, mathematical
knowledge is to be acquired in a decontextualized form — in a
classroom, not in the factory or supermarket. Thirdly, the general
context of mathematics schooling is ethnocentrism if not xenophobia:
the uses to which mathematical tools are to be put concern the
strengthening of the British economy and certainly not, for example,
the interrogation of the latter as a mechanism of domestic and global
neocolonialism.

This is a reading in a particular voice which is certainly critical
rather than celebratory of much of what is currently being said publicly concerning the National Curriculum; clearly, alternative voices are
possible. My intention in this chapter is to present two opposing
readings of discourse in mathematics education by focusing principally (but not exclusively) on *Mathematics in the National Curriculum*
(DES, 1989) and related documents. I shall first give some exposition
of the nature of these voices and then use them to produce readings of
mathematics education in relation to pronouncements on the nature of
mathematics and on the nature of the student. It is my contention that
despite the very different perspectives of the two voices, they generate
the same result which is heavily critical of mathematics education as
represented in the documents under consideration. However, the form
of criticism is distinctive in each voice, the first voice is forced by the
the internal contradictions of the reading into ironic self-destruction,
whilst the second produces a more conventional frontal attack. The
power of the second voice lies in its autocritical potential.

The Voice of Authority

This voice is that which surveys and pronounces firmly and finally,
the voice which sees no need to look behind its back to justify its

definitive statements and which, above all, denies the value of self-criticism. This is not to say that it necessarily ignores all the evidence, indeed the weight of evidence sometimes adds significantly to the power of this voice. This voice, however, defines and claims ownership over the evidence and its exclusive interpretation; it is immovable. This is the voice of party politics which denies debate and, instead, appeals directly to its supporters with all the subtlety of a chanting football crowd: will Chelsea's *'ere wi go . . .'* ever persuade Tottenham?

This is the voice with which the Secretaries of State[1] admonish the National Curriculum Mathematics Working Group on the contents of their final report:

> We are concerned that the suggested weightings give too little emphasis to the essential foundation of knowledge, skills and understanding which pupils need to tackle problems. There is a clear relationship between knowledge and application. (DES, 1988b: iii)

No need for evidence here. No need to worry that this constitutes a direct refutation of the advice that non-expert ministers have sought from 'expert' professionals.[2] This is a direct appeal to a pervasive 'commonsense'. No rational objection is possible.

The authoritative voice is also present in many governmental and quasi-governmental reports, although with rather less of the party political appeal. HMI rarely justify their pronouncements with anything other than their own observations, and the Cockcroft Report (1982) — less culpable than most in this respect — still seems to draw its 'Foundation List of Mathematical Topics' (§ 458) out of a hat. The National Curriculum Mathematics Working Party is, apparently, not quite as confident:

> In defining the levels of attainment appropriate for different ages and stages, we have relied mainly on our collective experience and knowledge of good teaching practice and on available research evidence. (DES, 1988b: 1)

Now, the reference to 'collective experience and knowledge of good teaching practice' is effectively a shut-out to the extent that it is not elaborated (and it isn't).[3] It might be expected, however, that the report would make clear precisely what 'available research evidence' referred to. Unfortunately, this seems not to be the case. Although the report presents a 'Selected Bibliography', including a reference to 'various unpublished works', nowhere is there any attempt to interpret 'available research evidence' in such a way as to validate the statements made in the Curriculum. Whether such a validation is or is not possible will, of course, remain an open question (unless and until it is achieved) and, indeed, remains of secondary importance in the present discussion. A brief consideration of the sorts of questions that such a validating process would have to address is, however, needed in order to establish the authoritarian nature of the report.

An academic validation might perhaps proceed by making explicit the deductive connexions — either direct or critical — between existing research and the specific statements of the report. One might start from a Piagetian form of stage theory, or a Vygotskian notion of concept formation, or a Brunerian sequence, or from work in the field of cognitive science, and develop their implications for curriculum construction to a level of specificity which is sufficient to indicate just how this work can be understood as informing the report.[4] Alternatively, one might take a more empiricist piece of research as a starting point and proceed in a similar manner. There is a suggestion that this latter strategy would be the one preferred by the Working Party as the research[5] mentioned in their 'selected bibliography' is of this form — for example, Hart (1981).[6] Again, however, although the connexions between empiricist work and a substantive curriculum might be expected to be rather easier to make, they are not made clear.

Rather than spend too much time reading research, the Working Party decided on a globetrotting junket to:

> ... discover why pupils in [the Netherlands, France, and Japan[7]] performed better in the mathematics tests of the First and Second International Mathematics Studies. (DES, 1988b: 105)

Again, the connexions between their observations and the results of their labour (Statements of Attainment, Attainment Targets, etc.) are not made explicit, however, as Brown and Dowling (1989) note, during their eight day study visit to Japan the team discovered that:

> ... there seems to be a great need and desire to conform with the attitudes and behaviour of others. This manifests itself in many ways, perhaps most notably in what appeared to us to be the virtual exclusion of the word 'no' and other contradictory and possibly antagonistic phrases from the daily vocabulary. (DES, 1988b: 113)

As Brown and Dowling point out:

> The report does not mention how many of their number were
> fluent in Japanese — which would, on the face of it, seem to be
> a prerequisite for making this sort of judgement — and it is
> certainly the case that Japanese history does not abound with
> examples of a lack of ability to say no. Nevertheless, should
> they be proved right, we should applaud this major contribu-
> tion to anthropology by a team which appears to exhibit very
> little in the way of qualification or experience in this field.
> (Brown and Dowling, 1989: 13)

The Working Party's generalization is a clear example of a pronouncement of the voice of authority, the voice through which the first of
each pair of sub-readings below is produced.

The Voice of Critique

In contrast to the voice of authority, this voice opens up the text to
critical scrutiny and, in particular, assumes that its own readings are
provisional. Most especially, those items of text closest to that which
is 'commonsense' (which always goes unchallenged in the domain to
which the voice of authority appeals) must be deconstructed and
rewritten. A general principle which would be consistent with this
voice is that the problem in curriculum design is not to produce the
correct solution, but to start from a critical appraisal of where we now
are, and to sustain a constant criticism (and, in particular, an auto-
criticism). In the field of practical education, it seems clear that self-
criticism must centrally involve the classroom teacher and the student
whom, it is hoped, will also be informed — but not dictated to — by
the work of HMI, academics, and others.

The idea of critique is advanced by Brown and Dowling (1989) as
an 'alternative to internationalism and monoculturalism in mathematics education': it is my intention to give the practice a broader
base, although emancipatory interests (Dowling, 1986) may still be
interpreted as foundational. The initiators of critical action may arise
out of a checklist (constantly under review) and/or out of questions
raised in the classroom ('what's the point of doing fractions?'), by a
scrutiny of examination results ('why did more boys than girls get
'A's), out of questions posed by professional and academic writing,
in-service courses, colleagues, parents, advisers — even politicians.

An essential feature of the voice of critique is that stability — in potentially all aspects of the curriculum — is very short term, although, clearly, not everything can change at once, and different aspects of the curriculum will change according to different time-scales.

The fluid notion of the curriculum advocated by the voice of critique is to be contrasted with the definitive (and frequently ground-less) pronouncements of the voice of authority. Whilst it is true that the 'Non-statutory Guidance' for the National Curriculum (NCC, 1989) emphasises the scope for flexibility and modification through feedback, the limits of this flexibility are clearly illustrated in its planning diagram (Figure 1). A consideration of the uni-directionality of the arrows, for example, makes it quite clear (as if it wasn't already) that the Programmes of Study and the Attainment Targets are not open to negotiation, and the Working Party's (almost unique) concession to modesty — 'It would be surprising [...] if we had got everything right first time' (DES, 1988b: 1) — is vacuous since, like the rest of their commentary and 'guidance' it is not enshrined within the legislation, no more is any clear mechanism for restructuring. Whilst this legislation remains on the statute books, the most that can be expected is revision on a long timescale and on a corporatist basis.

The voices through which mathematics education is to be inter-preted as readings having been described and contrasted briefly, I shall now proceed to the readings themselves, using two headings: the nature of mathematics; and the nature of the student.

The Nature of Mathematics: The Voice of Authority

A rather startling statement appears in the 'Non-statutory Guidance':

> Although mathematics does contain a hierarchical element, learning in mathematics does not necessarily take place in completely predetermined sequences. Mathematics is a struc-ture composed of a whole network of concepts and relation-ships, and, when being used, mathematics becomes a living process of creative activity. (NCC, 1989: A3)

This is startling, not because it cannot be reconciled with the voice of authority, but because it cannot be reconciled with *Mathematics in the National Curriculum* (DES, 1989); the statement is an example of the voice of authority saying (with authority, and without batting an

Figure 1 (from NCC, 1989, p. B4)

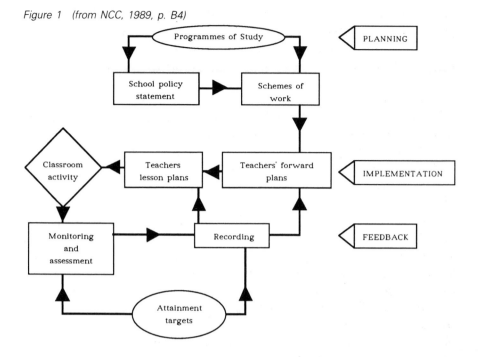

eyelid) 'I am a liar'. However, since the guidance (and the legislation) prioritise the Attainment Targets and Programmes of Study and not the guidance itself (another problem for Epimenides), I shall concentrate on the structure and content of the Attainment Targets.[8]

Firstly, school mathematics is atomisable into 296 Statements of Attainment — what Küchemann (in this volume) refers to as 'stoats'. As Küchemann points out, it is not entirely certain whether exactly 296 stoats make a curriculum, but at least 296 of them are sufficiently important and identifiable to be enshrined in law. Because the mathematics curriculum is defined in terms of statements of *attainment*, mathematics itself is being understood as a body of things that people *can do*. Indeed in an earlier document the Working Party seem to be suggesting that all knowledge is essentially reducible in these terms in advocating the development of 'a "can do" attitude to life's challenges' (DES, 1988b: 4); this is clearly spoken with the voice of authority which would never acknowledge that a 'should we do?' or a 'is it worth doing' or a 'what damage might it do?' approach might be appropriate.

Secondly, having been atomised into statements of attainment (stoats) or, to use a more familiar synonym, behavioural objectives (bobs?), school mathematics can be organized into 14 parallel hierarchies (two of which comprise the same stoats with different examples) most having ten levels, the Levels being linked across Attainment Targets by the association of ranges of Levels to student ages.[9] The Working Party originally left some of the cells blank so that, for example, Attainment Target 4, Level 7 originally contained 'Nothing new at this level' (NCC 1988: 35) and Attainment Target 6 had 'Nothing specific' at Level 1 (*ibid*; 40). Presumably, the Working Party were told off (by a higher authority) for such vagueness, and the final document includes a new stoat 'use the knowledge, skills and understanding attained at lower levels in a wider range of contexts' (DES, 1989: 16) at Level 7 of Attainment Target 4, whilst omitting Level 1 of Attainment Target 6 altogether; it is not at all certain whether the vagueness has been increased or decreased, but the result is certainly more assertively vague.[10]

Apart from the small number of stoats which make explicit reference to the existence of other stoats (such as the one above for Level 7 of Attainment Target 4) or which are clearly directly comparable (such as 'count, read, write and order numbers to at least 10 ...' and 'read, write and order numbers to at least 100 ...' and 'read, write and order numbers to at least 1000 ...' and 'read, write and order whole[11] numbers.' — Attainment Target 2, Levels 1, 2, 3 and 4 respectively) the relationships between stoats are defined by their respective positions in the matrix, rather than by any obvious (to me) logic. Thus within Attainment Target 2, Levels 5, 6 and 7 each contain stoats dealing with number:[12] integers, in the case of Levels 5 and 7; and rationals in the case of Level 6 (see Dowling, 1990a).

Looking across Attainment Targets, 'read, write and order whole numbers' (Attainment Target 2, Level 4) is equivalent — in some respect — to 'understand and use the probability scale from 0 to 1' (Attainment Target 14, Level 4), and 'reflect simple shapes in a mirror line' (Attainment Target 11, Level 6) is equivalent to 'solve simple polynomial equations by "trial and improvement" methods' (Attainment Target 6, Level 6).

The assertion that mathematics is useful has a long history in mathematics education, and is certainly a feature of the National Curriculum:

Mathematics provides a way of viewing and making sense of the world. It is used to analyse and communicate information and ideas and to tackle a range of practical tasks and real-life problems. (NCC, 1989: A2)

Learning skills, such as adding two numbers, calculating the area of a triangle or solving an equation, form a large part of pupils' work in school mathematics. Important though they are, such skills are only a means to an end, and should be taught and learned in a context that provides purpose and meaning. It is through, for example, handling money when shopping, analysing the results of a survey in geography or measuring fabric for a garment in design that the importance of such skills is seen. (*ibid*: A3)

However, the stoats and, in most cases, their respective examples, make virtually no reference to the precise uses to which mathematics is to be put. The Attainment Targets 1 and 9 — both entitled 'Using and Applying Mathematics' — do give some useful examples: 'Use handspans to measure the length of a table'; 'Test the statement: "If you add the house numbers of three houses next to one another you always get a multiple of 3", for various examples'; 'Decide where to put a telephone box in the locality'; 'Conduct an experiment to find the probability of a drawing pin landing on its base when dropped from a certain height; consider the factors that might affect the result'. However, it is clearly possible to abstract the essential mathematics from such everyday practices in order to present it as a matrix of stoats.

Essentially, then, the voice of authority produces a reading of school mathematics as atomisable into (at least) 296 behavioural objectives, which can be divided into 14 themes and hierarchically grouped into 10 levels within each theme and broadly equivalent across themes; the relationship between the elements is to be determined, principally, by their inscription in the resulting matrix rather than by any apparent logic. Furthermore, school mathematics has a utilitarian value with respect to both other school subjects and 'real-life'.[13]

The Nature of Mathematics: The Voice of Critique

Some of the problems associated with the selection, fragmentation and hierarchisation of the mathematics curriculum are discussed in some detail by Küchemann (in this volume),[14] and I shall try to avoid too much repetition. Part of the problem — and this relates to the particular categorization that I have chosen for this reading — is that the status that one attributes to fragments and hierarchies depends on whether they are being understood as features of mathematics[15] or as features of the way people learn and, if the latter, are we talking about the way people need to learn by virtue of the nature of the human brain, or about the way that people do learn simply because there seems to be a tendency for the authors of textbooks and the constructors of curricula in mathematics either to follow a similar pattern, or to copy one another?

Now, whilst there seems to be no evidence (at anything like the level of specificity required) that might suggest an essential psychological basis for a particular fragmentation and ordering of the mathematics curriculum, the popularity of individualized learning practices in, for example, the SMILE (ILEA) programme and in *SMP 11–16* (Cambridge University Press[16]) certainly questions the possibility of such a basis. Under these circumstances, it is not appropriate to assume that the organization of the Attainment Targets of the National Curriculum relates to psychology. On the other hand there is — as my authoritarian reading admits — no obvious mathematical logic to the organization of the Attainment Targets. Indeed the possibility of such a logic is itself open to question (Noss *et al.*, *op cit*).

We are left, then, with the possibility that the detailed hierarchical structure of the Attainment Targets is predicated upon practice in mathematics teaching, much of which currently involves the use of individualised schemes. Küchemann and O'Reilly (both in this volume) suggest that the Concepts in Secondary Mathematics and Science (CSMS) work (Hart, 1981) carried out in the 1970s was probably influential in the Working Party's deliberations, and this may have been the case[17] although, as I have stated above, the precise connexions are less than clear. Nevertheless, it may be that the Working Party's 'collective experience and knowledge of good teaching practice' (DES, 1988b: 1) may relate to teaching practice of the 1970s (before individualized approaches were widespread — at least in secondary mathematics). There again, it may be that this is attributing too high a level of professional conscience to the Working Party which is, after all, a committee: it may be that they were simply doing as they were told.[18]

Whether considered from a mathematical or *de facto* pedagogical point of view, the structuring of school mathematics is diverse; when considered from a psychological point of view it is at least *potentially* diverse since there is no evidence to suggest otherwise. The rigid structuring of the Attainment Targets is therefore a threefold reduction of school mathematics. The point is not that there should be an attempt to avoid making decisions on the selection, sequencing, and pacing of school mathematics — such decisions are clearly inevitable

— but that it is the activity involved in making the decisions, rather than the decisions themselves, which is illuminating and progressive; this is the essence of critique. The Attainment Targets, fixed by legislation, now become a set of givens, they define the limits of active reflexion by teachers and students. In fact, the Targets represent a particularly weak curriculum at this point in time because, as I have illustrated with respect to sequencing, they take inadequate account of current practices[19] and, where they appear to do so, they are reproductive rather than critical.

An example of this latter feature is the empiricist nature of Attainment Targets 1 and 9 — 'Using and Applying Mathematics'. The Statements of Attainment (or their clarification in the examples provided) concern the making and testing of conjectures, thus at Level 6 in Attainment Target 1:

> make and test generalizations and simple hypotheses; define and reason in simple contexts with some precision.

and the example is shown in Figure 2.

The approach being advocated is clearly inductive. The same Statement of Attainment in Attainment Target 9 is exemplified by:

> Make a hypothesis about children's weight in relation to their height and test it by reference to a scatter graph.

The expression 'test it by reference to a scatter graph' suggests that the scatter graph has already been drawn, and this is supported by the example for the previous Statement of Attainment ('use oral, written or visual forms to record and present findings'):

> Survey the class to find heights and weights and present the results in the form of a scatter graph.

The 'hypothesis' looks like an empiricist generalization — a conjecture generated inductively. At Level 8 — above the expected terminal attainment of the 'average' student — we are presented with the first occurrence of 'proof':

> make statement of conjecture using 'if ... then ...'; define, reason, prove and disprove.

Figure 2

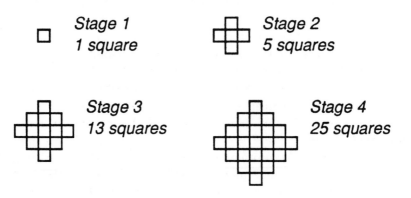

Explore the pattern:

Stage 1
1 square

Stage 2
5 squares

Stage 3
13 squares

Stage 4
25 squares

Use the difference method to extend the
pattern; determine a rule for the sequence and
test the rule.

In Attainment Target 1, the example includes a positive notion of proof:

> In exploring decimals and fractions with a calculator or micro-computer make statements of the type. 'If the denominator has prime factors other than 2 or 5, then the decimal will recur'; offer justifications, explanations and proofs of such statements.

Whilst the corresponding example in Attainment Target 9 permits a reversion to empiricism:

> Test the conjecture: 'a public car park will accommodate the same number of cars whatever their arrangement, where door-room and turning circles are standard'.

The examples at Levels 9 and 10 in both Attainment Targets suggest empirical testing of hypotheses (that in Level 10 of Attainment Target 1 also includes algebraic manipulation), all of the other examples in all of the Attainment Targets could be interpreted as suggesting either an empiricist or an algorithmic approach, except that at Level 10 of Attainment Target 6:

Simplify $\dfrac{1}{x + 2} + \dfrac{1}{x - 3}$.

Show that $x^2 - 6x + 10 = (x - 3)^2 + 1 \geq 1$,
(whatever the value of x).

There is a sense, of course, in which empiricism might be understood as a reaction against undue emphasis on an algorithmic approach to school mathematics, and we might find evidence of just such a re-action in an emphasis on experiential work in primary mathematics (Corran and Walkerdine, 1981) and in 'investigational' work in both primary and secondary schools; there is, in other words, nothing *new* in empiricism as a basis for school mathematics. On the other hand, empiricism itself is limiting in mathematics because it focuses on superficial pattern rather than on structure; it is from considering the latter that we might move from *school* mathematics to mathematics, that is, exploration of formal systems rather than of their analogues in the tangible world, and the introduction of *deduction* in addition to inductive processes.

Not that deduction is omitted from *writing* about school mathematics — see, for example, Mason *et al.* (1982) — but that, in my observation,[20] it is often absent from the classroom, where an 'investigation' is generally taken to have been 'successfully' completed when a conjecture has been stated and tested empirically. An example would be the ubiquitous 'billiard table' problem:[21]

Figure 3

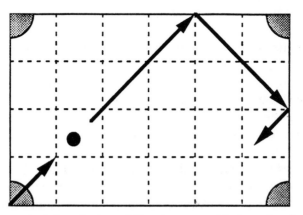

The ball is always struck from the lower lefthand corner, and it always travels, at 45° to the 'vertical' or 'horizontal', until it falls into one of the corner pockets. How many contacts with the edges of the table (including those with the starting and finishing pockets) will the ball make? Investigate for other sizes of table.

I have seen this used in secondary classrooms on a number of occasions. One of the most successful lessons centred around the use of a computer simulation of this problem[22] with a top set fifth year class. The lesson (run by a student teacher) involved whole class discussion, individual and group working, and the formulation and testing of conjectures. Somewhat fortuitously, the class arrived at 'the answer' (i.e. the relationship between the dimensions of the table and the number of contacts) almost right on the bell, and everyone left feeling that they had achieved something. What struck me about the lesson — apart from the undoubted success in terms of student and teacher participation and enjoyment — was that on only two occasions was the geometry of the table discussed: once when someone mentioned that there would be only two contacts for any square table, because 'the ball would go straight across'; and once when it was realized that there would be three contacts for any table that was twice as long as it was wide (or vice versa), 'because it's like two squares joined together'. The rest of the time, everyone was content to draw tables, count contacts, and make generalizations — which were then computer-tested in plenary discussions.

Furthermore, when I've given this 'investigation' to groups of student or practising teachers — groups which generally include a number of highly competent mathematicians — they have always approached the task in a similar sort of way, and when I've asked for a proof, the response has almost always been one of bewilderment.[23] The point being, that whilst mathematics is often thought of as essentially involving deductive processes, and to exhibit 'certainty' which is independent of empirical experience (see, for example, Howson and Wilson, 1986) deduction itself — as opposed to algorithmic working — is frequently entirely absent from school mathematics

The Statements of Attainment, in their celebration of empiricism, may articulate certain aspects of current practice in mathematics education, but certainly do not go beyond it. In other words, whilst a critical approach would involve development based upon a critical engagement with current practice, the National Curriculum appears to take an uncomfortable selection from current and previous practice and enshrine it in law.

A second example will serve to illustrate the potential dangers of any hierarchical ordering — potentially any ordering — in a curriculum; I've chosen to focus on fraction notation simply because I feel that it illustrates the point I want to make clearly. There would appear to be widespread agreement that the teaching of fractions should be ordered such that the drawing of an equivalence between a fraction and a shaded part of a simple plane figure ('a fraction is a piece of cake') should precede the addition of fractions; thus:

Figure 4

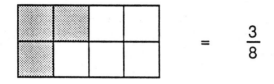

$$= \frac{3}{8}$$

should be introduced before:

$$\frac{3}{8} + \frac{2}{5}$$

This is the case in the National Curriculum, in which the addition of fractions appears only implicitly and not until Level 8 of Attainment Target 3 ('calculate with fractions'), and the same ordering appears in *SMP 11–16* — the most popular secondary scheme in England and Wales. David Pimm (1987) refers to relationships such as 'a fraction is a piece of cake' as metaphorical — the fraction is, in fact, something which is different from (though with some similarity to) a piece of cake; Valerie Walkerdine (1982) has described the task of mathematics teaching as stripping away these metaphors in order to reveal the true nature of mathematical activity as *metonymy*.[24] I want to suggest that Pimm's use of the figure 'metaphor' is inappropriate in the case of *school* mathematics and that it might be more accurate to refer to the relationship as *synecdoche*.[25] It is not correct, in other words to think of the fraction as something *different* from 'a piece of cake', on the contrary, 'a piece of cake' is always *part* of what we understand by the fraction — *I* still think of fractions in this way; indeed, it is perfectly correct to think of a fraction in this sense in many contexts; it is not something we can simply 'strip away'.[26]

However, if we now approach the addition of fractions using the 'piece of cake' synecdoche, we might produce:

Figure 5

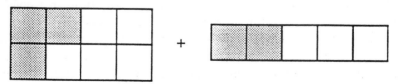

The most obvious interpretation of which leads us to the conclusion:

$$\frac{3}{8} + \frac{2}{5} = \frac{5}{13}$$

An alternative synecdoche which replaces the fraction $\frac{3}{8}$ with 3 marks out of 8 altogether on a test is likely to lead to precisely the same conclusion.

The dissonance between this result and the more conventional answer arises because the addition of fractions is linked to the addition of numbers rather than the addition (or combining) of areas of geometrical figures or examination marks. Some mathematicians might want to argue that the 'piece of cake' synecdoche is actually wrong, and might feel that they can explain why. But this is to assert some concept of school mathematics — and that's what we're talking about — which is separate from its institutionalization in, for example, school textbooks. The textbook produces a sequence of meanings for fractions, each of which is partial — all meanings are ultimately partial. Inevitably, one partial meaning contradicts another, and the choice between them is made at a higher level of discourse: higher, that is, in the curricular sequence; the level at which we decide that we really know what a fraction is.

I want to suggest — tentatively — that this difficulty is likely to arise whenever a curriculum is ordered on the basis of a gradual introduction to a set of 'concepts'. The 'truth' — the real thing — is promised, but perpetually deferred. Polemically, I would say the 'truth' is perpetually deferred because it doesn't exist as something which can be grasped in its tangibility; but this polemic is not necessary. Suffice it to say, that where a curriculum is internally contradictory, the price (to be paid by the student) of success is blind faith in the teacher or the textbook: potentially a remarkable system of control.

The notion that mathematics is useful as a problem solving tool and in communication, is the foundation upon which the compulsory status of mathematics is based. This largely goes unquestioned possibly because of the close association of 'mathematics' with reckoning or measurement and numeration, combined with the prevalence of numbers and quantities in our culture; mathematics is also closely associated with science and technology which seem to have status as the motor forces of 'progress'.

However, there is a growing amount of evidence which suggests a substantive separation between school mathematics and the social practices in which it might be presumed to be useful. In Dowling (1986; 1989), for example, I have considered the evidence of the three research projects, set up on behalf of the Cockcroft Committee, which looked at the uses made of mathematics in everyday life (Sewell, 1981) and in the workplace (Bath University, 1981; Shell Centre, nd). None of these projects found much in the way of evidence that people were *using* the mathematics that they had learned at school indeed, as one of the reports stated about its interviews:

> One of the principle things to emerge from these discussions is that few people, young or old, appear to have come out of school with a very clear idea of what the purpose of studying Mathematics might be (or education generally in many cases). (Bath University, 1981: 199)

Sewell (1981) pathologized those of her respondents whom she did not consider to be reporting the use of appropriately mathematical strategies in their everyday lives by referring to them as 'avoiding' mathematics. And individuals who were apparently quite competent in their working practices seemed completely disabled by the school context, Lindsay talked to Amanda, an invoice typist:

> I asked Amanda about tables. She said she used to recite them every day, and the Headmaster used to come and make spot checks to see if they were known but she doesn't really remember them now. I asked her if she knew what 8×9 were [sic] and she said 'it's 72 isn't it, or is it 74?' I asked what method she used to get this answer and she said 'Well I know that 8×8 are [sic] 64 and I want another 8, so that makes 72, doesn't it?' (Shell Centre, nd: 661)

These findings are entirely in accord with those of John Spradbery (1976) who was astonished to find a number of his class of mathematical failures engaging in what, to him, seemed to be highly mathematical practices in their pigeon-fancying activities. My interpretation of Spradbery's findings is that he is constructing a synecdoche for school mathematics — perhaps something similar to an examination syllabus or list of curriculum objectives — and projecting it onto pigeon-fancying, thus transforming and reducing the latter. The correspondence drawn between the two constructions ignores their embededness within highly specific practices, which contextualise and differentiate them.

Similarly, Jean Lave (1984; 1988) reports a disparity between the performances of shoppers on what she describes as arithmetic tasks within the context of shopping, and tasks constructed to be equivalent within the context of a paper and pencil test. Lave suggests that the shopping 'arithmetic' was performed within a dialectical process by which a purchasing decision was arrived at, whereas paper and pencil 'arithmetic' involved attempts to apply half-remembered algorithms from school mathematics. In fact, it seems very difficult to find evidence of anyone making much use of *school* mathematics at all.[27]

Now this is not to argue that it may not be possible to construct a school context within which school mathematics has a value, either as a domain of activity in its own right, or as a methodological approach to questions which arise outside of mathematics. My intention, however, is to raise serious doubts about the notion of a knowledge — any knowledge — which has a *generic* use-value.

My voice of critique thus challenges the vision of mathematics as an empiricist activity, as comprising tangible concepts which are to be developed as a sequence of pedagogic encounters, and as fundamentally useful — the vision of the National Curriculum. I have hinted at the possibility of an alternative vision, but what is being advocated in this paper is a critical approach: the detailing of such alternatives would therefore introduce an unwelcome dissonance.[28]

The Nature of the Student: The Voice of Authority

The voice of authority makes at least two forms of pronouncement on the nature of the student, the first constituting an attribution of essential qualities, properties which the student brings to the school or which develop independently of the school activities; these qualities define the limits of the school effectiveness by constituting a maximum potential which is measurable against hierarchically organized curriculum objectives. The role of the curriculum is to measure the qualities, and respond with an appropriate sequence of instruction so as to enable the fulfilment of the potential. The two principle qualities are 'level of ability' and 'age'. Thus, the Secretary of State writes, in his letter to the National Curriculum Mathematics Working Party dated 21st August 1987:

I am looking to you to recommend attainment targets which set out the knowledge, skills and understanding which pupils of different abilities should be able to achieve by the end of the school year in which they reach one of the key ages. They should allow scope for the very able, those of average ability, and the less able to show what they can do. So far as possible I want to avoid having different attainment targets for children of different levels of ability. (DES, 1988b: 94)

And the reality of these qualities is clearly accepted by the Working Party in their embracing of the structure provided by the Task Group on Assessment and Testing (DES, 1988a), illustrated in the statement and diagram in Figure 6.

We accept TGAT's rough estimate, illustrated by the graph below, concerning the spread of pupil performance about the mean at four reporting ages. As noted by TGAT, we might expect the most able 10 per cent of pupils to attain higher levels than those indicated by the dotted lines (e.g. Level 6 or higher at age 11). Similarly, some of the least able 10 per cent of pupils may have difficulty with, for example, Level 1 at age 7 and Level 2 at age 11. (*ibid*: 83)

There are two points of interpretation to be made concerning this diagram before any discussion of its implications. Firstly, the presentation of the graph on a ruled and scaled background is in some tension with the use of the expression 'rough estimate'. Nevertheless, we may assume that the assertion being made is that the form of the relationships embodied in the graph are correct, even if not the precise quantities involved; we must be duly circumspect regarding the level of precision of any quantitative inferences that we make. Secondly, the vertical scale is labelled conventionally as an ordinal scale, but this is contradicted by the positioning of the points showing the expected levels at key reporting ages, and by the use of a continuous line. Furthermore, the terminal level (i.e. at age 16) of the average student is indicated as 6/7, clearly indicative of a greater degree of continuity than the discrete labelling should represent; I have therefore presumed both scales to be continuous.

The graph represents a relationship between three variables: achievement (measured by Levels); age (measured in years); and ability (represented as a percentile within an ordered population). It

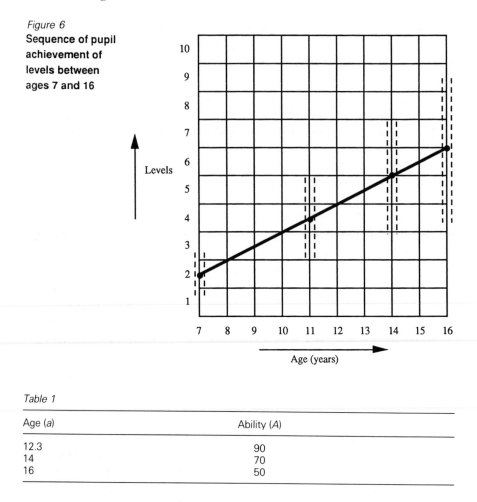

Figure 6

Sequence of pupil achievement of levels between ages 7 and 16

Levels

Age (years)

Table 1

Age (a)	Ability (A)
12.3	90
14	70
16	50

should be noted that age and achievement are directly measurable (the latter in terms of performance on stoats),[29] whilst ability is to be inferred.[30] Focusing on achievement level 6/7, and taking measurements directly from the graph,[31] the following table (Table 1) can be produced.

From which a least squares estimate generates the following relation between age and ability:

$$A = \frac{2213}{a} - 89$$

If we now substitute in the value of 10 for A, the formula produces 22 as the age (in years) at which a student with a level of ability at the tenth percentile (i.e. the lowest included on the graph) will be expected to reach the level of attainment equivalent to that of the median student at the end of compulsory schooling. On the other hand, a student at the 90th percentile of ability will complete 'normal' schooling by the age of 12.3 (from the graph); there is a real sense in which age and ability are interchangeable with respect to achievement. An 'equal opportunities' principle might therefore suggest that the school leaving age be reduced to (say) 14 for the most able students, in order to allow for the least able to remain in attendance until 22; it is interesting that current practice appears to adopt the opposite strategy.

The second form of pronouncement which the voice of authority makes on the student is the principle of unity. This is closely associated with the notion of utilitarianism, and can be summarised as follows: skills and knowledges which are elaborated in one context will be available to the student in (potentially) all other contexts; the student is in this sense a cognitively *unified* subject.[32] This often takes the form of a presumption of basic or generic skills, thus the Cockcroft Committee (recognizing the lack of evidence for the immediate utility of mathematics which had been provided by their research projects) stated that:

> However great the effort which is made, illustrations of the practical applications of mathematics within employment which are given to a group of pupils, whose members may enter many different types of job, cannot provide the immediacy of the actual job itself. Nevertheless, **it is important that the mathematical foundation which has been provided in the classroom should be such as to enable competence in particular applications to develop within a reasonably short time once the necessary employment situation is encountered**. (Cockcroft, 1982: 24; emphasis in original)

and the Secretaries of State:

> We are concerned that the suggested weightings give too little emphasis to the essential foundation of knowledge, skills and understanding which pupils need to tackle practical problems. (DES, 1988b: iii)

The principle of unity also provides the legitimate basis for the compilation of the Attainment Targets as decontextualized stoats.

Thus the voice of authority reads the National Curriculum as attributing to the student an essential ability and age — the former being fixed, and the latter progressing with time — and a consciousness displaying open-architecture.

The Nature of the Student: The Voice of Critique

It may be contended that the authoritarian inferences that are drawn from the diagram in Figure 6 are not valid, the diagram is not meant to be taken quite so literally, it is an allusion to a general structure, nothing more. The response of critique (authority does not respond to criticism) would be to ask 'if the graph does not mean what authority has described, then precisely why not, and precisely what does it mean?' In fact, the graph summarises the particular form of child-centredness which informs the National Curriculum, which, as authority has stated, delimits the effectiveness of the curriculum. The assumption is that performances (in terms of the statements of attainment) are produced by underlying competences which may develop, but only at a rate determined by some combination of the essential qualities 'age' and 'ability'; effective education should aim to maximise the development of these competences.

Furthermore, there may be different strategies or pedagogies which are deemed to be appropriate for different levels of 'age' and 'ability' (as seems to be implied by the references to pupils' 'needs' in the non-statutory guidance (NCC, 1989), these pedagogies are sometimes structured according to a fourth variable 'maturity'; an example will serve as an illustration. The third, fourth and fifth year course of *SMP 11–16* is divided into three tracks which the publicity material describes as follows:

> It is assumed that pupils will be grouped in sets in years 3, 4 and 5, and each series is designed for a different level.
> - **Green (G)** for those whose attainment level is below average — roughly below the 60th percentile*
> - **Blue (B)** with its upper branch **Red (R)** for the broad middle band–from about the 25th to the 60th percentile*
> - **Yellow (Y)** for the highest attainers — the top 20 — 25 per cent or so*

*These percentages will, of course, vary from school to school.[33]
(*SMP 11–16* publicity material, Cambridge University Press; my numbered footnote)

A brief comparison between the 'green'[34] and 'yellow' books will illustrate a possibility with respect to pedagogic differentiation. The 'yellow' series comprises properly bound books of around 150 pages each, and most of the pages give the impression of being full of words and symbols; the front cover of most of the books has an enigmatic design or photograph. The 'green' series are stapled books of around 60 pages, each page being far less densely covered in words and symbols; the covers generally show some aspect or act of measuring. The chapter titles of the 'yellow' series are simple and descriptive of their content — 'Negative Numbers and Equations'[35] — tasks very often include additional non-mathematical knowledge (information concerning the period and frequency of the vibrations of a fly's wing, for example), and references to school generally relate to the content of school lessons — frequently science. The chapter titles of the 'green' books include some more sensationalist headings — 'Cheapo rulers', 'Detective dice' — as well as the more mundane entries, many of the tasks include non-mathematical information which can hardly be referred to as 'informative', since it is clearly invented, and sometimes entirely fictitious (sometimes bizarre: 'Angle fish sleep nose down'), and references to school generally relate to organisation rather than content (the school timetable, for example).

The differentiation in pedagogy represented by these two series is startlingly redolent of the differentiation between the tabloid and the 'serious' press in the UK, the latter being associated with a readership differentiated in terms of socio-economic class (Tunstall, 1983). Furthermore, through their heavy use of comic strips, competitions and glittery advertisements, and their frequent tendency to celebrate 'naughtiness', certain tabloid newspapers might be described as constructing the working class — their principal readership — as childlike or 'immature' — at least intellectually. The 'serious' press, on the other hand, select only the most cerebral of *double entendres*, and generally emphasise independence, being informed, etc., constructing the middle class as 'mature'[36] and adult. This analogy suggests that 'maturity' might be an appropriate label for the pedagogic differentiation prescribed by SMP 11–16, 'maturity' being a function of 'ability' and 'age' such that 'immature' is applied to *either* low 'ability' or low 'age' (inclusive 'or'), just as it is applied to low socioeconomic status.

This potential link between class and 'maturity' — however speculative, and however tenuous — may be illustrative of a pedagogic practice which stereotypes the 'successful' student as essentially middle class, and the 'failure' as working class. An attribution to an individual student as having 'ability' — and even 'special needs' — presumes that this quality can be measured via assessment practices; but if these practices embody class-related stereotypes, then we may not be surprised if academic outcomes are socially structured. Ray Rist (1986) has provided illustrations of some of the possible mechanisms of such stereotyping in relation to socioeconomic class.[37]

The Mathematics Working Party has made explicit and positive reference to stereotyping:

> There is also evidence to suggest that some methods of assessment favour boys and others favour girls. Boys are more likely to do well when the assessment concentrates on timed written tests in which mathematical knowledge and skills carry more weight than communication skills. This is especially true when multiple choice items are included. Girls are more likely to do well when the assessment takes into account their progress over a longer period of time and gives recognition to the importance of communication skills and personal qualities such as perseverance. It is also reported that collaborative group work assists girls in overcoming their lack of confidence in tackling unfamiliar questions. (DES, 1988b: 86)

In other words, girls lack confidence and the ability to think quickly, but are good at working with people and will work very hard. These features are presumed to be essential qualities possessed by (all?) girls but not by (any?) boys;[38] if such stereotypical images are widely held, then we might not be surprised at the findings reported by Walden & Walkerdine (1985) and Walkerdine *et al.* (1989) to the effect that when students did succeed in mathematics, it was often believed to be the result of genuine ability, or flair in the case of boys, and hard work in the case of girls.

It is likely that assessment practices also involve race-related[39] and age-related stereotypes, and stereotypes relating to ablebodiedness etc. However, the Working Party simply lists 'some of the problems of children with special needs, and the groups with whom these problems are generally associated' (DES, 1988b: 88), and explicitly denies any responsibility in respect of antiracism:

... the key principle is that the attainment targets and programmes of study are the **same** for **all** pupils **regardless of
race**. (DES, 1988b: 87; emphasis in original)

suggesting that 'undue emphasis on multicultural mathematics [...]
could confuse young children' (*ibid*) and that:

... priority must be given to ensuring that [children] have the
knowledge, understanding and skills which they will need for
**adult life and employment in Britain in the twenty-first
century**. We believe that most ethnic minority parents would
share this view. We have not therefore included any 'multicultural' aspects in any of our attainment targets. (*ibid*; emphasis in original)[40]

Such a celebration of racism brings into relief the fundamental failure
of 'equal opportunities' approaches: precisely what the opportunities
are for is rarely questioned; and, since the opportunities are there,
there can be only one source of blame should they not be taken up,
and this must relate to some essential quality of the student.[41]

Pedagogic differentiation may also facilitate differences in performance in a more direct way, and this relates to the concept of
utilitarianism. If it is the case, for example, that students assessed as
having low 'ability' are directed towards a more mundane curriculum,
concentrating on 'everyday' activities such as the use of money, or the
school timetable, whilst students assessed as having high 'ability'
engage in a form of curriculum which is forever introducing more
exotic ideas, then we might expect a difference in respective 'success',
and certainly in respective motivation. As Lave has suggested (with
respect to the USA):

There is a widespread preoccupation with the responsibility of
schools in the preparation of children for life after school. And
further, there is an assumption that without such preparation
school alumni might be unable to do math. (Lave, 1988: 100)

A consideration of the pedagogic differentiation displayed in the *SMP*
materials suggests that such a 'preoccupation' relates to 'academic' life
after school for children with 'ability' and 'everyday' life after school
for those without. However, as has already been stated, Lave's empirical work with adults suggests a clear differentiation in performance

between quotidian maths and school maths: people are generally quite competent at the former (otherwise it would not be 'everyday'), even when not so with the latter; Spradbery's research (*op cit*) indicates that this may well also be the case for school students. We might therefore interpret the 'mundane' form of curriculum being presented to those with low 'ability' as an attempt to teach them something they already know how to do. Furthermore, since — following Lave — it is very likely that the methods used in school will be very different from those actually used in the relevant practices, the 'mundane'·curriculum is also tantamount to a statement that the students can't do what they nevertheless do do every day; such a dissonance does not, of course, arise in the more 'academic' curriculum.

The principle of unity espoused by the voice of authority clearly comes under some threat by the evidence that has been referred to concerning the differentiation of performances between school and non-school 'mathematical' activities. There is even some evidence that comparatively competent mathematicians do not 'transfer' their knowledge to other contexts which are academic but not mathematical (Trelinski, 1983). An alternative to the principle of unity is to understand knowledge as essentially contextualized, thus the labelling of a list of decontextualized skills as significant to one or more actual practices is, precisely, to distort and reduce these practices and fetishise the skills list. The human subject is, perhaps, more appropriately understood as fragmented, engaging in diverse sets of practices — diverse contexts — which each have their own rules (Dowling, 1986). It is clearly possible for a human subject to make metaphorical connexions between contexts, and this may be an element of creative work: but the structure and content of the Attainment Targets seems hardly likely to encourage creativity.

The voice of critique challenges the attribution of essential qualities to students, and directs attention onto the curriculum itself and, particularly, the assessment practices and resulting pedagogic differentiation within the curriculum. Again, the provision of specific alternatives would run counter to the project of this paper, and is left to another day.

Conclusion: The Shogun's Voice?

I have presented two readings of the National Curriculum in mathematics as it relates to the nature of school mathematics and to the nature of the student. The voice of authority asserts that mathematics is a corpus which can be minutely divided and sequenced, and which has use-values in diverse practices. On the other hand, the critical voice questions the bases for the fragmentation and ordering of mathematics, and finds none. Instead, it is found that the Attainment Targets and Statements of Attainment represent — at best — an uneasy alliance of memories of bygone teaching programmes together with the very worst of contemporary practice in which mathematics is imagined to be a collection of algorithms and empiricist exercises. Indeed, it is suggested that any hierarchising of a curriculum will involve the perpetual deferring of 'correct' concepts — which have no ontological bases — through representation as a sequence of potentially contradictory synecdochic images: emergence into the light of erudition is possible only through the suspension of rationality in favour of algorithmic obedience in deference to the superiority of the teacher.

The promised use-values never arrive. It is likely that those assessed as 'less able' in fact are able to see this before the others: their mundane curriculum simply offers them new and complicated solutions to problems that they can already solve far more simply; they can quickly see through the lie that is the principle of intellectual unity. Perversely, both differentiation in terms of pedagogy and universality in terms of objectives — the one asserting diversity of needs, the other, the identity of unquestioned goals — presume to attribute essential qualities to students, qualities which define the limits of curricular effectiveness, and which place the blame for failure onto the student her/himself.

The voices of authority and critique are entirely different in timbre, but ultimately, they sing the same tune: authority overinflates itself with its bombastic assertiveness, bursting in a whiff of flatulence under the atmospheric pressure of its inherent irony; critique resembles closer the unpeeling of the balloon. But there is a third voice which has not been heard for a while. It may be that, having learned mathematics, the Shogun soon realized that his power lay in maintaining his subjects in a state of perpetual — but possibly differential — ignorance. His methods of achieving this might have stopped (as far as mathematics was concerned) at giving the occasional display of his extreme knowledge by rattling off a line or two of jargon. On the other hand, he might have constructed a system of compulsory instruction, in which members of the population were fed little pieces of mathematics, in themselves decontextualized and irrelevant, he might have given them regular tests and promised — to the talented few — wealth and, best of all, enlightenment: the disappointment felt when enlightenment never came might be compensated by position and power. The Shogun would realise that no amount of mathematics made available in this way could possibly weaken his own position, any more than it could assist the population. Because he would have realised that his power and control lay, not in mathematics itself. The power of the Shogun lay in the discursive practices which partitioned, distributed, and rationed knowledge, whilst rendering as non-knowledge any understanding of the practices themselves: critical knowledge was, after all, never on the agenda. The Shogun could have made good use of the National Curriculum, especially in a society exhibiting the virtual exclusion of the word 'no'.

Acknowledgements

I would like to acknowledge the constructive criticism by Parin Bahl, Richard Noss and David Pimm on earlier drafts of this paper.

Notes

1 For Education and Science and for Wales.
2 And, of course, 'advisers advise and ministers decide'.
3 As an aside, the collective experience and knowledge of a working party can clearly be interpreted as relating more or less directly to someone else's (or some other group's) validating criteria, that is, to those of the individual or group responsible for selecting its membership (pointed out by Basil Bernstein in a private communication). See also Brown, in this volume, on the notion of 'good practice'.
4 It seems unlikely that any such deductive process from these starting points would be able to generate the National Curriculum in mathematics without considerable distortion of the original work.
5 As opposed to DES and associated bodies' publications, Local Education Authority Guidelines, books for teachers, etc.
6 This research is critically discussed in Dec O'Reilly's paper in this volume, and also in Noss, Goldstein and Hoyles, 1989.
7 They also visited the Federal Republic of Germany which (as they state) did not take part in these tests; it is not entirely clear why West Germany was added nor, indeed, why this particular selection of countries was made — see Brown and Dowling, 1989.
8 The Programmes of Study are, metaphorically, the Attainment Targets written across the page rather than down.
9 See the section below on 'the nature of the student'.
10 See also Noss, in this volume.
11 This is the first time that the qualifier 'whole' is used in this series (although it appears in a stoat at Level 3 concerning negative numbers);

it is not clear whether or not this implies that the earlier stoats are taken to include fractions and irrationals and possibly complex numbers; counting up to 10 in the rationals would be an interesting 'can do' achievement.

12 Levels 5 and 6 also contain stoats relating to ratio.

13 I find it intriguing that school is generally not considered to be 'real-life'.

14 And by Noss *et al.* (1989) with particular reference to the Graded Assessments in Mathematics Project (GAIM, 1987).

15 The Task Group on Assessment and Testing (TGAT; DES, 1988a) introduce the notion of intrinsic *difficulty* associated with the subject: it seems reasonable to resolve this conception into two components relating, respectively, to the logical structure of mathematics (in this case) and the psychology of the learner.

16 Who have informed me that the scheme is used in more than 50 per cent of secondary schools in the UK; this percentage would certainly be much higher if it related to England and Wales alone — the area covered (nominally) by the National Curriculum.

17 Especially considering the membership of the Working Party.

18 Which might direct us towards the criticisms made of the Report of the Task Group on Assessment and Testing (TGAT: DES, 1988a) by Goldstein (in this volume).

19 And no account at all of recent developments: see, for example, the chapters by Hoyles, Mellar, Sutherland, and Wolf in this volume.

20 I am not aware of any available classroom research in this area.

21 This problem is also mentioned by Wolf, in this volume.

22 Using a program in the SMILE scheme.

23 So far, only one student teacher has presented me with something which she claimed to be (and which looked like) the beginnings of a proof.

24 Selwyn (1980) offers an amusing example of mathematics being considered in this way.

25 Edmund Leach (1973) incorrectly defines 'metonymy' as the substitution of the part for the whole; he is, in fact, defining 'synecdoche' and, of course, I am using the term metaphorically.

26 This conclusion derives from an understanding of linguistic elements as lacking any positive quality or meaning in themselves, rather, meaning is a quality of the multiple relationships between elements. This understanding is to be attributed to work inspired by the structural linguistics of Ferdinand de Saussure (1972 edn); see, also, Culler (1976), Dowling (1990), Williamson (1978)

27 I am not denying the label 'mathematics' to shopping and other everyday, working, and even academic practices, although it is not immediately obvious that the use of this label serves any useful purpose. I am simply suggesting that the various occurrences of 'mathematics' arise out of distinctive social contexts: we cannot simply cut out the 'mathematical' bit and move it around (see Dowling, 1989).

28 Which is not to say that this should never be attempted — tentatively, of course: see, for example, Brown and Dowling (1989 and forthcoming).

29 Potential stoats (posts) at the time when the DES document was prepared.

30 There may exist some work which provides adequate support for the relationship between ability and stoat (or post) performance; unfortunately, I have been unable to locate it; in any event, evidence is not required by the voice of authority.

31 I've actually used the graph on page 83 of *Mathematics for Ages 5 to 16*, (DES, 1988b) and not the reproduction in Figure 6.

32 See Dowling (1986, 1990), Laclau (1984) and Williamson (1978) for some discussion of fragmentation in the subject.

33 Using the formula derived from the TGAT graph, students at the 60th percentile ($A = 40$) would need to stay at school until the age of 17, whilst those at the 20th could leave at 13.

34 Generally speaking, the books are not produced in a colour which matches the track: 'Green' Book 1 is, for example, orange.

35 Examples used here are taken from Books Y1 and G1.

36 A simplification is here being imposed on this term which is, in the context of education at least, highly slippery — see Walkerdine *et al.* (1989).

37 See, also, Heath (1986) and the seminal work of Bernstein (1971; 1977) with respect to linguistic mechanisms

38 And here is another example of a penchant for empiricism on the part of the Working Party: at no stage is there any attempt to provide any explanation for these differences.

39 See Brown and Dowling (1989) for a brief discussion of possible race-related stereotyping in teacher education.

40 It is also interesting that Kenneth Baker did not feel it necessary to admonish the Working Party for this failure to follow his instruction to 'take account of the ethnic and cultural diversity of the school population and society at large' (DES, 1988b: 96) — he was quick to respond critically in other respects. It is also unclear how many of the Working Party were associated with 'ethnic minority' groups: the list of names in *Mathematics for Ages 5 to 16* (ibid) is not encouraging.

41 See also Brown, in this volume, in relation to an equivalent pathologising of teachers.

References

BATH, University of, 1981, *Mathematics in Employment (16–19)*, Bath: University of Bath.

BERNSTEIN, B., 1971, *Class, Codes and Control, Volume 1: Theoretical Studies Towards a Sociology of Language*, London: Routledge and Kegan Paul.

BERNSTEIN, B., 1977, *Class, Codes and Control, Volume 3: — Towards a Theory of Educational Transmissions*, London: Routledge and Kegan Paul.

BROWN, A. and DOWLING, P.C., 1989, *Towards a Critical Alternative to Internationalism and Monoculturalism in Mathematics Education, working paper number 10*, London: Centre for Multicultural Education, Institute of Education, University of London.

COCKCROFT, W.H. *et al.*, 1982, *Mathematics Counts*, London: HMSO.

CORRAN, G. and WALKERDINE, V., 1981, *The Practice of Reason, volume 1: Reading the Signs*, mimeo, University of London Institute of Education.

CULLER, J., 1976, *Saussure*, London: Fontana.

DES AND WELSH OFFICE, 1988a, *National Curriculum Task Group on Assessment and Testing: A Report*, London: DES.

DES AND WELSH OFFICE, 1988b, *Mathematics for Ages 5 to 16*, London: HMSO.

DES AND WELSH OFFICE, 1989, *Mathematics in the National Curriculum*, London: HMSO.

DOWLING, P.C., 1986, *Mathematics Makes the Difference: A Sociological Approach to School Mathematics*, unpublished MA dissertation, Institute of Education, University of London.

DOWLING, P.C., 1989, 'The contextualizing of mathematics: Towards a theoretical map' in *Collected Original Resources in Education*, **13**, 2.

DOWLING, P.C., 1990, 'Some notes towards a theoretical model for reproduction, action and critique' in NOSS, R. *et al.* (Eds) *Political Dimensions of Mathematics Education: Action and Critique, Proceedings of the First International Conference*, London: Department of Mathematics, Statistics and Computing, Institute of Education, University of London.

DOWLING, P.C., 1990a, 'Mathematics in the marketplace: The National Curriculum and numerical control' in *Teaching London Kids*, 26.

FOUCAULT, M., 1981, 'The Order of discourse' in YOUNG, R. (Ed.) *Untying the Text: a poststructuralist reader*, London: Routledge and Kegan Paul.

GAIM, 1987, *Graded Assessments in Mathematics Development Pack: Teachers' Handbook*, King's College, University of London.

GEERTZ, C., 1973, *The Interpretation of Cultures*, New York: Basic Books.

HART, K.M., 1981, *Children's Understanding of Mathematics: 11–16*, London: John Murray.

HEATH, S.B., 1986, 'Questioning at home and at school: A comparative study' in HAMMERSLEY, M. (Ed.) *Case Studies in Classroom Research*, Milton Keynes: Open University Press.

HOWSON, G. and WILSON, B., 1986, *School Mathematics in the 1990s*, Cambridge: Cambridge University Press.

LACLAU, E., 1984, 'Transformations of advanced industrial societies and the theory of the subject' in HANNINEN, S. and PALDAN, L. (Eds) *Re-thinking Ideology*, Berlin: Argument-Verlag.

LAVE, J., 1988, *Cognition in Practice*, Cambridge: Cambridge University Press.

LAVE, J., MURTAUGH, M. and DE LA ROCHA, O., 1984, 'The dialectic of arithmetic in grocery shopping' in ROGOFF, B. and LAVE, J. (Eds) *Everyday Cognition: Its Development in Social Context*, Cambridge, Mass.: Harvard University Press.

LEACH, E., 1973, 'Structuralism in Social Anthropology' in ROBEY, D. (Ed.) *Structuralism: An Introduction*, Oxford: Clarendon.

MASON, J., BURTON, L. and STACEY, K., 1982, *Thinking Mathematically*, London: Addison-Wesley.

NATIONAL CURRICULUM COUNCIL, 1988, *National Curriculum Consultation Report: Mathematics*, London: NCC.

NATIONAL CURRICULUM COUNCIL, 1989, *Mathematics Non-statutory Guidance*, York: NCC.

Noss, R., Goldstein, H. and Hoyles, C., 1989, 'Graded assessments and learning hierarchies in mathematics' in *British Educational Research Journal*, **15**, 2, pp. 109–120.

Pimm, D., 1987, Speaking Mathematically, London: Routledge and Kegan Paul.

Rist, R.C., 1986, 'Student social class and teacher expectations: The self-fulfilling prophecy in ghetto education' in Hammersley, M. (Ed.) *Case Studies in Classroom Research*, Milton Keynes: Open University Press.

Saussure, F. de, 1972 edn, *Course in General Linguistics*, London: Duckworth.

Selwyn, J., 1980, 'Noitcarf numbers' in *Mathematics Teaching*, 90.

Sewell, B., 1981, *Uses of Mathematics by Adults in Daily Life*, London: ACACE.

Shell Centre for Mathematical Education, nd, *Report of Interviews for the Cockcroft Committee*, unpublished transcripts, University of Nottingham.

Spradbery, J., 1976, 'Conservative Pupils? Pupil resistance to curriculum innovations in mathematics' in Whitty, G. and Young, M.F.D. (Eds) *Explorations in the Politics of School Knowledge*, Driffield: Nafferton.

Trelinski, G., 1983, 'Spontaneous mathematization of situations outside mathematics' in *Educational Studies in Mathematics*, **14**, 3.

Tunstall, J., 1983, *The Media in Britain*, London: Constable.

Walden, R. and Walkerdine, V., 1985, *Girls and Mathematics: From Primary to Secondary Schools*, Bedford Way Paper no. 24, London University Institute of Education.

Walkerdine, V. and The Girls and Mathematics Unit, 1989, *Counting Girls Out*, London: Virago.

Walkerdine, V., 1982, 'From Context to text: a psychosemiotic approach to abstract thought' in Beveridge, M. (Ed.) *Children Thinking Through Language*, London: Arnold.

Williamson, J., 1978, *Decoding Advertisements: Ideology and Meaning in Advertising*, London: Marion Boyars.

Theme 2
Assessing assessment

3 The Fundamental Assumptions of National Assessment

Harvey Goldstein

Introduction

Of all the innovations in the 1988 education act, arguably the most important and most influential in the long term, will be the proposed system of National Assessment. The basic framework for this was the report of the Task Group on Assessment and Testing (TGAT), published in January 1988 (DES, 1988a). Most of the Report's major assumptions were accepted and are being implemented by the present government, through the Schools Examination and Assessment Council (SEAC), a government appointed body with wide powers to regulate and develop school examinations and assessments. Academic and research institutions have obtained contracts to prepare the details, principally in the form of 'standard assessment tasks' (SATs).

The speed with which the TGAT proposals were formulated and then operationalised has left little room for discussion of the more fundamental issues around a national assessment system and, this paper argues, has led to severe problems. In the paper I shall examine the notion of criterion referenced assessment, the proposals for teacher assessment, for the reporting of results, and the issue of gender and other 'bias'.

It is worth noting that the National Curriculum has been conceived in subject terms with little serious attempt to formulate genuine cross curricular structures. This has important implications for modes of learning and to some extent also for assessment. In particular, a cross curricular perspective would make the notion of 'learning hierarchies' more difficult to sustain and would also force assessments to take more account of contextual issues. This latter issue is discussed below, but space does not allow a more detailed exploration of all the implications of a subject based curriculum.

In the following sections I will argue that the surface plausibility which adheres to these issues begins to fall away when examined closely. I will also attempt to draw some conclusions and to suggest that there are more systematically rational approaches to assessment and 'standards' than so far have been proposed.

Criterion Referenced Assessment

Criterion referenced assessment ideas feature prominently in the arguments in the TGAT report. They also appear in the reports of the curriculum working parties which were set up to formulate the detailed structures of the National Curriculum in each subject.

The idea of criterion referenced assessment became articulated in the 1960s (Popham and Husek, 1969) as an attempt to link assessment to learning objectives. In the 1980s it has seen a resurgence in the UK; in grade criteria for the new 16 year old school leaving qualification, the General Certificate of Secondary Education (GCSE), in the graded assessment movement, in some of the early work on profiling and now in the attainment targets for the national curriculum. Often crudely interpreted in terms of 'can do' statements, it is promoted as a provider of practical information about what a pupil has 'learnt and mastered' (TGAT § 94). The report's claim is that 'Norm referenced approaches conceal changes in national standards.... Only by criterion referencing can standards be monitored.' (§ 222). The report provides no indication how such 'standards' are to be derived and communicated. In any case, the difficulty (if not impossibility) of measuring changes over time has little to do with the form of the assessment or the educational philosophy behind it. The difficulty arises from the fact that an assessment used at one time will generally need to be updated periodically to reflect curriculum changes, the introduction of new technology or language, and so forth. This means that the assessment instruments or tasks change over time and no 'absolute' standard or scale is feasible (Goldstein, 1983).

Attempts to produce descriptions of 'mastery' based on criterion referenced ideas have needed to operate at a level of generality which has demanded a set of 'context free' descriptions. Thus, for example, the report on Mathematics Attainment Targets in the National Curriculum (National Curriculum Council, 1988) quotes a specimen maths attainment target as: 'Select materials and the mathematics to use for a practical task'. In reality, the information upon which any such description can be based will be limited, and to make a decontextualised statement of achievement on such a base requires major assumptions. The single example for each target, given alongside, is hardly sufficient. In short, we have to assume that such statements can be applied in the far greater number of contexts which were not observed. What we do know is that in general this cannot be done. The work of the APU in mathematics, for example, has shown how something as simple as a change in presentation format can change performance markedly (APU 1986) and the same is true in language assessment (Thornton, 1986). There is now beginning to be some systematic research into this area, and this is exploring the ways in which learning and understanding are linked to the contexts surrounding the learner, her motivation and her perceptions of purpose (Wolf, 1987; Walkerdine, 1984).

The TGAT report, on the other hand, has no doubts. There is no recognition there that problems may exist and we are informed simply that 'the system is also required ... to play an active part in raising standards of attainment. Criterion referencing inevitably follows'. (§ 222).

Teacher Assessment and Moderation

There are two distinct kinds of assessment discussed in the TGAT report. One is a series of centrally designed 'standardized assessment tasks', both written and practical. The report spends time arguing in favour of 'innovative' and interesting tasks which can be incorporated into daily teaching. These tasks will be marked by teachers who will receive relevant training.

The other kind of assessment is that to be done by the teachers themselves on the basis of their pupils' general work and in the same 'profile component' areas covered by the centralized assessment. The report devotes much space to describing how the teachers' results are to be made compatible with each other and with the centralised assessment. The report recommends that 'teachers' ratings be moderated in such a way as to convey and to inform national standards.' (§ 62). It suggests that, if left alone, 'teachers' expectations (of what is normal) become the teachers' standards' (§ 65). The report recognizes that 'teachers' rank orders ... may vary systematically from rank orders provided by test users (§ 66)', and so the notion of teacher assessment adopted by TGAT is one where such differences are eliminated.

Where teacher assessment is a matter for discussion, negotiation and recording between pupil, teacher and parent, then there is no requirement to convey national standards, nor indeed for teachers to agree among themselves. Furthermore, such locally based assessment is in many respects more appropriate as the basis for decisions about curriculum provision, individualized teaching schemes and so forth. It is precisely its ability to reflect local conditions which makes it valuable. It is only where comparability is paramount that the above requirement is seen to be necessary. Yet neither the first report nor the supplementary reports recognize this distinction and by implication, therefore, would seem to place lower value on those elements of teacher assessment which do not accord with the centralized assessment. A likely consequence is that teacher assessment would become restricted to just those things which can also be measured by centralized tasks. Indeed, the report itself seems to envisage this when it recommends that 'support items, procedures and training be provided to help teachers relate their own assessments to the targets and assessment criteria of the national curriculum.' (§ 116).

Since the TGAT report, the role of teacher assessment seems to have been reduced in importance, while that of the SATs has increased. It is also becoming clear to many people that assessment instruments which are designed for public reporting of results are inappropriate for 'diagnostic' assessment of learning opportunities and difficulties. If teacher assessment becomes very strongly linked to the SATs and hence of the school reporting process, it is then not very relevant for diagnosis.

Reporting School Results

National assessment is a central feature of the 1988 Education Reform Act. The proposals to use these assessments to make comparisons between schools will also become the most important part of the system.

The TGAT report proposes that, for profile components, or groupings of these, each school should report its average level (or distribution of levels) at ages 11, 14 and 16. Although it recommends against publishing the results at seven years, this has been rejected by the Secretary of State for Education who strongly recommends that each school's seven year results should be reported (DES, 1988c). The report also suggests that at the same time, a report is attached describing the socioeconomic and other characteristics of the area surrounding the school. The implication of this is that parents and other users

Table 1 *Average LEA exam scores*

| | | Rank Orderings | | |
| LEA | Unadjusted | Adjusted | | |
		A	B	C
Harrow	1	1	1	4
Barnet	2	2	35	27
Coventry	59	5	7	1
Haringey	90	91	79	66

of these results will be able to make allowance for these factors when comparing the performances of schools.

Needless to say this is easier said than done. Apart from the obvious problem that there will often be a mismatch between the characteristics of a school neighbourhood and those of the children actually attending the school, it is unsurprising that the report fails to suggest precisely how the allowance is to be made. The various efforts by others in this area, notably the ILEA, have been unsuccessful. It has been known for some time that such attempts to 'adjust' or allow for influential factors solely using 'aggregated' data, are difficult if not impossible. For example, Woodhouse and Goldstein (1988) carried out such analyses for exam results aggregated to the LEA level, using data from the DES. The results, in Table 1, are based on an analysis relating average LEA exam results to socioeconomic and demographic factors.

The first column gives the rankings of the three LEAs shown using just the unadjusted exam results. Column A gives the results after adjustment for socioeconomic and demographic factors, as presented by Gray and Jesson (1987). Their statistical model was then slightly modified and column B gives the rankings thus obtained. Column C gives the rankings from a further modified model.

In terms of describing the observed data, all three models do equally well and there is no objective way of choosing between them. Yet the results for individual LEA's can vary markedly. It is, to put it mildly, somewhat optimistic of the authors of the TGAT report to suppose that very much sense could be made of its own proposals. This is especially so since the report ignores the single most important factor influencing achievement during schooling, namely the achievement of the pupils at time of entry to school. Indeed, it seems that the proposals cannot be implemented in their present form.

There is now a widespread interest in measuring school effectiveness, using a variety of procedures, qualitative as well as quantitative, but none of them is free of problems and there is no real consensus on how, or indeed whether, it can be done satisfactorily. Most recently, some workers have advocated the use of 'multilevel' statistical models (Aitkin and Longford, 1986), but these too have their problems and there is no guarantee that they would be able to supply convincing school comparisons, even if the resources were available to utilize them. Perhaps the most extensive analysis along such lines has been that of examination results in the Inner London Education Authority (Nuttall *et al.*, 1989). This confirms that analyses which use school averages can be highly misleading. The analysis also finds that schools differ along more than one dimension so that a single 'effectiveness' measure provides an incomplete picture. Thus, for example, the average difference in exam grades between those students who are in the top 25 per cent in terms of a verbal ability test score and those in the bottom 25 per cent on verbal ability, is just under 3 A grades at O-level.[1] This difference ranges from just under 2 A grades to just under 4 A grades across schools. The average difference between students of Pakistani origin and those originating from England, Scotland, Ireland or Wales, is about one A grade, but varies from zero to 2 A grades across schools. Likewise, the gender difference varies from school to school. All these differences are adjusted for the intake achievement (on verbal reasoning) and are only moderately intercorrelated.

In existing debates on the use of so called 'performance indicators' in schools (FitzGibbon, 1990) many of the same issues of using aggregated data arise. School examination and test results may well come to form the core of such indicator systems.

The importance of taking account of 'intake' achievement to a school and using multilevel analysis, is now widely recognized as the only secure starting point for comparing schools. Even so, the best that can be expected is that 'extreme' schools will be screened out. Such schools, whether apparently markedly good or markedly bad, would be available for further investigation by inspectors and advisors in collaboration with the schools and the Local Education Authorities. It would not be possible to say anything useful about the majority of schools which do not stand out, and in no way would it be legitimate for the results of such a screening programme by themselves to be used to pass judgement.

There is now plenty of evidence, much of it from the USA, that to use assessment results to compare schools promotes wasteful and unfair competition. It leads schools to concentrate on 'playing the assessment game', encouraging them to 'teach to the test' and to spend energy on finding ways to improve their test scores by means which are largely irrelevant to the true business of education. A spectacular example of this from the USA is the so-called 'Lake Wobegon' effect whereby every state in the USA was found to have an average test score above the national average! (Cannell, 1988).

Group Differences

Finally I would like to raise some problems of equity. I will discuss them in terms of gender, although the same general points apply to differences based on other classifications, for example ethnic groupings.

There are well known gender differences in various topic areas and according to test format. Thus, for example, girls perform relatively worse on multiple choice tests, and better on tests of 'verbal reasoning' at all ages. The scrutiny of test material for racial and sexual stereotyping is, by now, a standard procedure among test constructors.

Educational test constructors use the term 'bias' simply to refer to any item (or test) which shows differences between well defined groups. Thus, a multiple choice item might be described as biased in favour of boys if more boys obtained a correct answer, on average, than girls. Unfortunately, this procedure, which relies on the observation that some test items are more difficult for some individuals or groups of individuals, does not tell us what to do with those items. For example, should we regard the higher performance of girls on 'verbal' items as an indication of 'bias' or a 'real' reflection of girls' superiority? Should we eliminate multiple choice items on the grounds that they are biased in favour of boys?

Ultimately, the answers to such questions are political and ideological rather than technical. In general, by judicious selection, we can choose tests which on average will favour boys, or girls, or neither. We can also attempt to do this for ethnic group differences. In reality, of course, a choice always is made, even if unknowingly, for any assessment system. Often, this choice will be disguised by an appeal to historical precedent: namely that any new test should, broadly, reflect our current knowledge about matters such as group differences. The problem is that this 'knowledge' is essentially an historical accumulation of successive decisions of the same kind, and to a large extent therefore, reflects past cultural assumptions about such differences. Little research has been done in this area, so that we have no detailed account of how the process operates. Thus, it would be hardly surprising if the cultural assumptions and expectations of the early test constructors influenced their choice of test item contexts and hence gender differences. Gould (1981) demonstrates how a similar process influenced ethnic group differences on IQ tests.

Once such assumptions have become incorporated into existing tests it is not difficult to see how an historical determinism can be perpetuated. Unfortunately, the technical edifice which now supports the process of test construction tends to ignore such difficult issues, preferring to define the problems as technical rather than ideological or philosophical.

Essentially the same issue has been debated recently in the United States in the so called 'Golden Rule' case (Rooney, 1987). An out of court settlement in 1984 between the Golden Rule Insurance Company of Illinois, and Educational Testing Service (ETS) established the principle that, after following normal procedures for item selection in test construction, those remaining items which showed the smallest difference between blacks and whites were to be preferred.

In practice this procedure has led to difficulties in its implementation (Anrig, 1987). Nevertheless, one result has been that ETS have provided greater public access to their test construction materials and procedures. It is also interesting that the response of many psychometricians in the debate has been the standard one. Namely, to propose more refined statistical procedures for detecting statistical bias, to avoid, it seems, addressing the substantive issue which is largely political (see, for example, Anrig, 1988; Linn and Drasgow, 1987). A detailed discussion is given by Goldstein (1989).

Where the fate of individuals and institutions may depend on the results of such assessments, then equity suggests that the process of assessment design should be open to public scrutiny and debate, and it should, of course, be a debate principally about values, aims and consequencies.

Conclusions

This brief review inevitably is critical. None of the documents issued by the Schools Examination and Assessment Council, nor the TGAT report itself contain serious discussion of basic assumptions and major proposals are presented with an enthusiasm and conviction quite lacking in critical awareness.

While the idea that 'standards' will be raised appears throughout official pronouncements, there is little evidence for such a claim, nor is there much concern to define what is meant by 'standards'. Yet in some of the public debate there is a realization that there are different kinds of standards and different ways of changing them, most notably by providing extra resources.

Above all, as more of the 1988 Educational Reform Act comes into operation, so it becomes clear that the extreme haste in which many of its proposals were conceived, has produced undesirable consequences. Nowhere is this more apparent than in the area of assessment where the attempt to impose an elaborate structure upon an inadequately formulated theoretical base may eventually destroy the whole edifice.

Notes

1   The grading system for GCE and CSE is on a seven-point scale for each subject. The highest grade, 'A', receives a point score of 7, 'B' a score of 6 etc. Thus, for example, a difference of twenty-one points on the scale is equivalent to three extra 'A' grades. For each child, the total score is simply the sum of the separate subject scores.

References

AITKEN, M. and LONGFORD, N., 1986, 'Statistical modelling issues in school effectiveness studies', *Journal of the Royal Statistical Society*, A, **149**, pp. 1–43.

ANRIG, G.R., 1987, 'ETS on "Golden Rule"', *Educational Measurement, Issues and Practice*, **6**, pp. 24–7.

ANRIG, G.R., 1988, 'ETS replies to Golden Rule on "Golden Rule"', *Educational Measurement, Issues and Practice*, **7**, pp. 20–21.

Assessment of Performance Unit, 1986, *A Review of Monitoring in Mathematics, 1978–1982*, London: DES.

CANNELL, J.J., 1988, 'Nationally normed elementary achievement testing in America's public schools: How all 50 states are above the national average', *Educational Measurement; Issues and Practice*, **7**, pp. 5–9.

DES, 1988a, *National Curriculum: Task Group on Assessment and Testing, A report*, London: DES.

DES, 1988b, *National Curriculum: Task Group on Assessment and Testing, Three Supplementary Reports*, London: DES.

DES, 1988c, 'Kenneth Baker sets out principles for assessment and testing in schools', *Press Notice*, 175/88, June 7th 1988.

FITZGIBBON, C., 1990, *Performance Indicators — A dialogue*, BERA.

the hierarchies might not be universal but may depend on the school systems in which the tests are carried out. Finally, Hart's explanation of the test results in terms of recent topic exposure is an implicit admission that other differences could also be similarly explained, i.e. the differences in facilities used to construct the hierarchies.

Rather than explaining away the *Fraction* results as being atypical, we could ask whether they represent a more general consequence of the sampling methodology of the CSMS research, i.e. of the lack of control exerted over variables which could affect outcomes? There was, for example, no attempt made to allow for different teaching schemes as 'It soon became apparent that most teachers used a variety of source materials in their presentation.' (Hart, *et al.*: 1981). The research team did, however, analyse commonly used textbooks prior to the research 'in order that the researcher's view of the topic should not be at variance with the teacher's view of the same topic.' (Hart, 1980: 9).

The textbooks analysed were *SMP 1–4, SMP A–H, The Scottish Mathematics Project Group 1–5, Pattern and Power of Mathematics 1–7,* (Moakes, 1969) *Midland Mathematics Experiment GCE* and *CSE,* and *New Mathematics 1–4,* (Knight, 1967). Few, if any, of these are still in use today in their original form. Projects such as *SMP* have undergone several major revisions in response to the changing ideals and methods over the last decade. The question being raised here is whether a hierarchy constructed in the 1970s would be equally valid today?

Similarly, no attempt was made to compare styles of teaching 'since the research team did not observe the teachers.' (Hart, *et al.*, 1981: 6). She goes on to say that the researchers recognized that the effect of a teacher on how a child learns is very important but 'it was impossible to control for this particular aspect in the research being reported.' (Hart, *op cit*).

Given the aims of the research and the subsequent influence of its findings, one is struck by the lack of controls in a major research project of this nature: 'No attempt was made to control for socio-economic background of the pupils, size of school or the curriculum used in the school' (Hart, 1980: 56); another omission, is the absence of any data on the performance of girls. The failure to account for any input variables other than that of IQ is, I would suggest, a major weakness of the study and critically curtails the applicability of its findings concerning any general hierarchy of understanding.

Indeed, the APU surveys (APU, 1985) did take various background variables into account and found significant differences asso-

Figure 1

PROBLEM QUESTION 22
Shade in 1/6 of the dotted disc
What fraction of the whole disc
have you shaded?...........................

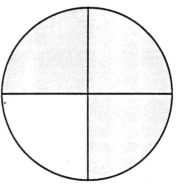

COMPUTATION QUESTION 10
$\dfrac{1}{6}$ of $\dfrac{3}{4}$.....................................

The correct responses were as follows:	P.22	C.10
CSMS	53%	23%
HASEMANN	30%	52%

ciated with many of them. Sex differences had an effect: 'In all five surveys at age 15, the mean scores of boys have been higher than the mean scores of girls in every sub-category with very few exceptions.' (APU, 1985: 698). Other variables such as the number of children taking free school dinners, school catchment area and regional differences were also found to exert significant effects on performance.

The Hierarchies

In the previous sections, I considered what might be termed the 'human elements' involved in constructing a hierarchy. In this section, I want to discuss the test items themselves i.e. the questions or part-questions which were used to form levels. I then want to look at the way these these levels were linked across topics to form stages.

The Levels: In order to produce a hierarchy, items were grouped into levels according to six criteria:

i)   they should be of approximately the same level of difficulty;
ii) the values of the homogeneity coefficient phi item/item should be at an acceptable level;
iii) the items should be linked (phi or Hij) with the items in both easier and harder groups;
iv) there should be some measure of mathematical coherence to the items;
v)   the groups should be scalable in the sense that a child's success (assessed as 2/3 correct) on a group entailed success on all easier groups;
vi) there should be no gross discrepancies when each age group's results were analysed in the same way.

This process was described by Hart as follows:

> To formulate a hierarchy, the items on each paper and pencil test were graded correct or incorrect, and were then ranked according to the percentage of right answers. This percentage is known as the 'facility' of an item. There was thus for each topic a list of ranked items. In order to form groups of items, a measure of association — the phi coefficient — was computed between every item and every other item on each test paper. This provided a guide to the items which tended to be solved successfully by the same individual children, and thus seemed to belong together. A criterion value of phi was arbitrarily decided upon and only items which reached this value with others in the same facility range were retained. (Hart *et al.*, 1985: 2)

Three observations are appropriate here. Firstly, it is not always clear whether the CSMS are writing about a hierarchy of questions or a cognitive hierarchy of children. The results of an empirical study are not sufficient in themselves to equate these distinct domains. Secondly, as Küchemann has acknowledged:

> There is no objective way of determining whether [phi] values of 0.4 and 0.6 are 'good'. The values are certainly significantly higher than would be expected by chance, but considering the

large number of children involved this does not say very much. (Küchemann, 1981: 303)

Finally, how mathematical coherence (criterion iv) was decided is not made clear.

Besides formulating levels of items, the aim was also to state that a child was 'at' a certain level. Attainment at any given level was defined as successfully solving about two-thirds of the items in that level and about two-thirds or more of the items in all easier levels. The two-thirds criterion was arbitrary, and in some cases the nearest fraction was taken. Thus a child is said to be 'at level 3' if he has scored at least two-thirds success on each of levels 1, 2 and 3, and not at level 4 or higher levels. The scalability of the hierarchy for each topic was tested by Guttman Scalogram Analysis, which counted the number of children who succeeded on harder levels without succeeding on all easier levels. Any grouping of items into levels which produced more than eight per cent of children succeeding on a harder level without succeeding on all easier levels was re-analysed.' (Hart *et al.*, 1985: 2).

The two-thirds criterion might be reasonable if there were many items at each level, but this is not always the case as Table 4 below indicates.

It can be seen that the number of items on a level ranges from as few as three to a maximum of twelve. It can also be observed that the criterion for being successful varies from 3/5 (60 per cent) to 4/5 (80 per cent).

Further criticisms of this procedure have been made by Noss, Goldstein and Hoyles (1989). Firstly, they point out that 'The grouping of items by difficulty and strength of association necessarily implies their subsequent scalability'. Furthermore, 'Items which did not fit, i.e. were not strongly associated with a group of other items, were omitted from the analysis'. On this second point the authors were in agreement with Ruthven (1986) who wrote 'The techniques of test design adopted by the researchers were such as to reduce the content validity of the tests, and to predispose results amenable to interpretation in hierarchical terms.' (p. 42)

In practice (see Table 5 below), between 26 and 57 per cent of the variables on every paper were excluded from the published hierarchies, and some hierarchies were not published at all.

Table 4   (From Hart et al., 1985)

Topic	Level:	1	2	3	4	5	6	7
				Attainment Levels and Criteria				
Algebra		4/6	5/7	5/8	6/9			
Fractions 1		2/3	7/10	7/11	3/4			
Fractions 2		7/10	5/8	2/3	3/5			
Graphs		5/7	4/6	7/11				
Measurement		5/7	5/8	3/5	3/5			
Place-value/Decimals		4/6	3/5	5/8	6/10	4/6	3/4	
Ratio/Proportion		3/5	3/5	4/6	3/4			
Reflection/Rotation		6/10	5/8	3/5	5/7	7/11		
Vectors		3/4	5/7	9/12	7/9	9/12	4/5	3/4

Table 5   (From Hart, 1980, Appendix 7 and Hart et al., 1985)

Topic	Total no of variables on CSMS tests	Variables excluded from final hierarchies — Number included in hierarchy	percentage excluded
Algebra	50	30	40
Fractions 1	60 (computations)	0	100
	42 (problems)	28	33
Fractions 2	65 (computations)	0	100
	45 (problems)	26	42
Graphs	56	24	57
Measurement	54	25	54
Place-value/ Decimals	73	39	47
Ratio	27	20	26
Reflections/ Rotations	56	41	27
Vectors	76	53	30
Number Ops.	14	(No hierarchy in monograph)	100
Positive/ Negative Nos.	57	36*	100
	Matrices core		
Matrices A	47 (3rd year)	26*	100
Matrices M	53 (4th year)	28*	100

* These test papers appeared in the original CSMS monograph but were not amongst those published by the NFER in The Chelsea Diagnostic Mathematics Tests, (Hart et al., 1985).

If one compares the number of variables which form the hierarchies in *The Chelsea Diagnostic Mathematics Tests* with the total number of variables in the original CSMS tests, one is struck by the scale of omission, i.e. out of 775 items, only 286 are retained in the hierarchies published by NFER. Given the six criteria which items had to satisfy before they were considered to form a group, one might reasonably expect that a number of items would be rejected. On the other hand, one might have expected a lower exclusion rate since the items used in the large scale-testing were themselves selected from those subjected to interviews and class tests.

Hart acknowledges the role of the items in the hierarchies:

> The hierarchies of understanding, by the very nature of their formulation, are dependent upon the items which appear in each of the ten tests. No claim is made to their uniqueness, but the demands of each level should assist teachers in planning the development of their schemes of work. (Hart *et al.*, 1985: 2)

As instruments of diagnosis, this is probably true. However, there is a danger that the 'levels of understanding' will become a way of prescribing rather than describing children's learning. Indeed, this would appear to be the function of the Attainment Targets in The National Curriculum.

The Stages: The age-related Attainment Targets in the National Curriculum in Mathematics have derived a certain degree of legitimacy from the CSMS research. Whether this is justified is another question. The research team state that all seven levels of understanding (for decimals) are found in each of years 1, 2, 3 and 4 of the secondary school, although the proportions differ from year to year. Therefore, 'It is not appropriate to recommend a programme of work for first year children followed by another for second years and so on.' (Hart, 1981: 64).

The four Key Stages in the National Curriculum also have counterparts in the four stages used by the CSMS to match hierarchies across topics. The justification given for this exercise was that 'A match between topic levels should enable a teacher to have an approximate guide to the comparative difficulty of topics' (Hart, 1981: 187). The methodology used to make this comparison was (i) to look at the performance on two tests of certain children and (ii) to match hierarchies based on the results of testing one group of children against the results of a second group who did a different test.

It was accepted that an exact match between topics was not possible given that 'i) the number of levels in each hierarchy varies from topic topic; and ii) the facility range of items within a level varies topic to topic.' (Hart *et al.*, 1981: 187). So an approximate guide to comparability was obtained by dividing the facility range into four 'stages'. These stages were formed on the basis of the third year tests only and generalized to the other years (See diagrams 1, 3, 6 and 8 on pages 191, 196, 203 and 207 respectively (Hart *et al.*, 1981).

Whilst one might appreciate the difficulties in matching levels across topics for the reasons given above, one might also expect that 'stages' implied well-defined boundaries, but this is not the case. If, for example, the stages derived from the third year sample are applied to the other years, levels with almost exactly the same facility range would appear in different stages. For instance, in year one, *Measurement* level 1 (facility range 66–78 per cent) would be in stage 1, whilst *Fractions* level 2 (facility range 66–80 per cent) would appear in stage 2. On the other hand, topics in the same stage could have wide variations in their facility range. For instance, applying the stages to the topics tested in year two, *Measurement* level 3 (facility range 39–48 per cent) would be in stage 2 but so too would *Fractions* 2 (facility range 68–79 per cent).[2]

In constructing 'levels of understanding', it is not entirely clear whether these should only apply to the years in which they were tested or to all of years 1 to 5. The use of stages exacerbates this problem. Hart (1981: 188) states that the contents for each stage are 'fixed for all ages in that Stage 1 for the 13-year-old sample contains exactly the same items as Stage 1 for the 15-year-old sample.' But 'Vectors', for example, did not appear at all in year two, whilst Measurement was absent from year four. The fraction levels which make up the stages for years three and four are not the same as those used for years one and two.

Of course, the stages are a simplification and at best an approximate match might be all that could be expected. However, as the above data indicates, the approximations are so rough as to be of little value in terms of comparability.

Contextual, Temporal and Societal Effects on the Hierarchies

Associating a facility level with a mathematical item and then using that facility level as a measure of a child's understanding requires, I would suggest, both great accuracy in the initial measurement and stability in any subsequent measurements. As we saw earlier, there are grounds for questioning whether the former has been achieved. There is ample research evidence for doubting whether the latter is attainable also. The APU have shown that the facility of an item is not stable but varies according to presentation, context, language, and even the

Table 6   *(From DES, 1985: 67)*

	Age 11	Age 15
$\begin{array}{r} 12.45 \\ 127.5 \\ +\quad 5.691 \\ \hline \end{array}$	78%	90%
12.45 + 127.5 + 5.691 =	37%	71%

Table 7   *(DES, 1985: 108)*

	Age 15
How many weeks will it take you to save up for a record which costs £4.50 if you save 25p each week?	88%
Jars of spice each weighing 25g are packed into a cardboard box. The jars weight 450g. How many jars are in a box?	79%
A 25kg bag of potatoes costs 4.50. What is the price of each kilogram of potatoes?	63%

position the item appears in the test. For example, the items in Table 6 indicate the effects of a change in presentation.

The effect of different contexts is shown by the examples in Table 7.

It is well known that the way a question is worded can affect the difficulties which children have in doing that question. The APU (1985: 36) found that the position of a question in a test or even having different accompanying items can also affect its facility. As they say 'Error rates and facilities for the same mathematical operation can vary in relation to incidental features of the task.' (APU, 1985: 826).

It is not suggested here that the CSMS authors were unaware of the effects of different contexts. The presence of the Fractions Computations test alongside the Fractions Problems test shows this clearly, as indeed does the format of the Ratio and other tests. What is argued however, is that their hierarchies are hierarchies of *items* in particular contexts rather than 'hierarchies of understanding' of concepts. In other words, if you rephrase the question, you get a different hierarchy.

The CSMS tests were designed mainly in a problem-solving format. From the children's responses, the researchers then constructed hierarchies in each topic. However, even if one accepts the hierarchies within these topics, it does not follow that there is an isomorphic relationship between the cognitive domain and the domain represented by what is being measured. Indeed, the difficulties in producing valid hierarchies of problem solving skills have been noted by other writers (e.g. Resnick and Ford, 1981: 57).

These examples illustrate the nature of the model being used by the CSMS. It is a model in which it is assumed that a child either can or cannot do the item, and no external factors will affect his or her performance in the test. The evidence suggests that this model is somewhat naive. Furthermore, it is a model based on conditions in England in the 1970s and neither accounts for changes in technology since then, nor societal differences.

Goldstein (1983) writes that 'Most tests of any value will eventually become outdated, and at least some of their items will require replacement' He argues that any falling off in test scores might just as easily be attributed to an increasing test difficulty as to a lowering of achievement in the population. For example, the advent of cheap electronic calculators may lead to a lowering of test scores in certain arithmetic operations because children no longer have to perform such operations.

> There is a clear duality between attributing change in an item parameter value to a change in the population response or in the characteristic of the item. The point, however, is whether the item should be regarded as an equally fair assessment of the educational system at each time, and it is here that judgement as well as empirical evidence is needed. (Goldstein, 1983: 374)

Such decisions he suggests, should be informed by changing curriculum content, social demands for knowledge and skills as well as information about item relevance for each child in terms of curriculum exposure or opportunity to acquire appropriate knowledge.

With regard to different societies, Lin (*op cit*) states that the results of the Taiwan ratio study showed a general consistency with the CSMS data in terms of the hierarchical grouping and sequencing of items of four levels of understanding. However, he adds (quoting an earlier paper) that

> From the children's point of view, the methods available to them for success on the items contained in each level are quite different. Therefore, the description of levels of understanding ratio are different too. (Lin, *op cit*: 490).

Table 8   *Correct responses (%)*

Item/Age	CSMS			MUT		
	13	14	15	13	14	15
(1)	94	94	96	70	73	77
(2)	95	95	96	72	78	80
(3)	85	84	88	54	59	67
(4)	75	75	79	52	58	66

According to Lin, the lack of encouragement in their primary and secondary schools means that the Taiwanese children do not develop their own methods. For the recipe item below the Taiwanese children have facilities which are roughly 20 per cent lower than their English counterparts (see Table 8), a difference Lin attributes to the latter's use of child methods.

> Onion Soup for 8 persons
>> 8 onions
>> 1 pint water
>> 4 chicken soup cubes
>> 2 dessertspoons butter
>> ½ pint cream
> a)   I am cooking onion soup for 4 people
>> How much water do I need? (1)
>> How much chicken soup cubes do I need? (2)
> b)   I am cooking onion soup for 6 people.
>> How much water do I need? (3)
>> How many chicken soup cubes do I need? (4)

However, he goes on to say that once Taiwan students have attained level 1, it is substantially easier for them to progress through the remaining levels, especially after they have learned the topic 'ratio and proportion'. The preference by the Taiwan students for the taught algorithm may account for this difference and their generally better performance at the higher levels. But, he adds (p. 495) 'The price Taiwan secondary mathematics students have paid is very high. For more able students, they might only learn "a set of recipes"'.

He points out (p. 491) that 'there is a marked difference in the facility bands defining the four levels of understanding, with the Taiwan levels spanning a narrower total range than the CSMS levels'. These are 19 per cent to 85 per cent and 12 per cent to 95 per cent respectively. He also highlights the facility gap between 50 per cent and 72 per cent in the CSMS study in which no item occurs and which acted as a watershed in that items above 72 per cent were grouped as level 1. Lin remarks that no such gap occurs in the MUT data.

In a recent article, Brown (1989: 126) writes that no claim is made that 'the levels we have described in various topics have any sort of objective existence in reality, let alone that they are necessarily innate or culturally independent'. But she also writes that the CSMS tests have been replicated in over 10 countries as 'culturally diverse' as Canada, Mongolia, Botswana, Taiwan and Greece, and although 'Individual items have differed in their relative facility, the data suggest that the levels themselves are surprisingly robust.'

I would certainly not disagree with the first of these statements since it supports much of what has been argued in this paper. But I would question whether the 'culturally diverse' countries mentioned have diverse mathematics curricula. Indeed, Howson (1986: 1) uses the expression 'canonical curriculum' to describe the 'astonishing uniformity of school mathematics curricula world-wide.' I also have serious reservations whether levels can remain robust in the light of changing facilities for individual items. It appears to me that the robustness of the levels may be partially accounted for by the methodology used which tends to aggregate out big differences in individual items. What the Lin study seems to show is that the hierarchies are not universal but are dependent upon the teaching methods used in different societies.

Conclusion

The CSMS study examined eleven topic areas which formed part of the secondary mathematics curriculum in this country at the time of the research (1975–1979), and eventually (Hart *et al.*, 1985) published diagnostic tests for eight of them. They did not cover all topic areas, e.g. Statistics, Probability, Trigonometry, Logic, Number Patterns, Sets, etc. were not studied. Nor did they study the whole of the secondary age-range for each topic.

Nevertheless, the CSMS research was a 'landmark' study of mathematical education. It gave us new insights into the difficulties which children face in learning mathematics. It made us aware that the methods which children use in solving problems — 'child methods' — may not be those which the teacher thinks are being employed. It also indicated the relative difficulties which children find with different aspects of the same topic. In this, the work of the CSMS research has been paralleled by that of the APU Surveys. Both add to our knowledge of how children learn mathematics. However, the CSMS research went beyond illumination by constructing a hierarchy of levels and stages from their empirical data and inferring that this was a 'hierarchy of understanding'.

In so doing, the authors have reinforced models both of mathematics and of how children learn mathematics. Thus, they have increased the danger that the descriptions will become a means of classifying children and controlling the mathematics curriculum. Indeed, the work of Lin (*op cit*) indicates that the more efficient the centralized curriculum is in inculcating techniques, the more closely do the measured responses approximate a continuous hierarchy. This may well be what the National Curriculum intends, but if so, it should be recognised as training — it is not mathematical education.

Notes

1 Two of the original eleven mathematical topics studied (Matrices and Positive/Negative Numbers) are omitted from this table.
2 See the criteria tables and the Facility Values for Measurement and Fractions in Hart, 1985.

References

APU, 1985, *A Review of Monitoring in Mathematics 1978–1982*, London: DES.
BELL, A.W., COSTELLO, J. and KÜCHEMANN, D., 1983, *A Review of Research in Mathematical Education Part A: Research on learning and teaching*, Windsor: NFER-Nelson.
BOOTH, L.R., 1981, 'Child methods in secondary mathematics', *Educational Studies in Mathematics*, **12**, pp. 29–41.
BOOTH, L.R., 1984, 'Misconceptions leading to error in elementary algebra', *Journal of Structural Learning*, **8**, pp. 125–38.
BOOTH, L.R., 1984, Algebra: Children's Strategies and Errors, Windsor: NFER-Nelson.
BROWN, M., 1981, 'Is it an add Miss?', *Mathematics in School*, **10**, 26–8.
BROWN, M., 1989, 'Graded assessment and learning hierarchies in mathematics — an alternative view', *British Educational Research Journal*, Vol. **15**, No. 2.
COCKCROFT, W.H. et al., 1982, *Mathematics Counts*, London: HMSO.
DENVIR, B., et al., 1987, '*Attainment Targets and Assessment in the Primary Phase*', London: DES.

DES, 1985, *Better Schools*, London: HMSO.

DES, 1987, *Mathematics from 5 to 16*, HMI Series, (2nd. Ed.). London: HMSO.

DES and WELSH OFFICE, 1988, *Mathematics for Ages 5 to 16*, London: HMSO.

DES and WELSH OFFICE, 1989, *Mathematics in the National Curriculum*, London: HMSO.

GOLDSTEIN, H., 1983 'Measuring changes in educational attainment over time: Problems and possibilities', *Journal of Educational Measurement*, **20**, 4, 369–77.

HART, K., 1980 *Secondary School Children's Understanding of mathematics (Research Monograph)*, A Report of the Mathematics Component of the CSMS Programme Chelsea College, University of London.

HART, K. (Ed.), 1981, *Children's Understanding of Mathematics: 11–16*, London: John Murray.

HART, K., 1981a, 'Hierarchies in mathematics education', *Educational Studies in Mathematics*, **12**, 205–18.

HART, K., 1984, *Ratio: Children's Strategies and Errors*, Windsor: NFER-Nelson.

HART, K. *et al.*, 1985, *Chelsea Diagnostic Mathematics Tests*, Windsor: NFER-Nelson.

HART, K., 1987, 'There is little connection', *Perspectives* **34**, 22–7.

HART, K., 1987, 'Where's the proof?', *Times Educational Supplement*, 2. October.

HASEMANN, K., 1981, 'On difficulties with fractions', *Educational Studies in Mathematics*, **12**, 71–87.

HOWSON, A.G. and WILSON, B., 1986, *School Mathematics in the 1990s*, Cambridge: Cambridge University Press.

KERSLAKE, D., 1986, *Fractions: Children's Strategies and Errors*, Windsor: NFER-Nelson.

KNIGHT, R.D., 1967, *New Mathematics*, London: Murray.

KÜCHEMANN, D.E., 1981, 'Cognitive demands of secondary school mathematics items', *Educational Studies in Mathematics*, **12**, 301–16.

KÜCHEMANN, D.E., 1983, 'Quantitative and formal methods for solving equations', *Mathematics in School*, 17–19.

KÜCHEMANN, D.E., 1985, 'Learning and Teaching Ratio', *Perspectives*, **34**, 28–47.

LIN, F.L., 1988, 'Societal differences and their Influences on children's mathematics understanding', *Educational Studies in Mathematics*, **19**, 471–97.

MOAKES, A.J., 1969, *Pattern and Power of Mathematics*, London: Macmillan.

MORTIMORE, P. *et al.*, 1988, *School Matters: The Junior Years*, Wells: Open Books.

NCC, 1988, *Consultation Report: mathematics*, York: NCC.

NCC, 1989, *Mathematics: non-statutory guidance*, York: NCC.

NOSS, R., GOLDSTEIN, H. and HOYLES, C., 1987, 'GAIM, Set, No Match', *Times Educational Supplement*, 11. September.

NOSS, R., GOLDSTEIN, H. and HOYLES, C., 1987 'GAIM Points', *Times Educational Supplement*, 13. October.

Noss, R. and Hoyles, C., 1988, 'The computer as a catalyst in children's proportion strategies', *Journal of Mathematical Behaviour*, **5**, 1–24.

Noss, R., Goldstein, H. and Hoyles, C., 1989, 'Graded Assessment and Learning Hierarchies in Mathematics', *British Educational Research Journal*, **15**, 2.

Resnick. L.B. and Ford, W.W., 1981, *The Psychology of Mathematics for Instruction*, Hillsdale: Lawrence Earlbaum Associates.

Ruthven, K., 1986, 'Differentiation in mathematics — A critique of *Mathematics Counts and Better Schools*', *Cambridge Journal of Education*, 41–5.

School Mathematics Project, 1967, *SMP Books 1–4*, Cambridge: Cambridge University Press

School Mathematics Project, 1969, *SMP Books A – H*, Cambridge: Cambridge University Press

Scottish Mathematics Group, 1965, *Modern Mathematics for Schools*, London: Chambers.

5 Ratio in the National Curriculum

Dietmar Küchemann

In this chapter I propose to look at the 'statements of attainment' in ratio in the mathematics National Curriculum. In particular I wish to examine their ordered and fragmented nature, and to consider the implications this might have for teaching and learning. I have chosen to look at ratio because it has an important place in any school mathematics curriculum and is an area that is well researched (e.g. Karplus and Peterson, 1970; Noelting, 1980; Hart, 1981; Vergnaud, 1983; Küchemann, 1989a). However, much of what is said in this chapter applies to any other area of mathematics in the National Curriculum.

Background

In July 1987 the then Secretary of State for Education and Science appointed a mathematics working group to advise the Government on how to establish

> ... clear objectives — attainment targets — for the know-
> ledge, skills, understanding and aptitudes which pupils of
> different abilities and maturity should be expected to have
> acquired at or near certain ages ... (and) programmes of study
> ... describing the essential content which needs to be covered
> to enable pupils to reach or surpass the attainment targets. (In
> DES, 1988b: 91)

The group was asked to submit an interim report by the end of November (DES, 1987) and a final report by the end of June 1988, less than a year after the group was constituted. The interim report was severely criticised by the Secretary of State; in his own words, he was

> ... disappointed that the group has not made more progress in their (sic) thinking about attainment targets and programmes of study. (In DES, 1988b: 99)

This led to the resignation of Professor R. Blin-Stoyle FRS, the chairman of the working group, who was replaced by Duncan Graham, at that time chief executive of Humberside County Council. The working group's final report (DES, 1988b) was received more favourably; though the Government asked for substantial changes to be made to the three attainment targets involving 'practical applications of mathematics', it was satisfied with the nature and overall content of the other twelve targets (on number, algebra, measures, shape and space, and handling data). The National Curriculum Council, for whom Duncan Graham was shortly to become chairman and chief executive, was asked to make these changes, and they were published in a report in December 1988 (NCC, 1988). The report contained two new attainment targets, to replace the previous three on practical mathematics; the other twelve attainment targets were kept, though minor modifications were made to some of the statements of attainment within them, such as changes in wording or shifts to a neighbouring level; occasionally a statement of attainment was dropped (for example, 'Determine the traversibility of networks'). The NCC report was followed soon afterwards by the document *Mathematics in the National Curriculum* (DES, 1989) which shows the attainment targets and programmes of study in mathematics in the form in which they were to be laid before Parliament in March 1989. The programmes of study are just a reiteration of the statements of attainment within the attainment targets, and the 1989 document shows no more changes to the latter,[1] other than further slight modifications to a few of the non-statutory examples.

Fragmentation

The National Curriculum in mathematics consists of 14 attainment targets, each of which is broken down into a series of statements of attainment (henceforth I propose to call these stoats). The stoats are classified into ten levels, in line with the recommendation of the TGAT Report (DES, 1988a). The use of the term 'level' implies an order (more of this later), and as a rough guide, a level is meant to correspond to 'two years of pupil progress' (DES, 1988b).

There are 296 stoats in the mathematics National Curriculum, which works out at an average of just over two stoats per level per attainment target. This might seem a large number, and indeed if the statements were little more than broad headings to define a syllabus, it would be — thus, for example, Duncan Graham (another one) and Christine Graham (1987), in their Letts Study Aid for GCSE Mathematics, use 136 headings (such as Angle, Area and Algebraic Graphs) to analyse the syllabuses of the various examination groups. However, the stoats in the National Curriculum are meant to be far more detailed, to allow for criterion referenced assessment (as recommended by TGAT; DES,1988a); as the mathematics working group puts it,

> Attainment targets in mathematics have to be very tightly defined to avoid ambiguity, and the degree of precision required gives a very clear indication of the 'content, skills and processes' associated with the targets. (DES, 1988b § 4.15)

In the event, the group got nowhere near avoiding the problem of ambiguity (as I will show). However, its descriptions of the attainment targets, in the form of the 296 stoats, are sufficiently tight to leave numerous gaps within the proposed curriculum. Thus for example, learning to calculate the area of a triangle, which according to the National Curriculum Council is the kind of activity that forms 'a large part of pupils' work in mathematics' (NCC, 1989: A3, § 2.4), is specified in none of the stoats. Ratio is explicitly referred to in only four of them (in the statements themselves and/or the examples used to illustrate them). (One other stoat refers to Proportion and there are perhaps a further ten stoats where a link with ratio is fairly clear, though left implicit — for example the statements on trigonometric functions, on scale, on geometric enlargement and on similarity).

Before looking at the ratio stoats in detail, it is interesting to consider why the mathematics National Curriculum has brought forth nearly 300 stoats. Unfortunately, as with many of the decisions of the mathematics working group and the NCC, no clear justification is offered. We know that ten was chosen as the number of levels of attainment because this was proposed in the TGAT Report, whose recommendations the working group was told to 'take account of' (DES, 1988b, § 1.4); we are also informed that the working group set itself the criterion that 'The number of attainment targets should be manageable by the schools' (*ibid*, § 4.5) and that therefore the number should be 'small'. However, we are given no further explanation of what is meant by manageable and small, or in what context the terms are being used; finally, when it comes to the number of stoats at each level for each target, no criterion is offered at all.

One can speculate, however. Since the construction of the National Curriculum is assessment driven, the aim being to provide a currency by which teachers and schools can be measured (see for example, Dowling, 1990), it is likely that the decision to have about 300 stoats is also based on assessment considerations. Given that pupils are to be tested at the end of four 'key stages' during the period of compulsory schooling, and given that only some of the ten levels of attainment are meant to apply to any one stage, it is perhaps thought that a total of 300 stoats is sufficiently small for it to be possible to test pupils on all appropriate stoats on each occasion that they are tested. This ties in with the recommendation that assessment should be criterion referenced, since if one wants to make statements about what pupils can do, it would be nice to tap *everything* they can do. However, this becomes absurd if the only way to tap 'everything' is to make it sufficiently small. (In fact the argument can be taken further: regardless of the total number of stoats, it is not possible to test a pupil's performance on even one stoat exhaustively, since it will always be possible to invent a new task to fit the description of the stoat but which produces a different performance from the pupil — see O'Reilly in this volume).

If it *is* the case that the number of stoats has deliberately been restricted for assessment reasons, then it might be argued that there are no gaps in the curriculum after all, it is just that not all the content of the curriculum is being tested (it is as if the stoats were just the tips of the curriculum iceberg). At times this seems to be the line taken by the mathematics working group, as in this strangely written piece of advice:

> For example, although the topic of time is not specified at Level 1 in the measures attainment target, it is essential that much preparatory work will need to be done to help children know the language of time by Level 2 and to read clocks by Level 3. (DES, 1988b, § 8.32)

More often though, a much closer correspondence seems to be being made between the attainment targets (and hence the stoats) and the content of the curriculum, as in this statement:

In essence the targets determine what is taught and what is assessed, but they do not, on their own, specify a mathematics curriculum. (*ibid*, § 8.3)

The latter is achieved by the programmes of study, which are defined in the group's terms of reference as

... the essential content which needs to be covered to enable pupils to reach or surpass the attainment targets. (*ibid*, § 4.13)

Now, it can be argued that the last two quotations still allow for programmes of study whose content is more extensive than that of the attainment targets themselves — indeed it is difficult to imagine how pupils could achieve a restricted set of targets without meeting other ideas that relate to them and form connections between them. However, as was pointed out earlier, in mathematics these programmes of study are simply a reiteration of the stoats. This came about as follows:

We approached the formulation of programmes of study after we had done the greater part of our work on attainment targets. This was logical since, following our terms of reference, the attainment targets represent curriculum objectives, while programmes of study are to describe the means of achieving these objectives. We found, however, that in the process of formulating attainment targets, and more particularly of formulating specific levels of attainment within targets, we had already defined in great detail the content, skills and processes that were to comprise the programmes of study. In other words, we found that the clear specification of the targets at several levels of attainment had in effect defined content, skills and processes. (*ibid*, § 4.14)

Note here the close identification of the attainment targets with the programmes of study, and the absence of any hint that the targets, in their level by level formulation, might represent only a subset of curriculum objectives, kept sufficiently small to suit the practicalities of criterion referenced assessment. In turn, there is no acknowledgement that the resulting curriculum, as represented by the programmes of study, is fragmented.

The absurdity of this fragmentation is immediately apparent when one considers the levels to which the statements of attainment refering explicitly to ratio have been assigned. As was mentioned earlier, there are just four such stoats, of which one is at level 5, two at level 6 and one at level 8. Presumably, it is only while pupils are working at these levels that they need make an explicit study of ratio. Presumably also, it means that pupils working below level 5 are assumed to know nothing about ratio (or what they do know can be ignored) and that pupils working above level 8 know all that they need to. And why is it deemed sensible for pupils working at level 7 to take a rest from studying ratio?

It might be argued that the picture I have drawn is so bizarre that no mathematics teacher would go along with it, even if it is a logical consequence of the way the mathematics National Curriculum has been constructed. I am not that optimistic, however, if only because the pressure on teachers to ensure that pupils perform well at a particular level is likely to deflect them from giving pupils work related to a more distant level (which, anyway, is the next teacher's problem). To illustrate this, I quote from a letter from the head of a school mathematics department to a publisher of mathematics text books. It was written in 1989 during the first term in which the mathematics National Curriculum was to be implemented, and as such it might represent just a panic reaction, but I doubt it.

> We are attempting to implement the National Curriculum and the Scheme we have adopted is to teach each Attainment Target for a period of two or three weeks at a level appropriate to the class concerned . . . For each class we will be teaching at a (predominantly) specific level. In the First Year, for instance, the low groups will be taught at Level 3, the middle groups at Level 4 and the high groups at Level 5. The levels will be increased each year.

Levels

As has been stated earlier, the statements of attainment in mathematics (and all other areas of the National Curriculum) are ordered into ten levels, on the recommendation of the TGAT Report and at the behest of the Government. Surprisingly, perhaps, it is far from clear whether this ordering reflects a belief in learning hierarchies or whether the ordering is seen as essentially arbitrary, imposed to satisfy the Government's professed desire for a curriculum that exhibits uniformity and continuity within and between schools. I will argue that the use of levels to order the curriculum is defensible on neither ground, but in the course of doing so it is of interest to examine TGAT's and the mathematics working group's views of the levels in more detail.

The members of TGAT state that they

> ... assume progress to be defined in terms of the national curriculum, and the stages of progress to be marked by levels of achievement as derived from that curriculum. *It is not necessary to presume that the progression defined indicates some inescapable order in the way children learn, or some sequence of difficulty inherent in the material to be learnt.* Both of these factors may apply, but the sequence of learning may also be the result of choices for whatever reason, which those for-mulating and operating the curriculum may recommend in the light of teaching experience. (DES 1988a, § 93; emphasis added)

Here the approach is clearly a pragmatic one, with the levels seen as essentially arbitrary, to be determined by the practicalities of devis-ing a curriculum that is to define and thence be used to measure 'progress' (incidentally a worryingly circular aim).

It is worth adding that the group's approach to the order in which pupils are to *learn*, rather than be assessed, seems equally clear, namely that though there is no *inescapable* order, an order will be laid down, to conform to the way progression is defined in the curricu-lum. Interestingly, the NCC in its non-statutory guidance issued in June 1989, quotes the same extract from the TGAT report, but inter-prets it quite differently, as offering clear advice against adopting

> ... an over simplified view of the programmes of study and associated levels, as a sub-divided and strictly hierarchical model for pupils' learning. (NCC,1989: C2, § 2.3)

Though there is a lack of precision in the TGAT statement, this interpretation by the NCC seems little short of an attempt to rewrite history. It suggests that in the cold light of day the NCC has begun to recognise that the curriculum it helped to create suffers from the shortcomings discussed in the previous section. This is an astonishing turn-around, but as an attempt to negate the logic of the National Curriculum it has surely come too late.

The mathematics working group does not refer to the extract

from the TGAT report, but on the report's recommendation that a ten point scale be used to record pupils' progress, it states

> We believe that this model is a good one: it is flexible enough to allow all pupils ... to progress through the levels at their own rate, while at the same time setting clear age-related targets. (DES, 1988b, § 1.4)

It is perhaps just conceivable that such a comment is being made about a curriculum in which the material (within each attainment target, at least) is presented in a fixed, but arbitrarily chosen order; however, the reference to *progress through the levels* and to *age-related targets* strongly suggests that the group has a hierarchically structured curriculum in mind. At first sight, this would seem to be contradicted by this later comment however:

> The mathematical development of each pupil is different and is difficult to predict. Mathematical concepts form a network through which there are many different paths. Different pupils will need to take different paths through the network, and approach learning from a variety of perspectives. (DES, l988b, § 8.16)

This is repeated in the NCC guidelines (NCC, 1989: B8, § 5.3) and would seem to blow apart the whole notion of a curriculum that is ordered into levels, unless the references to different development and different paths apply *across* attainment targets but not within them — in other words, that an individual pupil might be at different levels for different attainment targets, but that for a given attainment target, all pupils will progress through the levels in the same order (note also that the reference to paths, even individualised ones, is still restrictive in that it implies *direction*: it does not embrace the notion of mathematical development occuring through the development of concepts that mutually inform each other). It is regrettable that the group does not make its position clear, though further evidence to suggest that it does subscribe to a hierarchical view of the levels comes from its discussion about how the levels are defined. For example, the group states that

> In defining the levels of attainment appropriate for different ages and stages, we have relied mainly on our collective ex-

perience and knowledge of good teaching practice and on available research evidence. (*ibid*, § 1.6)

This suggests that the order of the levels is not regarded as arbitrary, though again there is a regrettable vagueness about the group's criteria: we are not told what research evidence was relied on, beyond the listing of a select bibliography in an appendix, nor what the group regards as good practice.[2] Disarmingly, the group continues with this statement:

> It would be surprising therefore if we had got everything right first time. It is likely that at some points we will have pitched the levels of attainment for particular age bands too high; at other points we may have underestimated what pupils are capable of. The only way that this can be tested is empirically. (*ibid*, § 1.6)

Here is a clearly expressed belief that there *is* a right order; however, the statement is disingenuous as well as disarming, since the outcomes of a curriculum based on the notion of levels is likely to be self-fulfilling, to the extent that pupils learn what they are taught and do not learn what they are not taught.

In the bibliography, the group cites work by the CSMS project (Hart, 1981) and by the APU (e.g. APU, 1980). Amongst other things, these studies provide performance data on a large range of mathematics items, and it is likely that this helped inform the group in the task of assigning levels to statements of attainment. However, it is worth pointing out that most of this work is now well over ten years old, so that a reliance on it to set attainment levels will tend to ossify the curriculum rather than opening it to the best of present and future practice.[3] More importantly perhaps, there is no reason why the order of difficulty of a set of tasks should determine the order in which they are taught. Unfortunately, this appears to be a widespread practice in mathematics classrooms (see for example the lessons of experienced and committed teachers cited in Johnson, 1989), which all too often seems to lead to work that is perceived as purposeless by the pupils and with learning outcomes that are transitory (e.g. Bell and Bassford, 1989). The mathematics National Curriculum, in which there is a direct correspondence between the levels of attainment and the order in which material is to be taught (the programmes of study), is just such a curriculum.

As well as providing data on individual items, the CSMS work classified items in selected areas of the mathematics curriculum into levels and it is likely that this was seen as providing support for the use of levels of attainment in the National Curriculum, though this is not acknowledged by the mathematics working group. The CSMS project (and some of its successors) is to a large extent responsible for this interpretation of its work, although it should be pointed out that the use of levels sprung from the framework adopted by the project — its aim was not to test their validity. It is also worth noting that the CSMS levels are defined by sets of specific test items, in contrast to the much broader terms used to describe the levels in the mathematics National Curriculum. The difficulty with this is discussed shortly.

The Ratio Statements of Attainment

The four explicit ratio stoats are shown below (as a shorthand, I will refer to them as AT2.5, AT2.6, AT3.6 and AT3.8 respectively). I propose first to discuss their ordering *within* attainment targets (does it make sense to place AT2.5 before AT2.6, and AT3.6 before AT3.8?), then their ordering *across* attainment targets (does it make sense to place AT2.6 at the same level as AT3.6?); last I will consider whether it makes sense at all to assign levels to individual stoats.

AT2 Number (Understand number and number notation)

| Level 5 | use unitary ratios | *Use a ratio of 1:50 for drawing a plan of the classroom.* |
| Level 6 | understand and use equivalence of fractions and of ratios; relate these to decimals and percentages | *Show that lengths 8 cm and 12 cm in a drawing are in the ratio 2:3.* |

AT3 Number (Understand number operations and make use of appropriate methods of calculation)

| Level 6 | calculate using ratios in a variety of situations. | *Adapt a recipe for 6 people to one to one for 8 people; enlarge a design in a given ratio.* |
| Level 8 | calculate with fractions. | *Divide a 3 m strip of wood into two parts in a given ratio.* |

AT2.5 and AT2.6. Other things being equal, there is probably broad agreement that unitary ratios are easier to deal with than ratios

like 2:3. Thus, in terms of assessment, it might make sense to place AT2.5 before AT2.6. However, when it comes to teaching and learning, the situation is not so obvious.

The use of unitary ratios seems to be widespread when solving ratio problems. Thus, for example, the unitary method was the most commonly used method to solve the item below amongst a group of 40 PGCE mathematics students at the Institute of Education [18 students used the unitary method (one person needs one-and-a-half eggs), 14 students used some version of rated addition (six people need half as many eggs again . . .), 5 students used the rule of three, and 3 students did not clearly describe their method].

This omelette recipe is for 4 people. **Omelet Germiny**
6 eggs
1 handful of sorrel
2 handfuls of spinach

How many eggs are needed for 6 people? . . .
etc.

Similar results have been found amongst school students (e.g. Küchemann, 1989b). This apparent accessibility of the unitary method, together with its considerable power, suggests that it would be a viable and worthwhile aim to teach pupils to use it, which would include developing a familiarity with unitary ratios. However, this does not mean that unitary ratios should be studied 'before' other ratios. Though this is the approach adopted by most school text books (Küchemann, 1989a), it ignores the possibility that pupils already possess strategies (e.g. rated addition) that enables them to tackle tasks involving more complex ratios; also, it all too frequently leads to tasks that are trivial and purposeless [such as 'In this picture each man has 2 horses. We say the ratio of horses to men is 2 to 1. . . . (From this second picture,) The ratio of girls to dogs is __ __ __' (SMP, 1983)]. It would seem far more sensible to study unitary ratios in the context of solving tasks like the omelette item, where the value of using a unitary ratio is immediately apparent.

AT3.6 and AT3.8. The statement of attainment AT3.8 (calculate with fractions) is clearly not just about ratio. However, as far as the example is concerned (*Divide a 3 m strip of wood into two parts in a given ratio*), it is difficult to see why this should necessarily come after AT3.6 (indeed, four years after). It would be a simple matter to devise tasks fitting AT3.6 that are substantially harder than tasks fitting AT3.8. The ordering of the two stoats is thus essentially arbitrary, and at best one could argue that this has been done to produce a curriculum that is uniform within and between schools. However, such an ordering is not well suited to a subject like mathematics, which the devisers of the curriculum themselves acknowledge is 'a network of ideas in which the various parts are interrelated to form a coherent whole' (DES, 1988b, 2.9), and which means that pupils who are working at one level are bound to run into ideas that have been placed at other levels. It is absurd to suggest that at a certain age pupils should apply ratio to recipes but not to strips of wood till four years later. More generally, such an ordering can only have a stultifying effect on the curriculum and on pupils' thinking.

AT2.6 and AT3.6. For pupils to develop a broad understanding of ratio, it is important to tackle ratio tasks in a variety of settings. This importance is perhaps underlined by having AT2.6 and AT3.6 assigned to the same level, since AT2.6 is illustrated by a geometric example, while AT3.6 is illustrated by one involving recipes (as well as another geometric example). However, from the point of view of assessment, it is far from certain that tasks involving different settings will be of comparable difficulty. Thus for example, in a study mentioned earlier (Küchemann, 1989b), it was found that while 49 per cent of a sample of secondary school pupils could successfully cope with a recipe item involving the relationship $6:7 = 15:?$, only 22 percent could successfully cope with a geometric item involving the same relationship. On the other hand, the geometric example used to illustrate AT2.6 (*Show that lengths 8 cm and 12 cm in a drawing are in the ratio 2:3*) does not require pupils to recognise the need for a ratio relationship, and so might prove to be substantially easier than the kind of recipe task suggested for AT3.6.

Assigning levels to individual statements. It has just been pointed out that changing the setting of a ratio task can have a substantial effect on its difficulty. The same is true for numerical content. Thus for example, the two items below had facilities of 85 per cent and 38 per cent respectively for comparable samples of secondary school pupils (*ibid*).

A packet of 5 chocolate biscuits weights 15 ounces.
How much does a packet of 2 chocolate biscuits weigh?

A packet of 15 biscuits weighs 25 ounces.
How much does a packet of 9 biscuits weigh?

The mathematics working group and the NCC seem to have been aware of this issue, since the geometric example used to illustrate

AT3.6 was originally given as *enlarge a design in the ratio 3:5* (DES, 1988b), then as *enlarge a design in the ratio 2:3* (NCC, 1988), and finally as enlarge a design in a given ratio (DES, 1989). As a general aim, this last version is perfectly sensible, as is the overall statement for AT3.6 (calculate using ratios in a variety of situations). However, the result can hardly be said to satisfy the mathematics working group's own requirement, quoted earlier, that 'Attainment targets in mathematics have to be very tightly defined'. Rather, the statement 'calculate using ratios in a variety of situations' is of such generality that it fits tasks suitable for pupils throughout the 5–16 age range. It makes no sense to target the statement on the average 15 year old, which is the age at which pupils are meant to be able to cope with level 6.

The same argument applies to any other statement of attainment, since the difficulty of any task used to exemplify it can be substantially altered by changing the numerical content or setting. The situation is further compounded by differences among pupils — for example, though there might be firm evidence to suggest that many pupils find ratio tasks in a geometric setting more difficult than in a recipe setting (other things being equal), this might not be true of all pupils, or of individual pupils at all times.

The only satisfactory way out of this dilemma is to abandon levels as a way of structuring the curriculum. The alternative, of producing more tightly defined stoats, would result in their further proliferation (though without making pupils any more 'consistent') or in an even more fragmented curriculum.

Notes

1 Apart from the replacement of statements of the form 'nothing specific at this level': see papers by Dowling and Noss in this volume.
2 See chapters in this volume by Brown and Dowling on the notion of 'good practice'.
3 See O'Reilly, in this volume.

References

APU (Assessment of Performance Unit), 1980, *Mathematical Development: Primary Survey Report No. 1*, London: HMSO.
BELL, A. and BASSFORD, D., 1989, A conflict and investigation teaching method and an individualised learning scheme — a comparative experi-

ment on the teaching of fractions, *Proceedings of PME 13*, Paris, July 1989.

DES AND WELSH OFFICE, 1987: *National Curriculum: Mathematics Working Group, Interim Report.*, London: DES.

DES AND WELSH OFFICE, 1988a, *Task Group on Assessment and Testing: A Report.*, London: DES.

DES AND WELSH OFFICE, 1988b, *Mathematics for Ages 5 to 16*, London: DES.

DES and WELSH OFFICE, 1989, *Mathematics in the National Curriculum*, London: DES.

DOWLING, P.C., 1990, 'Mathematics in the marketplace: The National Curriculum and numerical control', *Teaching London Kids*, 26.

GRAHAM, D. and GRAHAM, C., 1987, *Revise Mathematics: A Complete Revision Course.*, London: Letts.

HART, K., 1981, 'Ratio', in HART, K. (Ed.), *Children's Understanding of Mathematics: 11–16*, Murray: London.

HART, K. (Ed.), 1981, *Children's Understanding of Mathematics: 11–16*, Murray: London.

JOHNSON, D.C. (Ed.), 1989, *Children's Mathematical Frameworks 8–13: A Study of Classroom Teaching*, Windsor: NFER-NELSON.

KARPLUS, R. and PETERSON, R., 1970, 'Intellectual development beyond elementary school II: Ratio, a survey,' *School Science and Mathematics*, **LXX**, 9.12. 70.

KÜCHEMANN, D.E., 1989a, 'Learning and teaching ratio: A look at some current textbooks, in ERNEST, P. (Ed.), *Mathematics Teaching, the State of the Art*, Lewes: Falmer.

KÜCHEMANN, D.E., 1989b, 'The effect of setting and numerical content on the difficulty of ratio tasks, *Proceedings of PME 13*, Paris, July 1989.

NOELTING, G., 1980, 'The development of proportional reasoning and the ratio concept 1 — Differentiation of stages', *Educational Studies in Mathematics*, **11**, pp. 217–53.

NCC, 1988, *Consultation Report: Mathematics*, York: NCC.

NCC, 1989: *Mathematics: Non-statutory Guidance*, York: NCC.

SMP, 1983, *SMP 11–16: Ratio 1*, Cambridge: Cambridge University Press.

VERGNAUD, G., 1983, 'Multiplicative structures', in LESH, R. and LANDAU, M. (Eds), *Acquisition of Mathematics Concepts and Processes*, London: Academic Press.

Theme 3
Lost Opportunities

6   Neglected Voices: Pupils' Mathematics in the National Curriculum

Celia Hoyles

It is, in fact, nothing short of a miracle that the modern methods of instruction have not yet entirely strangled the holy curiosity of inquiry; for this delicate little plant aside from stimulation, stands mainly in need of freedom; without this it goes to wreck and ruin without fail. (Einstein, 1949: 19)

The National Curriculum in Mathematics

The National Curriculum in Mathematics is a matrix of 14 attainment targets organised into 10 levels. The subject knowledge is reified, objectified and 'rationally' ordered. Attainment targets purport to encapsulate clear behavioural objectives or specific cognitive-based strategies: for example 'pupils should understand congruence of simple shapes' (attainment target 10, level 5), 'pupils should construct, read and interpret block graphs and frequency tables' (attainment target 13, level 2).

Different views of the way children learn in schools and their motivation to learn stem from different psychological paradigms. These have been characterised by whether knowledge is seen as text or whether it is seen as context (Steinbring, in press). The National Curriculum presents knowledge as text. It assumes a linear sequencing of knowledge development and hierarchies of concepts. Pupils are expected to master mathematical knowledge, skills and applications and it is assumed that the achievement of this mastery can be pinpointed; an assumption obviously crucial for assessment purposes.

The individual pupil's behaviour is the pertinent and unique unit of analysis. Pupil behaviour is seen as a set of performances structured by the conceptual frameworks of the individual. Pupils interact with the knowledge as a series of required tasks, perceived only as part of their own interpersonal context. Obstacles to learning stem from pupil misconceptions which after diagnosis must be remediated. It is also assumed that the context in which the mathematical activity is embedded, although needing to be described, can be separated from the issue of knowledge and conceptual development. Ultimately and inevitably, mastery of knowledge is decontextualized and domain independent. Context is needed merely to provide illustration; for example, Brown argues 'criteria should be accompanied by examples both to communicate the meaning to fit the criterion and the types of context intended' (Brown 1989: 125).

So what is the relationship of the National Curriculum to class-room practice? It is very evident that the task of schools is to deliver or implement the National Curriculum. The task for the teacher is to transmit the mathematical knowledge specified. It is carefully stated in the Non-Statutory Guidance that 'The matrix (of attainment targets and levels), in itself, does not constitute or define a scheme of work. Rather it provides a series of reference points or features which should be reflected in a school's plans' (National Curriculum Council 1989, 2.11: A4). Undoubtedly however, the 'conceptual levels' in the matrix will have a strong influence on teaching sequence. Tests are to be designed for formative as well as summative evaluation of pupil performance. Regular assessment is also expected to enhance pupil motivation through mastery of short term goals, and 'knowing clearly where you are and where you are going'. Close and Brown (1987), for example, argue that a sequenced approach will improve attitudes of both teacher and pupils. Finally the tests will fulfil a selection function and a means of grading schools and teachers. It is this function of tests which undoubtedly is their primary purpose and which will have the most pervasive influence on pupil learning as well as on the curriculum, teachers' role, and teacher/pupil relations.

As far as equal opportunities is concerned, the position of the National Curriculum is that pupils are essentially alike and equal opportunities are guaranteed provided all pupils undertake the same work and the same assessments. This attitude is encapsulated in the proposals of August 1988 (DES, 1988b) concerning ethnic and cultural diversity, '. . . the key principle is that the attainment targets and programmes of study are the *same* for *all* pupils *regardless of race*' (§ 10.23: 87, their emphasis). Similarly, with regard to gender it is stated 'in framing attainment targets we have not therefore sought to devise targets with girls (or boys) in mind. To do this would only help perpetuate the gender stereotypes which currently inhibit girls' attainment' (§ 10.17: 86). Thus the pupil and the pupil's individuality is absent from the argument.

Critique of the National Curriculum

1. Validity of the Hierarchies

In mounting a critique of the National Curriculum in mathematics let us first consider the validity of the matrix of knowledge as set out in the documents. Immediately it is obvious that there is a lack of clarity underlying the statements of attainment. What does it mean to understand congruence of simple shapes? What is 'understanding'? What is 'simple'? By pointing to these ambiguities, I am not arguing that the attainment targets are written badly (which may or may not be the case but is of little relevance here). More fundamentally I am suggesting that it is impossible for the attainment targets and associated statements to be unambiguous and completely explicit. School mathematics is a social activity and its characteristics and meanings (of say 'simple') must be defined and clarified in context.

In an earlier paper (Noss, Goldstein and Hoyles, 1989), we argued that the need to have the same number of levels for each attainment target (emanating from the TGAT[1] model) implies necessarily that there is a meaning for, for example, a 'level 5 task' across topics. However, it seems clear that 'the claim for criterion-referencing within a particular knowledge domain must necessarily rule out the possibility of equivalence on the basis of any theoretical justification' (Noss *et al.*, 1989: 115). Why for example is: 'distinguish between rational and irrational numbers' (Level 9, Attainment Target 2, Number) the same level as 'use the knowledge, skills and understanding attained at lower levels in a wider range of context' (Level 9 Attainment Target 3, Number)?[2] It is all too easy to ridicule the specification of the attainment targets, not because the working group did badly, but simply because the targets cannot sustain at a logical level any underlying validity. This point is essentially accepted by Brown who wrote, with reference to GAIM,[3]

> Nor would we argue that the levels we have described in various topics have any sort of objective existence in reality, let alone that they are necessarily innate or culturally independent. (Brown, 1989: 126)

It follows that different orderings, both horizontally and vertically could have been enshrined in the National Curriculum documents if there had been different participants in their development with different agendas and different intentions. There is some empirical evidence giving data leading to performance hierarchies (see for example Hart, 1981) but this evidence is patchy in relation to a whole curriculum. Moreover it is important to stress that *empirical* hierarchies are not necessarily *cognitive* hierarchies. or indeed learning hierarchies.

So what can we do as mathematics educators faced with this situation? We could merely accept the matrix as a reasonable description of pupil performances, laugh at its foolishness, and do our best in the circumstances — but by so doing, in my view, we are relinquishing our academic integrity. We must unpick the assumptions concerning the *nature* of mathematics and the *nature* of mathematics learning which underlie the National Curriculum. A major question posed by van Oers must be faced — that is, whether the elements of mathematics can be safely taken apart and ordered according to their psychological theory for the purpose of instruction (van Oers, 1990, my emphasis). I will argue that this transformation destroys both the essence of mathematics and the potential for pupil mathematical activity. Thus, I question the validity of presenting mathematics as text as suggested in the National Curriculum — it is, in my view, neither academic mathematics nor pupils' mathematics.

2. Intuitive and Contextual Influences

Now let us turn to the separation of knowledge, skills and applications from intuitive and contextual factors — a separation which is inevitable and necessary from a political perspective given the need for a universal set of standards against which pupils and schools can be measured. In relation to the role of intuition, Fischbein (1980) has argued that 'at every level of mathematical reasoning the intuitive aspect must be considered' and that 'there are processes of elaboration which cannot be reduced to algorithms, that is to successions of elementary steps, logically consistent and explicitly formulated'. There is a subjective interpretation of concepts — so the 'same concept, the same operation, may evoke in different persons different intuitive meanings according to their age, education, personal experience — or may not evoke any intuitive meaning at all' (Fischbein, 1990). He gives as an example the following two problems:

1. One litre of juice costs $0.75. What is the price of 2 litres?
2. One litre of juice costs $2. What is the price of 0.75 litres?

In both cases, the embedded mathematical rule is: total cost = unit price × quantity. The numbers to be multiplied are the same but the function of the numbers is different with the effect, according to Fischbein, that the intuitive interpretation of the problems and the respective intuitive solutions are different; for problem 1, the intuitive (correct) solution is multiplication; for problem 2, the intuitive (incorrect) solution is division.

Let me now take an example from our own work which points up the influence of context as well as intuition on pupil response. As part of our work to evaluate a ratio and proportion microworld,[4] we designed written tests to probe pupils' intuitions and understandings about ratio and proportion through a paper-and-pencil format. The questions did not explicitly mention ratio and proportion but were set in the form of word problems which necessitated multiplication operations for their solution. The tests included questions where a response had to be constructed in two contexts; one, concerning mixing paint (*paint context*) (see Figure 1) and the second, concerning enlarging photographs of rugs (*rugs context*) (see Figure 2). We were interested in how far the context provoked the pupils to respond in proportional ways. Qualitative information concerning this issue was obtained by interviewing a group of case study pupils following the written tests. These interviews were crucial as a means of probing pupil *meanings* and not merely their *responses*. Our findings pointed to the different strategies adopted by the pupils according to the different contexts. Pupils were more likely to relate their response to the setting of the question in the rugs context, where they were influenced by visual cues than in the paint context. Moreover, 'We found that pupils with no idea as to the meaning of 'in proportion' or who did not pick up context clues as to the structures underlying the question, adopted a pattern-spotting approach. In the numerical paint context the pattern-spotting in integer questions tended to be *adding*, while in a rug context it tended to be *non-adding*, (Hoyles, Noss and Sutherland, 1990, my emphasis).

We can illustrate some of these effects with extracts from pupil interviews. Christopher's responses were incorrect for all the paint questions but he obtained three out of four of the rugs questions correct. It was very clear on interview that although the underlying mathematical structures were identical, Christopher adopted com-

Figure 1   Paint Question

Jo and Pat are painting the garden shed. They want it to be grey. The shop only has small tins of white paint and small tins of black paint.

Jo mixes ten tins of white paint with fifteen tins of black paint. Pat has two tins of white paint. Here is a table showing these amounts:

	Amount of white paint	Amount of black paint
Jo	3	9
Pat	2	?

How many litres of black paint must Pat use to get the same shade of grey? Pat needs ....tins.

Figure 2   Rugs Question

You collect photographs of rugs. You have just received a new set of photographs to add to your collection. You need to enlarge or shrink them to fit into the spaces in your catalogue. One of the 'new' lengths is unknown. Find the missing lengths (marked '?') on each diagram.

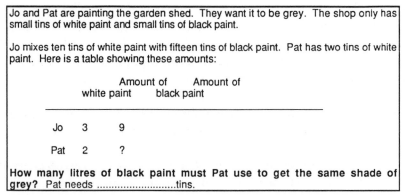

Missing length is.....................

pletely different approaches in the two contexts. For the paint questions, Christopher wanted to use a 'totalling' strategy, that is making the total number of tins of paint used by Jo and Pat the same regardless of paint colour. So for example when the total number of tins of paint that Jo used was 12 and Pat had used two tins of white paint (as in Figure 1), 10 tins of black paint was given as the missing answer. When asked why he used this strategy Christopher said he didn't know 'its just what I thought'. Obviously this strategy was not generalisable. When Christopher came to the next question he was immediately in trouble because the number of tins of paint that Jo used was 10 and Pat had already used 12 tins of white paint! Christopher in this situation just guessed.

When faced with the rugs questions, Christopher exhibited an intuitive feel for the operation that had to be used and consistently adopted a multiplicative approach. For example for the question in Figure 2 he described his strategy as:

> C.   Twelve divided by four is three, then I did nine divided by three ... no, nine times three to get twenty-seven.

His answer to the following question, though wrong, was in fact obtained by a correct strategy using an approximation of 2.5 for 2.33.

> C.   I divided three into seven which gave me 2.5 and multiplied 2.5 by 15.

In summary, Christopher had a sense of the necessary relationships within the rugs context but not at all in the paint context, where it was clear that he did not think the strategy he used mattered. It is interesting that nowhere did he explicitly mention the context as a means of assistance in his responses; *yet the context did make a difference in his performance.*

A similar pattern of responses was obtained from another pupil, Samantha. For the paint questions, Samantha answered randomly with a slight preference for addition. Her decision was made on 'what the type of number was' and when she did not see 'a pattern of numbers' she either added or subtracted. In contrast in the rugs questions, Samantha *never* added. When she could not see how to multiply or divide she used an approximate method. In response to one question for example, she said:

> S.   Three nines are twenty seven and then ....
> um....... I must have put.... No.... that one.......
> because that was three threes are nine so it can make up to ten.
> I think I just put three down because that was the nearest.

Ignoring intuition and the cultural setting assumes that the pupil is engaging in the activity as prescribed by the teacher. Did Christopher have a misconception or was his behaviour in the face of the paint questions a result of thinking that the activity was an investigation where you have to find any number that fits the pattern? If we cannot be sure, what is the meaning of diagnosis? Diagnosis assumes a deficit

matrices and their rows and columns as a strategy for guiding the achievement of the nation's children is in question. (Romberg *et al.*, 1989).

Approaches that rely on extrinsic motivation and train narrowly-focused skills are inevitably at odds with those that rely on the natural dynamics of social influence and induce long-term developmental advance in conceptual insight. It is not so much that the two have different areas of concern but that the two reflect different values about the aims of education. In many cases, we contend, the former approach reflects an unexamined set of aims deriving from the conventions of schooling — conventions which often have evolved through economic necessity and tradition over the past century and a half rather than through informed judgment about the optimal instructional context for students' cognitive development. We believe that schools can do better, and must do better if they are to meet today's formidable challenges. (Damon and Phelps, 1990: 16)

Notes

1   TGAT: Task Group on Assessment and Testing (DES, 1988a).
2   This latter statement is repeated at Level 10.
3   GAIM: Graded Assessment in Mathematics; a scheme which can be seen to have influenced the National Curriculum.
4   The microworld was designed and evaluated as part of an ESRC research project, The Microworlds Project 1986–1989 (Hoyles, Noss and Sutherland 1990).
5   In the context of this chapter, the questions would be placed at the same 'level' of the National Curriculum.
6   Computer tools also impose their own constraints and present new conceptual obstacles (with respect to graph plotting see Goldenberg, 1989).

References

APU, in press Mathematics Monitoring 1984–1988 (Phase 2).
AMABILE, T.M., 1987, 'The motivation to be creative', in ISAKSEN, S. (Ed.), Frontiers in Creativity: Beyond the Basics, Buffalo, NY: Bearly Limited, pp. 223–54.
BOEKAERTS, M., 1988, 'Introduction to emotion, motivation and learning', International Journal of Educational Research, **12**, pp. 229–34.

Brousseau', G., 1984, 'The crucial role of the didactical contract in the analysis and construction of situations in teaching and learning mathematics', in Theory of Mathematics Education Occasional Paper 54, November, Institut für Didaktich der Mathematik IDM, Universität Bielefeld, pp. 110–19.

Brown, M., 1989, 'Graded assessment and learning hierarchies in mathematics — An alternative view', British Educational Research Journal, **15**, 2, pp. 121–128.

Close, G., and Brown, M., 1987, Graduated Assessment in Mathematics, Report of the SSCC Study, Part I Summary and Evaluation, London: DES Publications.

Cobb, P., Yackel, B., and Wood, T., 1988, 'Curriculum and teacher Development: psychological and anthropological perspectives', in Fennema, E., Carpenter, T.P. and Lamon, S.J. (Eds), Integrating Research on Teaching and Learning Mathematics, Madison: Wisconsin Center for Education Research, University of Wisconsin, Madison, pp. 92–131.

Cockcroft, W.H. et al., 1982, Mathematics Counts, London: HMSO.

Damon, W., and Phelps, E., 1990, 'Critical distinctions among three approaches to peer education', in Webb, N. (Ed.), 'Peer Interaction, Problem-Solving, and Cognition', International Journal of Education Research, **13**, 1, pp. 9–19.

De Corte, E., 1990, 'Learning with New Information Technologies in Schools: perspectives from the psychology of learning and instruction', *Journal of Computer Assisted Learning*, **6**, 1, 69–87.

DES, 1988a, Task Group on Assessment and Testing, London: DES.

DES, 1988b, Mathematics for ages 5–16, Proposals of the Secreatry of State for Education and Science and the Secretary of State for Wales, London: DES and the Welsh Office.

Dweck, C.S. and Elliott, E.S., 1983, 'Achievement motivation', in Mussen, P.H. (Ed.), Handbook of Child Psychology, Volume 4, New York: Wiley.

Einstein, A., 1949, Autobiography quoted in Annabile, T.M. 'The motivation to be creative', in Isaken, S. (Ed.) 1987 Frontiers in Creativity: Beyond the Basics, Buffalo, NY: Bearly Ltd.

Fischbein, E., 1990, 'Intuition and information processing in mathematical activity', *International Journal of Educational Research*, **14**, 1, 31–50.

Fransson, A., 1977, 'On Qualitative Differences in Learning: — effects of intrinsic motivation and extrinsic test anxiety on process and outcome, British Journal of Educational Psychology, **47**, pp. 244–57.

Goldenberg, P., 1989, 'Seeing beauty in mathematics', Journal of Mathematical Behaviour, **8**, 2, August, pp. 169–204.

Hart, K.M., 1981, Children's Understanding of Mathematics: 11–16, London: John Murray.

Hoyles, C., 1985, 'What is the point of group discussion in mathematics?', Educational Studies in Mathematics, **16**, pp. 205–14.

Hoyles, C. and Noss, R., 1989, 'The computer as a catalyst in children's proportion strategies', *Journal of Mathematical Behaviour*, **8**, pp. 53–75.

Hoyles, C., Noss, R. and Sutherland, R., 1990, *The Microworlds Project*, Final Report to ESRC.

LEPPER, M.R., 1988, 'Motivational considerations in the study of instruction', *Cognition and Instruction*, **54**, pp. 289–309.

MARTON, F. and SALJÖ, R., 1984, 'Approaches to learning', in MARTON, F., HOUNSELL, D.J., and ENTWISTLE, N.J. (Eds), *The Experience of Learning*, Edinburgh: Scottish Academic Press.

MCBRIDE, M., 1990, 'A Foulcauldian analysis of mathematical discourse', *For the Learning of Mathematics*, **9**, 1, pp. 40–47.

MURRHY, P., 1989, 'Assessment and Gender', *Education Review*, **3**, 2, pp. 37–41.

NATIONAL COUNCIL OF TEACHERS OF MATHEMATICS, 1989, *Curriculum and Evaluation Standards for School Mathematics*, Reston, V.A.

NATIONAL CURRICULUM COUNCIL, 1989, *Mathematics Non-Statutory Guidance*, York: National Curriculum Council.

NOSS, R., GOLDSTEIN, H. and HOYLES, C., 1989, 'Graded assessment and learning hierarchies in mathematics', *British Education Research Journal*, **15**, 2, pp. 109–20.

OWEN, D., 1985, None of the Above: *Behind the Myth of Scholastic Aptitude*, Boston: Houghton Mifflin Co.

ROMBERG, T.A., ZARINNIA, E.A. and WILLIAMS, S., 1989, *The Influence of Mandated Testing on Mathematics Instruction: Grade 8 Teachers' Perceptions*, National Center for Research in Mathemaical Science Education, University of Wisconsin-Madison.

SELIGMANN, M.E., 1975, *Helplessness*, W.H. Freeman and Company.

SLAVIN, R.E., 1983, *Cooperative Learning*, New York: Longman.

STEINBRING, H., 1990, 'Interaction and knowledge in mathematics teaching' *Recherches en Didactique des Mathematiques*, in press.

TURKLE, S. and PAPERT, S., 1990, 'Epistemological pluralism: Styles and noices within the computer culture', *Signs*, **15**, 1.

VAN OERS, B., 1990, 'The development of mathematical thinking in school: A comparison of the action-psychological and the information-processing approaches, *International Journal of Educational Research*, **14**, 1, 51–66.

WALKERDINE, V., 1988, *The Mastery of Reason: Cognitive Development and the Production of Rationality*, London: Routledge.

VOIGT, J., 1989, 'Social functions of routines and consequences for subject matter learning', in PERRET-CLERMONT, A.N. and SCHUBAUER-LEONI, M.L. (Eds) 'social factors in learning and instruction', *International Journal of Research*, **16**, 3, pp. 647–56.

WEBB, N.M. (Ed.), 1989a, 'Peer interaction, problem-solving and cognition', *International Journal of Education Research*, **13**, 1.

WEBB, N.M., 1989b, 'Peer interaction and learning in small groups', in WEBB, N.M. (Ed.) 'Peer Interaction, Problem-Solving and Cognition', *International Journal of Education Research*, **13**, 1, pp. 21–39.

7   Testing Investigations

Alison Wolf

Introduction

The most notable innovation in the mathematics syllabus in recent years has been the introduction of extended coursework or investigations into Mathematics GCSE. While in many other subjects, coursework did not involve any substantive changes in syllabus content or teaching methods, mathematics investigations were new to the vast majority of teachers and pupils alike. They were also seen as the major vehicle for establishing the new orthodoxy: namely that mathematics teaching needs to give far more emphasis to the application of mathematics, and its use in practical, problem-solving situations.

This same view inheres in the National Curriculum documents on mathematics: most notably in the final report of the Mathematics Working Group, but also in later documents such as the National Curriculum Council's non-statutory guidance. It is therefore worth examining how investigations have actually evolved and operated. It is a salutary tale — both for those who believe that Standard Achievement Tasks in mathematics can really be new and exciting creatures, and for those interested in the future of 'teacher assessment' within the National Curriculum.

The New Orthodoxy

The new orthodoxy in mathematics education dates from the publication of the Cockcroft report, Mathematics Counts (1982). That report enunciates the growing awareness that 'mastery' of an algorithm, in the sense of being able to manipulate symbols, is not at all the same thing as being able to use it appropriately. For example, 'knowing' that $9 \times 7 = 63$ is not the same as the ability to calculate how many hours one sleeps in a week, given nine hours of sleep a night. And 'knowing' how to calculate 5 per cent of 70, or 50 per cent of 600, certainly is not the same as being able to monitor whether the wastage rate in a restaurant falls within a set target, or determine the effect on costs of a 150 per cent rise in component prices. (See e.g. APU 1982; Ekenstam and Greger 1983.)

If people have enormous trouble in identifying the mathematical structure of problems, and in using their mathematics appropriately., it seems logical that students should have more practice in just this area. Hence the Cockcroft report's argument that 'no topic should be included unless it can be developed sufficiently for it to be applied in ways which the pupils can understand' (para 451) and insistence on 'the need ... to relate the content of the mathematics course to pupils' experience of everyday life' (para 462).

Within GCSE mathematics, coursework was originally identified as an ideal mechanism for delivering on these good intentions. The following excerpts are taken from the SMP11–16 Training Package issued by the Midland Examining Group: but parallels can be found in the background notes for any of the groups and syllabi which explain the nature of coursework assignments.

> In school mathematics a great deal of time is devoted to acquiring facts and ideas, becoming familiar with terminology, and practising skills and routines.... The kinds of work assessed by coursework are of a quite different kind. The emphasis is shifted toward mathematical thinking of a more general kind, the sort of thinking that will enable pupils to tackle, with confidence, the solving of novel kinds of problem that require more than just the application of standard techniques.... Certain types of work, notably investigational work, practical work and work requiring the pupil to collect and select appropriate data from the real world cannot be adequately assessed by written papers. (Midland Examining Group: 1)

Turning to the report of the National Curriculum Mathematics Working Group (DES, 1988), we find this perspective on mathematics education well entrenched. Thus, at the very beginning of the discussion on the nature of mathematics (para 2.1), the report notes that:

The special power of mathematics lies in its capacity not just to describe and explain but also to predict — to suggest possible answers to practical problems. (DES, 1988: 3)

and a little later (para. 2.10):

We have said that the power of mathematics in tackling practical problems from everyday life and world of work justifies its position in the school curriculum. However, that power will not be fully realised if the ability to apply mathematics effectively to unfamiliar problems is not developed through the mathematics curriculum. The nature of the relationship between mathematical skills and techniques and their practical use is not self-evident to some children. It has to be learned, just as much as the skills and techniques have to be learned. Learning to communicate with and about mathematics is an important aspect of learning to use mathematics to tackle problems. But developing the ability and confidence to use mathematics in this way will also foster other important qualities: perseverance; imagination and flexibility; self management and team working skills; and, perhaps above all, a 'can do' attitude to life's challenges. ... (Our) report presents detailed proposals for ensuring that the mathematics curriculum realizes its potential in these respects. (DES 1988: 4)

The working group also describes in some detail their visits to other countries to examine principles of mathematics teaching. In all of them, they registered an apparent consensus among educators — if not the population at large — that greater emphasis on practical applications was desirable.

The group's report proposed that the mathematics curriculum be divided into three 'profile components', one of which would be concerned directly with practical applications of mathematics (and carry 40 per cent of the assessment loading.) However, the Government — or, strictly speaking, the Secretaries of State for Education and Science and for Wales — expressed 'concern' about this approach, arguing both that this gave too much weight to applications compared to the 'foundation of knowledge, skills and understanding'; and that, where possible, targets for practical applications should be combined with other targets. Consequently, the National Curriculum is, in this area, a quintessentially bureaucratic fudge. 'Practical applications' no longer stand alone with a heavy assessment weighting. However, two related targets are included. Of the 14 attainment targets for the subject, 12 concern topics: — number, algebra, measures, data handling or 'shape and space'. Targets 1 and 9 however, are concerned with the 'use and application' of mathematics and specifically with its use in 'practical tasks and real-life problems' (DES, 1989). In the non-statutory guidance of 1989, the NCC pronounces that:

> Using and applying mathematics, as represented in Attainment Targets 1 and 9 and the associated elements of the programmes of study, should stretch across and permeate all other work in mathematics, providing both the means to, and the rationale for, the progressive development of knowledge, skills and understanding in mathematics. (NCC, 1989, Section D 1.5)

It would seem, therefore, that within the mathematics teaching profession and the examining groups, general agreement prevails. Effective teaching and learning demand an enormous increase in the use of 'practical' examples. The mathematics curriculum consequently should be informed on a day-to-day basis by its relevance to everyday life.

From all this, we might predict first, that the contemporary classroom will indeed differ markedly from its predecessors in its emphasis on applications; second, that GCSE coursework will emphasise strongly the application of mathematics to 'real-life' situations; and third, that these trends will continue under the National Curriculum. If so, we would be wrong. Neither of the first two statements holds true, and in explaining why, we can see how unlikely it is that our third prediction will be correct.

'Investigations' Crystallize

Extended coursework within mathematics GCSE is intended to include two very different sorts of activity. On the one hand, students are asked to explore abstract mathematical situations and puzzles, many of which seem to be lifted directly from the collections of mathematical recreations beloved by the Victorians (e.g. Ball 1892). On the other hand, they may be presented with tasks in which mathematics is related to objects and activities from the world outside school.

Teachers following SMP (School Mathematics Project) courses

recently have been issued detailed guidance on compulsory 'open ended tasks' (sic). Here, the SMP 11–16 examiners state that:

> There are two basic categories of open-ended task, called practical and investigational. Practical tasks offer opportunities to apply mathematical thinking to 'real' situations; investigational tasks refer to the mathematical explanation of more abstract contexts. (Midland Examining Group: 20)

Not all the examining groups would use 'practical' in exactly this way, or make a formal distinction between types of task. However, operationally, the difference is clear enough. The former group embodies the 'applications' philosophy of which current documents are redolent: the latter provides extensions of 'pure' mathematics.

These two types of task also represent two different influences on the philosophy of GCSE. The idea that open-ended investigation is desirable developed separately from the concern with applications: and in principle one could have had coursework requirements concerned with either one or the other. In fact, however, no-one seems to have queried the desirability of letting coursework assignments cover both.

One might suppose, however, that, over the last few years, there would be increasing use of practical/applied tasks as examiners and teachers build up expertize in their development and administration. Not so. Surveying the range of tasks offered by, and submitted to, the examining groups, one finds:

a) an increasing preponderance of 'investigations.'
b) the correct perception by teachers that 'investigation' tasks offer able pupils greater opportunities to display the type of work required to obtain high grades: and that, by implication, the 'practical' tasks are more suited to less able pupils entering for less demanding papers.
c) chief examiners identifying greater problems with the way in which 'practical' tasks are tackled and completed by candidates.

If this is the case for GCSE coursework, what can we expect for the National Curriculum's Standard Assessment Tasks, produced and administered under far greater time pressure and with the need to 'score' numerous, differentiated targets, defined in mathematical terms? And why has the heralded shift to 'real life' coursework never occurred?

added.). To dieters, of course, that is exactly what calorie counting is: and to pupils unaware of what they 'ought' to be doing, it would reasonably have appeared likewise. Why should it occur to them to import unnecessary mathematics techniques into apparently sensible questions?[2]

Contingent Disappointment? Or Necessary Failing?

Faced with the choice between abstract 'investigations' and practical tasks which often seem tedious, as well as ill-suited to 'higher' mathematics, there seems an obvious riposte: improve the coursework tasks. Given the general chorus of approval for the idea of applying mathematics, the observer may wonder why one cannot simply devise better assignments, in which the use of, say, algebra represents a natural and appropriate response to the problem.

So far, as noted earlier, this has signally failed to occur. Nor, we would suggest, is it likely. And this in turn bodes ill for the chances of a National Curriculum which is truly imbued with targets 1 and 9 — the 'use' and 'application' of mathematics to real-life situations.

From the point of view of the pupil, there is actually a good reason to expect that less 'advanced' mathematics will be used in more realistic or anchored tasks than in purely mathematical investigations. If we define more 'advanced' simply as more recently learned, then we know that such techniques are less likely to be used in problematic or difficult situations, where people fall back on familiar and fully internalized methods (Sewell, 1982; Wolf, 1984). Equally, we know that applied problems involving a given algorithm are more difficult than manipulation in the abstract (APU, 1982; Hart, 1981). That is, after all, precisely the point from which the current advocacy of mathematics applications began! We should therefore expect, on theoretical grounds, that pupils will use fewer of the less familiar skills — such as algebraic formulations — in 'applied' coursework problems than in investigations of comparable difficulty which are presented within an entirely mathematical framework.

This is not to say that 'practical' tasks are necessarily boring for pupils, closed-ended or unchallenging. Within the school curriculum, for example, subjects such as Design and Technology or Physics throw up problems which can be developed into successful mathematics coursework (Wolf and Grey, 1988). From the point of view of a maths examiner, however, realistic and 'practical' tasks, whether drawn from the school curriculum or elsewhere, have two enormous disadvantages.

First, they require a considerable amount of non-mathematical knowledge. You cannot identify and create tasks derived from problems in technology; or construction work; or food processing unless you know a considerable amount about these areas. And of course, what a mathematics examiner or teacher knows about is mathematics. . . .

The second problem may, ultimately, be even more decisive. It is that most 'real-life' situations in which mathematics is used in any cumulative or symbolic way tend to be rather large and unwieldy. They do not fit neatly onto two sides of A4 paper, but call on large quantities of data, and — very often — the work of more than one individual. An examining group, on the other hand, must not assume prior non-mathematical knowledge on the part of a candidate; is setting a task which probably accounts for only 10 per cent of the marks in one of eight subjects; and is cost-cutting to boot. A recent NEA task on 'House Plans', using authentic estate agents' details, ran to eight pages — and left one with far too little information for any statistical analysis to make sense.

It is thus hardly surprising that, three years into GCSE, 'applications' in any meaningful sense are on the retreat, not the advance. The prognosis for the National Curriculum is surely worse still. Most of the examining groups have moved away from an itemized marking scheme for coursework, recognising that, for integrated tasks, this is unworkable. It is thus at least theoretically possible for them to treat applied tasks differently from abstract ones, and recognize that a script is not at a lower level simply because it contains fewer 'skills'. The National Curriculum, however, is built around just such itemised disaggregated checklists of targets and levels. There will be even more pressure on pupils to 'score' a level 9 on measures ('lengths of arcs, areas of sectors and segments of circles') or a level 8 on algebra ('manipulation of simple algebraic expressions: rules of indices for fractional and negative values').

The Secretaries of State had a point in their failure to be convinced by the original argument presented in favour of 'practical applications' for it reflected a fundamental incoherence in the new orthodox rhetoric. As Richard Noss has pointed out in another paper in this volume, the sole 'practical' example which the mathematics working group provided is in fact a completely non-real problem, selected entirely because it allows for a mathematical range of solutions. What we have now, however, is a curriculum in which developing the 'inherent' applications commended by Targets 1 and 9 has almost nothing going for it — and a lot against.

Lessons for Teacher Assessment

While the main concern of this article is with the way coursework content evolves, GCSE experiences also illustrate clearly the pressures which will inevitably attend attempts to implement TGAT recommendations. Within the coursework component, there is offered, under GCSE, a possible 'dual' scheme — and, predictably, it is the scheme in which teachers have the greater control which has been 'problematic', and 'unsatisfactory'.

With the exception (until 1991 entry) of SMP, the examining groups have offered schools two options in those mathematics syllabi involving coursework. Either they can use the group-set tasks for coursework, or they can use and submit tasks which they have devised themselves. However, very few schools have availed themselves of the second option (and while no exact figures are kept, numbers seem to be declining, not increasing.) This is sensible on their part. The LEA inspector who informed us that 'candidates entering non-standard coursework appeared to be disadvantaged' had encapsulated the examining groups' perception, which is that centre-set topics are generally disappointing and/or mathematically undemanding. As one Chief Examiner remarked, 'Accuracy of assessment from the centres tended to be better on the Group-set tasks than on ones set by the centres themselves'.

Deliberate sabotage of the centre-led option is again too simple an explanation. On the one hand, it was not necessary for the groups to offer the option in the first place: on the other, examiners and staff consistently express regret at not finding in these submissions fresh ideas they could adapt. Instead, we need to look at processes inherent to centrally administered and 'standardized' assessment: processes which will apply, quite as strongly, to the proposed National Curriculum system.

Ultimately, the model of what is being tested, and of what constitutes different levels of achievement, exists in a chief examiner's head (Orr and Nuttall 1983). He or she can pass it on through the shared experiences of marking and discussing borderline scripts: but it is not, ever, fully conveyed by written syllabi or grade criteria. That is why, whether in GCSE, A-level, 'criterion-referenced' vocational tests, or university finals, the candidate (and teacher) find out what they really have to know and do by looking at the assessments set.

Centre-set tasks are, by definition, not a direct product of the chief examiner's own mental model. In some subjects (notably English), this situation seems to have been sustainable — presumably because the subject culture is uniform and shared. In maths, however, the very area in which coursework tasks were introduced was the one which was new to the subject, and where no such shared consensus had or could have evolved. In this situation, a mismatch between centre-set tasks and what the examiners felt 'should' be produced, was almost inevitable.

The process of marking produces corresponding pressures. Here, groups have adopted a variety of approaches. The early SMP tasks carried work schemes of the most rigidly traditional kinds, including the notorious 'pages of the novel' task, which asked candidates to look at ways of estimating the number of words in a book! Most groups started by asking for separate scores for different objectives — e.g. 'reason and make deductions', 'communicate'. This proved unworkable on a task-by-task basis because the demands and opportunities varied so between tasks. Thus, LEAG, for example, now ask simply for an overall mark, while NEA still requests separate marks for each of its six 'Objectives' but with one score per candidate, extracted and summed over all coursework tasks.

Whatever method is used, when faced with scripts which may have taken very different approaches to a topic, examiners and teachers alike tend to start with a more or less comprehensive ranking. That is, they use their general, integrated model of what different grades 'should' look like to put things in approximate order. Teachers tend to be rather defensive about this: experienced moderators less so. One of the latter emphasised to us the fact that in GCSE, the same script would get different marks according to the paper for which it was entered. In this situation, he felt, the human brain could only function if the scripts were placed in some overall order first.

Such a ranking process also helps to clarify what a particular grade script 'ought' to look like for a particular task. Examiners can and do argue that they can recognize a GCSE 'C' script — or an 'alpha' script in university finals — even when it stands alone. However, this supposed facility does not extend equally to every question or task. However experienced one may be in setting questions, there are always some which turn out to be harder, or easier, than one would expect. Hence, quite inevitably, what an 'A' or an 'F' script looks like becomes, in good part, a reflection of the scripts submitted by people who are 'obviously' 'A' or 'F' candidates. This is not to imply that exam marking is simply a question of rank ordering: on the contrary as Good and Cresswell found (1988), in GCSE harder questions tend to be marked more severely. Nonetheless, this 'norm-referencing' process is very important in crystallizing, for teacher-assessors and for moderators, the nature of 'criterion' scripts.

The more scripts one sees, the easier it becomes to create — again, largely unconsciously — a generalized model of 'appropriate' responses for different grades on a given task. Similarly, if tasks are set by the same chief examiners, year by year, and if teacher training uses answers to questions set by these same examiners, it will become increasingly easy for the teachers to discern what an 'A', 'C' or 'F' script 'should' be like.

If, however, a centre sets its own tasks, the teacher-assessor and the moderator are immediately placed in very different situations from each other. The model, now, is in the teacher's head, not the chief examiner's or (through shared marking), the moderator's. The small number of scripts involved also makes it harder for the moderator to discern what the teacher's general underlying model/grade criteria are. He or she is more likely to fix on what are from the teacher's viewpoint, 'distractors', or relatively unimportant features — and see them as evidence of inappropriate grading on the teacher's part. The situation in fact makes evident the basic incoherence in the idea that completely different tasks or exams can be equated through reference to freestanding 'criteria'. However, what the exam groups perceive to be happening is that centre-set tasks are less reliable and less accurately marked than tasks set by the examining group.

The parallels with the National Curriculum are clear. There will be moderation of teacher assessments — i.e. assessments which used teachers' own assessment tasks — to adjust and account for any differences between these and pupils' results on the SATs. Harvey Goldstein has noted, elsewhere in this collection, that if the SAT results are to be treated as definitive, then the teacher assessments are strictly superfluous. But even if there were no such formal hierarchy in the weight given to each set of marks, the history of GCSE investigations suggests that the SAT scores would inevitably win the day. As established carriers of standards, familiar to everyone, SATs will be seen not only by moderators but also by other teachers as the reference tests to which their colleagues' unfamiliar tests and marking schemes must necessarily refer. Any attempt to move away from the exemplars institutionalized in guidance documents will, whatever the rhetoric and intentions, tend to disadvantage pupils and teachers alike.

Notes

1 Referring to GCSE grades.
2 See also Dowling, in this volume.

References

ASSESSMENT OF PERFORMANCE UNIT (APU), 1982, *Mathematical Development: Secondary Survey Report No. 3*, London: HMSO.

BALL, W.W. Rouse, 1892, *Mathematical Recreations and Essays*, London: Macmillan

COCKCROFT, W.H. *et al.*, 1982, *Mathematics Counts*, London: HMSO.

DES AND WELSH OFFICE, 1988, *Mathematics for ages 5 to 16*, London: HMSO.

DES AND WELSH OFFICE, 1989, *Mathematics in the National Curriculum*, London: HMSO.

EKENSTAM, A. and GREGOR, K., 1983, 'Some aspects of children's ability to solve mathematical problems', *Educational Studies in Mathematics*, **14**, 369–84.

GOOD, F. and CRESSWELL, M., 1988, *Differentiated Assessment: Grading and Related Issues. The Full Report of the Novel Examinations at 16+ Research Project*, London: Secondary Examinations Council.

HART, K.M. (ed.), 1981, *Children's Understanding of Mathematics 11–16*, Oxford: John Murray.

LONDON and EAST ANGLIA EXAMINING GROUP (LEAG), nd, *Mathematics GCSE Coursework*, London: LEAG.

MIDLAND EXAMINING GROUP (in association with the London and East Anglian Group on behalf of all GCSE Examining Groups), *SMP 11–16 Training Package*, MEG.

NCC, 1989, *Mathematics: Non-Statutory Guidance*, York: NCC.

NORTHERN EXAMINING ASSOCIATION (NEA), nd, *GCSE Mathematics Coursework Exemplar Material: 1991*, NEA.

ORR, L. and NUTTALL, D.L., 1983, *Determining Standards in the Proposed Common System of Examinations at 16+*, London: Schools Council.

SEWELL, B., 1982, *Use of Mathematics by Adults in Daily Life*, Advisory Council for Adult and Continuing Education.

SOUTHERN EXAMINING GROUP (SEG), nd, *GCSE Mathematics Coursework Exemplar Material*, SEG.

WOLF, A., 1984, *Practical Mathematics at Work*, MSC Research and Development Monograph no. 21, Sheffield: Manpower Services Commission.

WOLF, A. and GREY, A., 1988, 'Maths and TVEI: Right for the job' *Times Educational Supplement*, 30 September.

8 The Changing Role of Algebra in School Mathematics: the potential of computer-based environments

Rosamund Sutherland

Introduction

Algebra is the language of mathematics, a language which can be used to express ideas within mathematics itself, or within other disciplines. It is an abstract language which has developed over the centuries from its first introduction as a tool to solve equations in which a letter or symbol represented a particular but unknown number, to classical generalized arithmetic in which symbols are used to represent relationships between variables. Within modern mathematics, algebra is not only a language for generalized arithmetic but also a language which enables the similarities in structure between different mathematical systems to be made explicit. An essential aspect of the algebraic language is that it enables referential meaning to be suspended. Meaning can lie within the constraints of the algebraic system and this is what causes most confusion amongst pupils. In this respect algebra is different from natural language:

> While stressing the linguistic aspect of algebra, one should not overlook an important feature by which the instruction of the language of algebraic formulae is distinguished from other linguistic instruction. To a high degree the language of formulae can be handled autonomously, independent of the understanding of the content. Such an autonomy does not apply to everyday language. (Freudenthal, 1973: 311)

Within the new National Curriculum for mathematics algebra is the main focus of three attainment targets. Attainment Target 5 is predominantly concerned with algebra as a means of expressing general patterns. Attainment Target 6 deals with functions, formulae, equations and inequalities and Attainment Target 7 focuses on graphical representations of algebraic functions. The algebra curriculum is now set out very precisely within these attainment targets and the main focus of this chapter will be to consider whether this curriculum reflects the potential of computer-based environments to change pupils' use and understanding of algebraic ideas. There are two main reasons why the influence of the computer could radically change the ways in which pupils learn algebra. The first is that computer-based experiences can provide pupils with a background of using and manipulating formalisms which offers the potential of a new entry point into algebra. The second is that mathematics itself is being influenced by the computer, as illustrated by the present interest in non-linear feedback systems which result in chaotic behaviour.

Within this chapter I shall firstly discuss the development of the teaching and learning of algebra since the beginning of the century, in order to understand how these have influenced the algebra components of the National Curriculum.

Influences on the Algebra Components of the National Curriculum

Since the beginning of the century the teaching of algebra has been a central concern of mathematics educators, who have always been aware of the inherent difficulties in the subject. At this time school algebra placed an emphasis on definition and notation and all the text books deriving from the period introduced algebra by means of a series of definitions:

> Algebra, like arithmetic is a science which treats of numbers. In Arithmetic numbers are represented by figures which have determinate values. In Algebra the letters of the alphabet are used to represent numbers, and each letter can stand for any number whatever, except that in any connected series of operations each letter must throughout be supposed to represent the same number. Since the letters employed in Algebra represent any numbers whatever, the results arrived at must be equally true of all numbers. (Smith, 1921: 1)

Figure 1

Examples

1. Find the numerical values of the following expressions in each of which $a = 1$, $b = 2$, $c = 3$, and $d = 4$.

    (i) $5a + 3c - 3b - 2d$,   (ii) $26a - 3bc + d$,
    (iii) $ab + 3bc - 5d$,   (iv) $bc - ca - ab$,
    (v) $a + bc + d$ and   (vi) $bcd + cda + dab + abc$.
                                              Ans. 0, 12, 0, 1, 11, 50.

2. If $a = 3$, $b = 1$ and $c = 2$, find the numerical values of

    (i) $2a^2 - 3b^2 - 4c^2$,   (ii) $2a^2b - 3b^2c^2$,

                                   (iv) $a^2 + 3ac^2 - 3a^2c - c^2$,
    (iii) $\frac{16}{1}c^2 - \frac{2}{1}b^2$,

and (v) $2a^4b^2c - 3b^4c^2a - c^4a^2b$.   *Ans.* 19, 6, 0, 1, 0.

Algebra was synonymous with generalised arithmetic and, after being presented with a series of definitions, pupils were introduced to algebraic symbolism in the context of evaluating general algebraic expressions for specific values (see for example Figure 1).

The four rules of arithmetic were progressively introduced in an algebra context with references being made to the similarities between arithmetic and algebra and the emphasis was on repeatedly practising algebraic ideas by working through a multitude of exercises (see for example Figure 2). Already in 1933 this method of introducing pupils to algebra was criticised:

> The 'Four Rules' method is unsatisfactory, not because it is difficult, but because it is uninteresting and leaves the boy in a very bad position for further progress. He will have learnt to regard the new subject as meaningless and artificial, and this is the most difficult of all defects to remedy. (Mathematics Association, 1933: 88; in Mason *et al.*, 1985)

That school algebra should not descend into meaningless manipulations of symbols has been a recurring fear of mathematics educators, as illustrated by this more recent comment by Küchemann:

> Mathematics teaching is often seen as an initiation into rules and procedures which, though very powerful (and therefore

very attractive to teachers) are often seen by children as meaningless. (Küchemann, 1981: 118)

In order to overcome this seemingly meaningless manipulation of symbols, algebra began to be introduced in the context of solving practical problems deriving from practical geometry, physics and mechanics as illustrated by the problem in Figure 3.

These types of 'practical' problems were considered to constitute a new approach to the teaching of algebra, although teachers were warned that in solving problems 'there is a danger that the boy may learn first to regard the idea of x as representing an unknown in an equation as more important that the idea of x as a variable' (Mathematics Association, 1933). From our present day position these 'practical' problems seem rather contrived, may only appeal to certain pupils, and could in most cases be solved without the use of algebra.

What might motivate students to learn and like algebra would be a glimpse of its problem-solving power, but the only problems that can be solved with the algebra taught in a first algebra course are either trivial or better solved by other methods. (Lee and Wheeler, 1987: 13)

However this quest for meaning from 'practical' as opposed to more abstract ideas continues and is nowadays reflected in the general trend to link mathematics to the problems of every-day life.

The teaching of algebra remained essentially unchanged until the mathematical reform movement, starting in the 60s and spearheaded in Britain by the School Mathematics Project. This movement reflected the changing role of algebra for mathematicians, placing an emphasis on algebra as a language for representing structures. Functions, mappings and isomorphisms became a strong focus and pupils' first introduction to algebra was now likely to be in the context of set theory. Freudenthal maintains that the new mathematics had a disastrous effect on the teaching of algebra and is particularly critical of the ways in which letters were now used to denote both sets and members of sets (e.g. x ϵ {a,b,c}) and that pupils used letters in this context before using the idea of a letter as representing a variable. 'Sets of letters are of course quite legitimate ... but sets of letters are dangerous ... the use of letters in mathematics was already settled in ancient times' (Freudenthal, 1973: 289). The effect of the new mathematics movement has also been criticised by Chevellard (1984)

Figure 2

EXAMPLES

6. Add $m^2 - 3mn + 2n^2$, $3n^2 - m^2$ and $5mn - 3n^2 + 2m^2$.
7. Add $3a^2 - 2ac - 2ab$, $2b^2 + 3bc + 3ab$ and $c^2 - 2ac - 2bc$.
8. Add $\frac{3}{2}a^2b - 5ab^2 + 7b^2$, $2a^3 - \frac{1}{2}a^2b + 5ab^2$ and $3b^3 - 2a^3$.
9. Subtract $3a - 4b + 2c$ from $a + b - 2c$.
10. Subtract $\frac{a}{2} + \frac{3}{2}b - \frac{5}{3}c$ from $c - \frac{1}{2}a - \frac{2}{3}b$.
11. Subtract $3x^2 - 4x + 2$ from $4x^2 - 5x - 7$.
12. Subtract $5a^4 - 3a^3b + 4a^2b^2$.

Figure 3

2. How much can the water-level rise in each of the glasses shown in Fig. 3 before the water overflows?

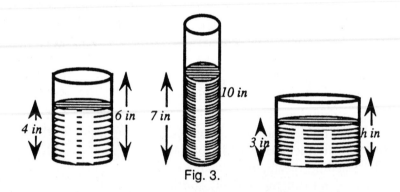

Fig. 3.

How much if   (i) a glass 5 inches high contains water *d* inches deep;
                (ii) a glass *h* inches high contains water *d* inches deep?

who maintains that what has been lost since the reform is the dialectic between arithmetic and algebra which was so heavily prevalent in the earlier algebra text books. He stresses that this dialectic existed even before the construction of the algebraic language and that in Greek times there existed two arithmetics, a computational arithmetic (logistica) and theory of numbers (arithmetica).

When we study the new National Curriculum almost all traces of the 'new mathematics' seem to have been removed. As with many educational swings, ideas introduced have now been whole-heartedly rejected, in part because the more abstract nature of the new mathematics was found to be inaccessible to most pupils. However the algebra components of the new National Curriculum have not returned to the situation which existed before the 'new maths' movement and the close interrelationship between algebra and arithmetic is predominantly missing. There are some traces of this link within Attainment Target 5 (Number/Algebra) but the emphasis is more on number patterns arising from a whole range of situations, as opposed to number patterns arising from the rules of arithmetic. There is very little explicit mention of the structure of arithmetic and the fragmented nature of the National Curriculum means that it is unlikely that teachers will be able to reconstruct this for themselves.

Perhaps the most obvious influence on the new National Curriculum for mathematics is the outcome of research concerned with pupils' difficulties with the use of letters (Collis, 1974; Küchemann, 1981; see also Kieran, 1989 for a review of this research). This research highlighted the difficulties which pupils have with the use of letters in algebra. In Britain research was spearheaded by the CSMS study (Hart, 1981) which made attempts to link pupils' difficulties with algebra to Piagetian sub-stages (see O'Reilly in this volume). One effect of this research on the algebra curriculum is that many pupils in Britain are (just before the advent of the new Curriculum for mathematics) introduced to algebraic ideas at a later stage of their secondary schooling and with more caution than they were some years ago. This seems to be a direct consequence of i) the finding that pupils have difficulty with algebra and ii) a belief in Piaget's theory concerning formal operations and the related idea that pupils will not be able to cope with algebra until they reach the stage of formal operations. These beliefs are so strong, that in the early stages of our work with the computer (Hoyles and Sutherland, 1989) the secondary teachers we worked with were reluctant to introduce pupils to the idea of variable in Logo.

I suggest that the difficulties which pupils develop with algebra will at least be partly related to the ways in which algebra has been introduced to them in school. It seems surprising therefore that a major study, the CSMS algebra study, did not in any way attempt to describe or link the algebraic practices from which these difficulties stemmed, especially since at the time of the study it is likely that some schools were using the 'new mathematics' approach and others a more traditional approach. This is also discussed by O'Reilly (this volume).

In Booth's study (1984), which followed on from the CSMS study, she also identified pupils' difficulties with the use of letters but made the additional point that:

> many of the difficulties which children have in algebra are not difficulties in algebra as such, but are rather difficulties in arithmetic. Many children i) do not explicitly consider method in arithmetic, ii) may in fact use procedures which are not formalised, iii) tend to interpret expressions in terms of context so that the need for precision and rigour in the form of mathematical statements is not appreciated, and iv) even in the case of those mathematical procedures of which they are explicitly aware are not always proficient in their symbolisation. (Booth, 1984: 89)

This finding seems to be directly related to Chevellard's concern that the new maths movement effectively destroyed the close interrelationship between arithmetic and algebra.

During the 1980s and influenced by the CSMS research findings the emphasis within algebra teaching gradually changed. The introduction of symbol manipulation was delayed and pupils first introduction to algebra was more likely to be in the context of expressing generality (see for example Figure 4).

The idea of algebra as a means of expressing generalities is also strongly reflected in work emanating from the Open University (Mason *et al.* 1985). These authors point out that:

> ... rearranging and manipulating algebraic expressions is what most people associate with algebra, and in particular, solving equations. It is certainly an important aspect but it can be over-emphasised at the expense of more delicate perceptions. (Mason *et al.*, 1985: 54)

They stress that 'the central feature of algebra is that it is an ideal medium through which one can see and express general statements (*ibid*: 1). This emphasis has been preserved within the new National Curriculum in Attainment Target 5: Pupils should recognise and use patterns, relationships and sequences and make generalisations.

Another general trend in mathematics education in the 80s is an emphasis on the mathematics of 'everyday life' (See Wolf, this volume). This search for 'real life' meaning within mathematics is often quite inappropriate within the realm of algebra, and has resulted in algebra taking a seemingly 'back seat' within school mathematics. However, as Alison Wolf points out (this volume) within 'practical' GCSE mathematics investigations the expectation is that the successful pupils will finally use algebra to solve the problem and this is how the

Figure 4

2a) Complete the mapping diagram by looking for a pattern in the squares.

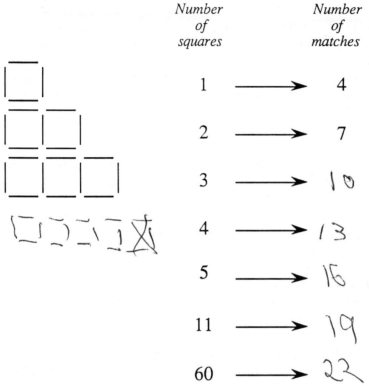

Number of squares		Number of matches
1	⟶	4
2	⟶	7
3	⟶	10
4	⟶	13
5	⟶	16
11	⟶	19
60	⟶	22

b) Write down a **rule** which explains how you got the second number from the first.

c) If possible write down the **rule** in algebra.

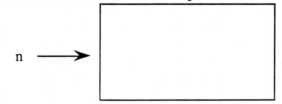

n ⟶ [ ]

highest marks are obtained. That this is not usually made explicit to the pupils themselves seems to result from a dishonest or muddled view of the role of algebra within school mathematics. This view has not been clarified within the new National Curriculum and algebra still seems to be part of the 'hidden curriculum' within the Using and Applying Mathematics (Target 1) strand of the document. In the introduction to this Attainment Target it says 'Pupils should use number, algebra and measures in practical tasks, in real-life problems and to investigate within mathematics itself'. However algebraic ideas are nowhere explicitly mentioned within the statements of attainment of Attainment Target 1, apart from a vague reference in Attainment Level 10 'Use symbolism with confidence'.

So, to summarise, the most clearly identifiable influences on the algebra components of the National Curriculum for Mathematics are:

- the suppression of symbolism as a reaction to the methods of teaching algebra deriving from the beginning of the century, a time when mathematical concepts were taught by reference to the authority of the teacher, which was linked to the authority of mathematics as an abstract and powerful symbolic system.
- an emphasis on algebra as a means of expressing generality with generalising being more important than symbolising. This is related to the dual aims of giving meaning to algebra and making algebra more accessible to a larger number of pupils.
- the loss of the dialectic between arithmetic and algebra resulting from the influence of the 'new maths' movement on the teaching of algebra.
- algebra as the 'hidden curriculum' within practical mathematics.

These influences can be summarized as both a search for meaning and the suppression of symbolism. However there is an inherent paradox in this search for meaning within algebra, because what gives algebra its power is the potential to work with symbols without reference to 'external' meaning. The meaning can lie within the algebraic system itself:

> ... algebra is a detour; Students must give up the temptation of calculating the unknown as quickly as possible, they must accept operating on symbols without paying attention to the

meaning of these operations in the context referred to. (Vergnaud and Cortes, 1986: 320)

There are many who believe that operating on the unknown is the
most crucial and most difficult aspect of algebra (Filloy and Rojano,
1989). In other countries pupils are faced with this idea when they
solve algebraic equations. Algebraic equation solving has been de-
emphasised within the National Curriculum for mathematics and we
need to ask whether or not equation solving had a crucial role in
helping pupils accept the important algebraic idea of operating on the
unknown.

Computer-Based Environments: the potential

It is ironical that at a time when many secondary pupils' introduction
to algebra is both being delayed and restricted the use of computers in
schools is increasing. To interact with most computer environments it
is necessary to use a formal language and this is particularly the case
for programming languages and other powerful computer programs
(for example spreadsheets and databases). Studies have shown that
pupils can use these computer-based formal systems (Noss, 1986;
Sutherland, 1989; Thomas and Tall, 1986) and there are many reports
of pupils being able to work with the formal computer-based systems
in ways which are far more sophisticated than that which is normally
expected of them within school algebra (see Healy *et al.*, 1990). This is
not to suggest that pupils' use of these computer-based formal systems is unproblematic but only that with appropriate support pupils
can use them in ways which far exceed their use of school algebra.
Whether this is because these systems are qualitatively different from
'paper and pencil' algebra or whether it is because expectation of
pupils' performance within school algebra is restricted, are questions
which are being addressed by an on-going project (Sutherland, 1990).

I shall firstly discuss the potential of the Logo programming
language from the point of view of developing algebraic understandings. One important feature of Logo is that it is an interactive language in which variables are locally named and operated on within a
procedure (see Figure 5). This provides pupils with the opportunity to
develop a dialectical relationship between the process of generalizing
and the process of formalizing. In addition, Logo is a functional and
recursive programming language, both important algebraic ideas. Like
algebra, Logo is a formal system with precise syntax and rules and

Figure 5

```
TO  P  :SIZE
FD  :SIZE  *  3
RT  90
FD  :SIZE
RT  90
FD  :SIZE  *  1.5
RT  90
FD  :SIZE
LT  90
FD  :SIZE  *  1.5
LT  180
END
```

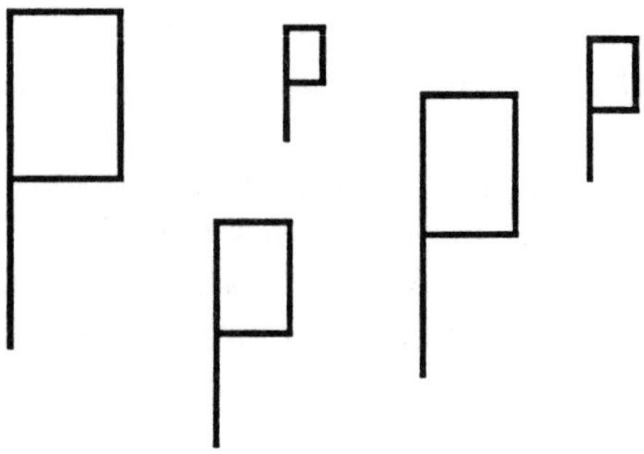

pupils must perceive it as such before they can use it in any meaningful way.

One of the difficulties with 'traditional' algebra in that it is not easy to find introductory problems which need the idea of variable as a problem solving tool. Many introductory algebra problems can be solved without using algebra. This is not the case in the Logo programming context. Logo is a language for expressing generalities and in order to express the generality it is essential to name and operate on a symbol as representing a variable. This is illustrated by the procedure P which was written by two 12 year old pupils (Figure 5). In order to write the general procedure they used the naming of the variable (SIZE) in the title line of the procedure as a means of structuring the problem and referred to this variable as they discussed the nature of the generalisation. These pupils used the variable name SIZE but were well aware that they could have used any name and at other times used single letter names (e.g. S, X). Because of the suppression of letters as symbols within the algebra curriculum, we were initially cautious about using single letters to represent variables. We found however that most pupils eventually chose for themselves to use single letter variable names because this saved time when typing into the computer. In the Logo context pupils are not frightened or alienated by the use of symbols.

Recent studies (Sutherland, 1989) focusing on the crucial aspects of programming in Logo from the point of view of developing algebraic understandings have found that:

Pupils are able to use symbols in Logo to negotiate and express complex mathematical relationships. Moreover pupils can successfully write procedures in Logo which use algebraic variables without any prior experience of 'paper and pencil' algebra.

Pupils accept that a variable in Logo represents a range of numbers. This seems to derive from constructive experiences of using variable in Logo. 'Range of numbers' can include decimals and negative numbers if use of these has been part of the Logo experience.

Pupils can accept unclosed variable-dependent expressions (for example X + 5) as objects. This is a crucial step in using and operating on these variable dependent expressions.

Pupils can define and use functions in Logo and explore relationships between functions, including inverse and composite functions.

The role of symbols to construct a generalization in Logo is paramount; this is in stark contrast to the decreasing role of symbols in the algebra curriculum. I suggest that the acceptance, use and manipulation of abstract symbols is an essential part of algebra practice and that Logo provides access to these processes which have previously been relatively accessible for the majority of pupils.

Spreadsheets have also been found to be valuable from the point of view of developing algebraic understandings (Capponi and Balacheff, 1989; Healy and Sutherland, 1988; Healy *et al.*, 1990). Spreadsheets were primarily designed for manipulating 'business data', but have recently taken on a new role within mathematics education. In some senses a spreadsheet can also be thought of as similar to a programming language (although it is more similar in structure to BASIC than Logo). The following example of two pupils using a spreadsheet to generate the triangle number sequence, provides an example of the potential of a spreadsheet environment from an algebraic perspective.

Penny and Nadine are two second-year pupils from a mixed North London comprehensive school. During their third session of using spreadsheets (after about two and a half hours experience of

Figure 6

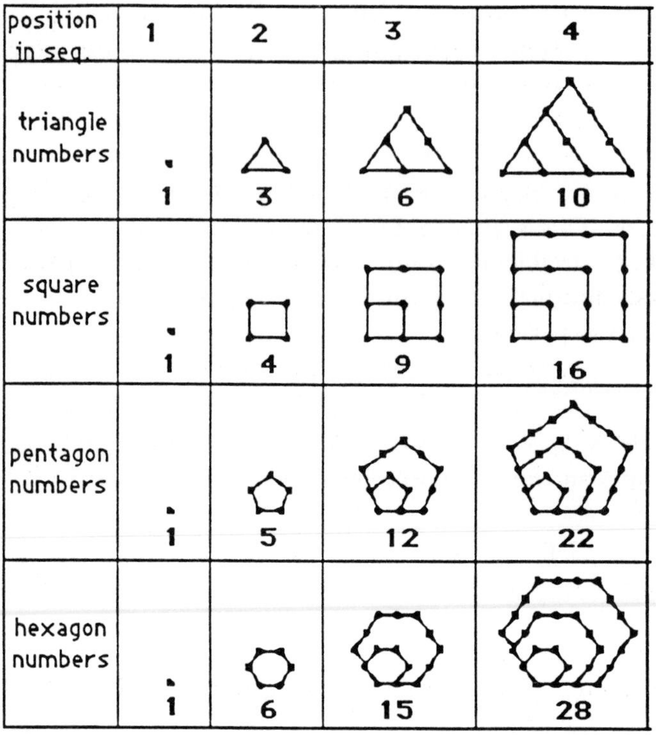

position in seq.	1	2	3	4
triangle numbers	1	3	6	10
square numbers	1	4	9	16
pentagon numbers	1	5	12	22
hexagon numbers	1	6	15	28

Excel) they were asked to generate the polygon numbers (Figure 6). They started with the problem of generating the triangle numbers.

Without any difficulty they entered the natural numbers into their spreadsheet by replicating the rule 'add 1 to the cell before' which they had already used during their previous spreadsheet sessions.

Their initial strategy was to attempt to define a recurrence relation in which each term of the triangle numbers was generated solely on the basis of the term before it (e.g. the 5th term is defined in terms of the 4th term). After unsuccessfully looking for a rule using this strategy, Penny tried out rules which were derived from the position of the triangle number in the sequence. As Penny continued to try out these rules, moving between looking at the term before and the position in the sequence she suddenly stopped in the middle of a sentence, paused, and finally announced her discovery of a pattern.

Penny: it's 3, 2 times 6 take away 3, yeah it's 3 hang on, 2 times 2 minus 1 equals 3, 3 times 2 minus 1, na, 3 times 3

equals 9, minus itself, no ....
1 2 3, hey look, look, I've found something look, here
to get the next number you add 2, here to get the next
number you add 3, and there to get the next one you
add 4, how do we write that into a formula ...... ah
I've got, it's this one add this one, that one add that one
equals that one, that one add that one equals that one.

Without any teacher intervention they write down on paper the following general rule:

trig. Δno. = no. before + position.[2]

At this stage they have written down the rule using their own representation system. We suggest that it would not be difficult for them
eventually to use the equivalent algebraic representation:

$$T_n = T_{n-1} + n \text{ (where } T_n \text{ is the nth triangle number)}$$

Having generated the triangle numbers they were able to work out
rules to generate all the other polygonal numbers. Their final spreadsheet is shown in Figures 7 and 8:

Figure 7

	A	B	C	D	E	F
1	position	1	2	3	4	5
2	triangle no.	1	3	6	10	1
3	square no.	1	4	9	16	
4	pentagon no.	1	5	12	22	
5	hexagon no.	1	6	15	28	

Figure 8

	A	B	C	D	E	F
1	position	1	=B1+1	=C1+1	=D1+1	=E1+1
2	triangle no.	1	=B2+C1	=C2+D1	=D2+E1	=E2+F1
3	square no.	1	=(B3+C1)+B1	=(C3+D1)+C1	=(D3+E1)+D1	=(E3+F1)+
4	pentagon no.	1	=(3*B2)+C1	=(3*C2)+D1	=(3*D2)+E1	=(3*E2)+
5	hexagon no.	1	=(4*B2)+C1	=(4*C2)+D1	=(4*D2)+E1	=(4*E2)+

Unlike other programming languages, naming and declaring a variable is no longer a focus in a spreadsheet environment and within a 'mouse driven' environment a mathematical relationship can be encapsulated by physically moving the mouse without explicit reference to the formal spreadsheet language. The environment allows pupils to test out mathematical relationships without having to take on board all the complexities of a formal language. The 'algebraic' relationships are likely to be closely related to arithmetic and in this sense a spreadsheet provides a context for generalizing from arithmetic. The spreadsheet environment can be thought of as some sort of intermediary between natural language and formal algebra. Pupils have to be aware of the constraints on a system before they can express it using the cells of a spreadsheet. They can use the mouse (or the arrow keys) to express the relationship between cells but can also see that this relationship is represented formally in the spreadsheet language (see for example Figure 7).

Function/graph plotting computer-based environments are also a relatively new educational development which could substantially influence the teaching of functions and graphs in schools. Recently there have also been substantial developments in the area of software which link symbolic and graphical representations. In Function Analyser, for example, a pupil can transform a graph and watch the algebraic symbolism change or alternatively manipulate the symbolism and watch the graphical representation change. Kaput claims that:

> ... the dynamic nature of the medium supports dynamic changes in variable values that renders the underlying ideas of variable and function more learnable, which should make them accessible to a younger population, and which in turn makes possible a much more gradual and extended algebra curriculum, beginning in the early grades. (Kaput, 1989: 192)

Most of these developments are taking place in the USA and have, as yet, had little impact on our educational system (possibly because most of the hardware available in schools is incompatible with most 'good' international software). Many people within the mathematics education community are wary of these 'multiple representation' environments, although it seems that increasingly software packages confront the user with multiple representations of data (e.g. the spreadsheet package EXCEL).

There is much debate about just which skills of algebraic manipulation should be preserved in the curriculum. Tall maintains that 'the manipulation of algebra to solve equations will be less important for that class of problems for which a numerical solution is appropriate and for which simple numerical algorithms on the computer will suffice' (Tall, 1989: 91). Certainly computer programs are now able to do much of the algebra manipulation which is part of beginning algebra (Nicaud, 1989). As far as I know there has been no research on the implications of these developments on school algebra practice. Undoubtedly the curriculum will eventually react as it has always done in the past but given the constraints of the National Curriculum it seems unlikely that the reaction time will keep up with the pace of technological change.

Implications of the National Curriculum on the Teaching and Learning of Algebra

Firstly I must stress that I welcome the fact that within the National Curriculum the role of algebra is relatively emphasised and the need for pupils to start working with algebraic ideas in the junior school is recognised. I suggest that delaying the teaching of algebra disadvantages all pupils because some pupils will be completely excluded from algebraic experiences and for the others 'waiting until they are ready' is, in my opinion, misconceived. During the last 20 years the role of algebra has been gradually underplayed in secondary school, which is surprising when taking into account the importance of algebra for many scientific, technological and computer based professions. An emphasis on 'child methods' and a desire to make mathematics less threatening and more enjoyable for the majority seems to have resulted in this majority being excluded from the study of A' level mathematics within which algebra still plays a crucial role. This in its turn has the effect of excluding these pupils from professions in which A-level mathematics is an entry criterion (e.g. engineering, computer science).

My first major criticism of the algebra components of the National Curriculum is that the role of symbolism is undervalued and that this undervaluing has failed to take into account the effect which experience of symbol manipulation within computer-based environments will have on pupils developing algebraic understandings. I have argued earlier that this rejection of symbolism is linked to a rejection of the authoritarian nature of approaches to algebra teaching in which definition and symbolism played a crucial role. It also reflects a very pervasive view amongst mathematics educators that symbolism is somehow grafted-on to an understanding which can be expressed in natural language (this is also linked to the Piagetian view that natural language can be grafted-on to a deeper conceptual understanding). 'Algebra is not what we write on paper, but it is something that goes on inside us. So as a teacher, I realize that notation is only a way of representing algebra, not algebra itself' (Hewitt, 1985). This view is reflected in the hierarchies of the National Curriculum. So we have for example in Attainment Target 5:

- Level 4: generalize, mainly in words, patterns which arise in various situations.
- Level 7: use symbolic notation to express the rules of sequence (mainly linear and quadratic)

and in Attainment Target 6:

- Level 3: deal with inputs to and outputs from simple function machines
- Level 5: express a simple function symbolically.

This idea of symbolising being a final stage in the generalising process is inherent in many of the algebra materials being used in schools at the present time (see for example Figure 4). Walkerdine has pointed out that for Piaget the role of the signifier was merely one of representing the signified. In contrast to this Walkerdine (1982), when discussing pupils' learning of arithmetic, puts forward the idea that the crucial moment of understanding lies in the fusing of the signifier and signified, a position which if applied to the area of algebra would seem to imply that the language of algebra cannot in some way be separated from the algebraic processes and grafted- on as a final step. Our detailed research with both the computer environment Logo and spreadsheets supports this view. For many pupils the computer-based symbolism is an essential tool in their negotiation of a generalization. Our work suggests that the use of symbols is inextricably linked to the generalization process. Now this may only be a characteristic of computer environments but I know of no evidence which suggests that expressing a mathematical relationship in natural language necessarily comes before being able to express it in symbols. My experience suggests that many pupils who are considered 'gifted' in mathematics have difficulty in expressing mathematical ideas in natural language.

Kaput has discussed this 'abhorrence' of symbols amongst mathematics educators in the context of the development of multiple representation systems within computer environments.

> Our initial attention to symbol systems should not be misread as an assertion that mathematics is, and hence the curriculum should be, about symbols and syntax. On the contrary, our ultimate aim is to account for the building and expressing of mathematical meaning through the use of notational forms and structures. (Kaput, 1989: 167)

He goes on to say that 'meanings are developed within or relative to particular representations or ensembles of such' (Kaput, 1989), a position which is strongly related to the ideas of post-structuralist thinkers.

> We assume the process of signification has travelled from signified to signifier: the writer knew what he wanted to say, then decided how exactly he should say it. We are upset if we asked to believe the opposite, that the author had first decided how to say and only then discovered what 'it' was; this reversal of our habits seems degrading to the whole notion of authorship. (Sturrock, 1989: 67)

Of course we do not often observe pupils using symbols to negotiate meaning within school algebra but this may be more related to the fact that pupils do not have a fluency with symbols than that they use them to negotiate. Certainly more work needs to be done in this area, and there are two important questions which future research studies needs to address.

- Could pupils use algebraic symbols to negotiate meaning in a similar way to their use of Logo symbolism, if different approaches were found to introduce pupils to algebraic symbolism?
- If pupils already have experience of using and manipulating symbols in computer-based environments, what effect could this have on their developing understandings within a paper-based algebra context?

Another related mathematical idea which is relegated to a 'later stage' within the National Curriculum is the idea of mathematical proof.

This even more than algebra, has been out of fashion within mathematics education for some time. Mathematical proof does not only have to be concerned with formal proof (see Balacheff, 1988 for more discussion of this issue). Within computer environments pupils are even more likely to believe in the 'correctness' of the computer response and so it seems important to introduce the ideas of convincing and counter-examples at a similar time to ideas of formalising and generalising.

My second major criticism of the National Curriculum is that it does not adequately take into account the influence of the computer on developments within mathematics. One area of mathematics which is heavily dependent on computers is the study of chaotic behaviour in seemingly ordered and determined feedback systems of the form $x_{n+1} = f(x_n, c)$. Totally predictable equations can produce unpredictable behaviour. None of this seems to have been considered in Attainment target 5: level 10

- use a calculator or computer to investigate whether a sequence given iteratively converges or diverges.

Many iterative sequences (e.g. $t_{n+1} = 1 - at_n$) exhibit behaviours which cannot be categorised as converging or diverging (e.g. oscillate between two points, break down to chaos) and these behaviours can easily be investigated using for example a spreadsheet package. Attainment Target 5,10 will mislead teachers who, in their turn, will mislead their pupils. As long ago as 1976 the biologist Robert May wrote:

> I would therefore urge that people be introduced to say, (the Verhulst[3] equation) early in their mathematical education. This equation can be studied phenomenologically by iterating it on a calculator ... its study does not involve as much conceptual sophistication as does elementary calculus. Such a study would greatly enrich the student's intuition about non-linear systems. Not only in research, but also in the everyday world of politics and economics, we would all be better off if more people realised that simple nonlinear systems do not necessarily possess simple dynamical properties. (quoted in Peitgen and Richter, 1986: 11)

Conclusions

Within this chapter I suggest that there are two interrelated influences on the algebra components of the National Curriculum. The first is the suppression of symbolism which arises partly as a reaction to the more authoritarian teaching methods prevalent at the beginning of the century and partly as a response to research findings which highlight pupils' difficulties with symbols. The second is the search for referential meaning with the aim of making algebra more accessible to pupils. I argue that this search for meaning is paradoxical because the power of algebra lies in the suppression of referential meaning.

I have argued that algebraic symbolism is presented as a final add-on to the algebraic process within the National Curriculum. Similarly computer-based activities within the National Curriculum are viewed as a final add-on to existing school algebra practices. This fundamentally fails to take into account the nature of technological change and the impact which computer-based environments could have on the teaching and learning of algebra. Within this chapter I have discussed the potential of a small number of computer environments and I predict that these environments will seem archaic in ten years time. We need a coordinated effort between curriculum developers, researchers and classroom practitioners if we are to ensure that classroom practice reacts to technological changes. We not only need to ask questions like 'What mathematics can pupils learn when using a computer package' but we also need to ask the question 'What mathematics will pupils need to know to effectively use such a package'.

Notes

1 Figures 1–5 were submitted by the author as photocopies of originals; they have been redrawn by the editors (eds).
2 This was, of course, originally written in handwriting (eds).
3 The Verhulst equation is of the following form $x_{n+1} = (1 + r)x_n - rx_n^2$ and can be used to model population growth.

References

BALACHEFF, N., 1988, 'Aspects of proof in pupils' practice of school mathematics', in PIMM, D. (Ed.), *Mathematics, Teachers and Children*, London: Hodder & Stoughton.

Booth, L., 1984, Algebra: *Children's Srategies and Errors*, Windsor: NFER-Nelson.

Capponi, B. and Balacheff, N., 1989, 'Multiplan et Calcul Algébrique', *Educational Studies in Mathematics*, **20**, 2, 147–76.

Chevellard, Y., 1984, 'Le Passage de l'arithmetique a l'algebre dans l'enseignment des mathematiques au college', Petit X, 5, IREM de Grenoble, pp 51–95.

Collis, K.F., 1974, 'Cognitive Development and Mathematics Learning', paper prepared for *Psychology of Mathematics Education Workshop*, Centre for Science Education, Chelsea College, London, 28 June.

Durrell, C.V., 1937, *School Certificate Algebra 'An Alternative Version of 'A New Algebra for Schools'*, London: G Bell & Sons Ltd.

Filloy, E. and Rojano, T., 1989, 'Solving equations: The transition from arithmetic to algebra', *For the Learning of Mathematics*, **9**, 2, 19–25.

Freudenthal, H., 1973, *Mathematics as an Educational Task*, Dordrecht: Reidel.

Hart, K., 1981, *Children's Understanding of Mathematics 11–16*, London: John Murray.

Healy, S., and Sutherland, R., 1988, 'Using spreadsheets for Mathematics', *Computers, Learning and Mathematics Education: A Reader*, Department of Mathematics, Statistics & Computing, Institute of Education, University of London.

Healy, S., Hoyles, C., and Sutherland, R., 1990, *Peer Group Discussion in Mathematical Environments: Final Report to the Leverhulme Trust*, Institute of Education, University of London.

Hewitt, D., 1985, 'Equations', *Mathematics Teaching*, **111**, June, pp. 15–16.

Hoyles, C. and Sutherland, R., 1989, *Logo Mathematics in the Classroom*, London: Routledge.

Kaput, J., 1989, 'Linking representations in the symbol systems of algebra', in Wagner, S. and Kieran, C., *Research Issues in the Learning and Teaching of Algebra*, Hillsdale: LEA.

Kieran, C., 1989, 'The early learning of algebra: A structural perspective', in Wagner, S. and Kieran, C., *Research Issues in the Learning and Teaching of Algebra*, Hillsdale: LEA.

Küchemann, D.E., 1981, 'Algebra' in Hart, K. (ed.) *Children's Understanding of Mathematics: 11–16*, London: Murray.

Lee, L. and Wheeler, D., 1987, *Algebraic Thinking in High School Students: their conceptions of generalization and justification*, Dept. of Mathematics, Concordia University, Montreal.

Mathematics Association, 1933, *Report on The Teaching of Algebra in Schools*, MA.

Mason, J., Graham, A., Pimm, D. and Gowar, N., 1985, *Routes to Roots of Algebra*, Milton Keynes: The Open University Press.

Nicaud, J.F., 1989, 'APLUSIX: un supreme expert pedagogique st un environment d'apprentissage dans le dumaire du raisonnement algebrique', *Technique et Science Informatiques*, **8**, 2 pp. 145–155.

Noss, R., 1986, 'Constructing a Conceptual Framework for elementary algebra through Logo programming', *Educational Studies in Mathematics*, **17**, 4, pp. 335–57.

Pietgen, H. and Richter, P., 1986, *The Beauty of Fractals*, New York: Springer.

Smith, C., 1921, *A Treatise on Algebra*, London: Macmillan & Co.

Sturrock, J., 1989, *Structuralism and Since*, Oxford: Oxford University Press.

Sutherland, R., 1989, 'Providing a computer-based framework for algebraic thinking', *Educational Studies in Maths*, **20**, 3, pp. 317–44.

Sutherland, R., 1990, 'The Gap between Arithmetical and Algebraic Thinking: computer effects'. Proposal to the Economic and Social Research Council Project, Department of Mathematics, Statistics and Computing, Institute of Education, University of London.

Tall, D., 1989, 'Different cognitive obstacles in a Technological Paradigm', in Wagner, S. and Kieran, C., *Research Issues in the Learning and Teaching of Algebra*, Hillsdale: LEA.

Thomas, T., and Tall, D., 1986, 'The value of the computer in learning algebra concepts', *Proceedings of the Tenth International Conference for the Learning of Mathematics*, London.

Vergnaud, G. and Corte, A., 1986, 'Introducing algebra to "Low-Level" 8th and 9th Graders', *Proceedings of the Tenth International Conference for the Psychology of Mathematics Education*, University of London Institute of Education.

Walkerdine, V., 1982, 'From Context to Text: A psychosemiotic approach to abstract thought', in Beveridge, M., (Ed.) *Children Thinking Through Language*, London: Edward Arnold Ltd.

9   Creating Alternative Realities: computers, modelling and curriculum change

Harvey Mellar

Introduction

Computational modelling has been a growing interest within education since the late 1970s, and strong claims have been put forward for the role it can play in supporting students' learning. By 1989 modelling had still made relatively little impact on the curriculum though research and development was going ahead in a number of institutions directed towards making it's use in schools a more viable proposition. This slow process of gradual dissemination was then rather suddenly overtaken by Government dictat, for modelling now features prominently in the National Curriculum.

This paper examines what the National Curriculum says about modelling and puts this into context by looking at the way in which modelling has developed in education over the last ten years, and at the influences that seem likely to affect it in the near future. I shall argue that the National Curriculum view of modelling as a set of techniques to be learned and applied is a very restricted view of the role of modelling within the curriculum, it is a view derived from the role of modelling within industry and commerce, rather than from the past history of modelling within education. I shall argue that modelling with computers can open up exciting new ways for students to express their own ideas, and hence to develop their own understandings, but this will not be possible if the process of learning to model is turned into a series of hurdles to be jumped over.

Modelling in the National Curriculum

Computational modelling forms a major part of the attainment target for information technology (IT) capability in the National Curriculum (DES and the Welsh Office, 1990) and yet, surprisingly (at least for those whose look for consistency within the National Curriculum), there is no explicit mention of modelling in the Mathematics National Curriculum (DES and the Welsh Office, 1989c). That there are those in the DES who do see a link between the two is evident from the HMI document Information Technology from 5 to 16 (DES, 1989b) which lists the mathematical skills important for simulation and modelling as:

— how to investigate and detect mathematical relationships and draw conclusions from them;
— how to use IT tools to represent statistical information;
— how to check that results obtained using IT are sensible;
— how to formulate a problem in ways which allow the use of IT in the solution.

The Design and Technology working group envisage that IT will be taught across the curriculum rather than as a separate subject, indeed they suggest that 'pupils should be required to take SATs which cover the IT attainment target in maths or science or design and technology and in English or geography or history' (DES and the Welsh Office 1989a: 84). In other words, they thought that there should be SATs covering computational modelling in mathematics.

Within the National Curriculum for Mathematics the Attainment Targets 'Using and applying mathematics' provide plenty of opportunity for modelling. Spreadsheets, databases, programming languages and statistical software are all mentioned in statements of attainment, and they provide adequate means for computational modelling. The National Curriculum documents do not however explain what the motives for putting computational modelling in the curriculum might be. In their document Information Technology from 5 to 16 (DES, 1989b) the HMIs develop their argument for modelling in education from a consideration of simulations. A major advantage of simulations is, they say, that they save time and money (sic), but, they argue, if students are to make good use of simulations they should know that there is a computational model underlying a simulation, and that they should realize that this model is not a true representation.

The modelling examples given by the Design and Technology working party (DES and the Welsh Office, 1989a) indicate something of their approach to modelling. Here are some of the examples:

— modify a turtle graphics procedure or its parameters to draw a variety of shapes and transform them;
— model and investigate the growth of bacteria;
— develop a system to aid the management of assessments and pupils' records of achievement in a school and produce suitable reports and summaries;
— a system for monitoring the performance of a central heating system in order to plan a system for a house or school;
— develop a system for notifying parents that their child's immunisation is due.

Notice the implicit appeal to the world of work and to efficient management in these last three examples. These examples together with the statements of attainment at the various levels (described below) suggest that modelling within the National Curriculum is viewed as a set of techniques to be learned and then applied, rather than as a process of coming to greater understanding. Moreover, modelling is seen as an activity independent of the domain that is being modelled, that is, it is seen as a transferable skill. As a result of much research mathematics educators have recently begun to give up (or at least considerably modify) their claims for the transferability of mathematical concepts such as those of arithmetic from one domain to another. Information technology educators, having much less research evidence to trouble them, seem to be still quite willing to make wide ranging assumptions of transferability for concepts such as modelling.

The National Curriculum goes on to lay down a modelling curriculum, a sequence of stages through which children will pass in learning to model. There is research underway looking at the way in which children might be introduced to modelling, and what kinds of reasoning children can do with various types of computational tools, but as yet little is known about how children learn to model. Little daunted, the authors of the Information Technology profile component tell us that children should be able to do the following things at the indicated levels:

level 4   use a model in order to detect patterns and relationships;

level 5   use a model in order to explore patterns and relationships;

level 6   vary the data and rules in a model and assess the
outcomes;

level 7   design construct and use a specified model of a specified
situation;

level 8   represent a specified situation with variables as a model,
and show the relationship between the variables;

level 9   evaluate a model;

level 10   decide how to model a system, design, implement and
test the model.

Let me propose a curriculum for another technologically aided activity, namely photography, based on this imaginative structure. Students should be able to do the following things at the indicated levels:

level 4   examine a photograph in order to detect patterns and
relationships in the image;

level 5   examine a photograph in order to explore patterns and
relationships in the image;

level 6   change the aperture and time settings for a photograph
and assess the effects;

level 7   take a specified photograph of a specified object and
examine it;

level 8   take a series of photographs of a specified object; and
display appropriately;

level 9   appraise a photograph;

level 10   choose an object to photograph, take photographs of it,
and appraise the photographs.

I am aware of the dangers I run in proposing this; it is certain to get
taken up eventually as the National Curriculum for photography. Just
remember, you read it here first.

This approach to a modelling curriculum divides modelling into a
series of techniques, and fails to present it as a whole. Before they
arrive in school young children are already constructing their own
models in their own minds, on paper, and with other materials, even
if not already on a computer. Computational modelling can be used
by children to express their own views, and thus to hold their ideas up

for examination by themselves and others. However, instead of beginning from the children's models and what they already know about the modelling process this curriculum begins by presenting children with an adult's models, and it is these adult models that are to be transferred to the computer screen, rather than the children's models. After this it will be very difficult for the children to make the link between their own models and the adult models that they are presented with and as a result the possibilities that could be opened up by allowing children to express themselves computationally are lost.

The concept of a modelling curriculum found in the National Curriculum neither examines the nature of models themselves, or the process by which people create models. By way of contrast it is worth looking at the very different approach to teaching modelling proposed by Mason (1988). Mason puts forward a number of suggestions to teachers that could well form the basis of a viable modelling curriculum:

— stimulate pupils to ask their own questions;
— practice exploring and developing metaphors;
— genuinely work with pupils;
— present completed models, but stress the generic aspects and the modelling process, and play down technical details;
— present incomplete models and invite development and criticism; draw explicit attention to the movement from particular to general and vice versa.

Modelling in Education

This section describes something of the history of modelling in education over the last ten years. The word 'model' is unfortunately a very overworked concept that is used in many ways. However, I intend to follow the fine example set by Humpty Dumpty, who tells us: 'When I use a word it means just what I choose it to mean — neither more nor less'. I shall take the concept of a model to have three features: structure, boundedness, and purpose.

A model is a representation of structure. There are many kinds of models: a model might be a physical object, or it might be a structure of related ideas, which might be expressed informally in words or diagrams, or which might be expressed more formally. Logic, algebra, differential equations, and computer programs have been some of the common formalisms for expressing these formal structures of ideas.

A model is bounded, it only represents certain aspects of the situation being modelled, and the relationships within a model often depend on assumptions that only hold over a limited range of situations. Modelling is not a process of trying to get closer and closer to some 'reality'. A map of the world that was as big as the world would be too big to be useful. Corollary: it is what is NOT included in a model that gives it its power.

A model is defined by its purpose, those aspects of the situation which are represented in a model are those thought to be useful for that specific purpose. Models, therefore, always contain implicit value judgements.

Computers have been used for modelling since they were first built, and a number of programming languages have been developed specifically for writing models (for an account of some of these languages, see Bronson, 1985). Early computational modelling was mainly restricted to technological fields, but the development of system dynamics by Forrester and his associates at MIT (Forrester, 1968) led to the development of computational modelling in the social sciences as well.

Personal computers when combined with spreadsheets provide a powerful resource for certain types of modelling (particularly in the area of economics), and this has been the cause of much of the success of PCs in the commercial world. More recently, however, worries have begun to be expressed in the business world about the use of spreadsheets for economic modelling. Levy (1988), for example, argues that economic models generally (and especially spreadsheet models) are more often used to persuade than to explain, and more often used to hide assumptions than to reveal them. Levy recounts the sorry tale of a certain Ronald Reagan who on his election as US President planned to lower taxes and raise defence expenditure. The President's budget advisor had an elaborate computer model of the US economy, which indicated that massive deficits lay ahead if this course was to be followed. This was clearly too embarrassing a prediction to be revealed to the President elect, so the assumptions in the economic model were rewritten to include a dramatic surge in US productivity which nicely eliminated the prediction of deficits. It is with great sadness that we have to report that the economy turned out to be harder to manipulate than the model had been.

There has been a growing interest in mathematical modelling in schools over the last ten years — see, for example, Burkhardt, 1981;

Berry *et al.*, 1984; Pimm, 1988; Houston, 1989. At the start of this period computers were not playing any significant role in mathematical modelling in schools because of their scarcity, but since that time computers in schools have become much more common, and in mathematics education generally there has been something of a swing away from symbolic methods towards the greater use of numerical methods, particularly the use of iterative and difference methods supported by calculators and computers.

Computational modelling had its first impact on secondary schools in the late 1970s with the appearance of a variety of simulation programs for science, geography and economics education produced by the National Development Programme in Computer Assisted Learning (Hooper, 1977). The Computers in the Curriculum group at King's College London continued this production of educational simulation programs from 1973 onwards. At the heart of these simulations are models which are created by the authors of the programs and then hidden away within the program code. Teachers and students who used these simulations complained that they could not get at the models in order to examine them and change them, and as a result of this dissatisfaction a number of teachers began to explore the possibilities of building their own computational models.

One way to build your own computational model is to use a general purpose computer language. Since BASIC was readily available on school computers, this was the first language to be used for modelling in education, but it was soon found to be rather unsuitable for the purpose. The Dynamic Modelling System (DMS) (see Wong, 1987a, b) grew out of this early experience of writing models in BASIC. DMS used a BASIC-like syntax in order to express the rules of the model, but it provided a much more convenient environment in which to run the model than was provided by BASIC. The use of DMS was supported in schools by the Computers in the Curriculum Group who developed a large number of example models and a quantity of teaching materials to accompany it. In re-thinking the design of DMS, Holland and Ogborn created the Cellular Modelling System (CMS) which moved away from a BASIC-like syntax towards a spreadsheet like format.

BASIC, however, was not the only choice as to a general purpose language, Logo offered an attractive alternative programming language for exploring modelling (Howe, 1979). The creation of Logo microworlds such as the Newtonian Microworld (see, for example, Burns and Smart, 1989) opened up further interesting possibilities that lie between pre-written simulations such as those produced by the

Computers in the Curriculum group (in which the model is given and unchangeable) and a general modelling system such as DMS. In the Newtonian microworld students are provided with a set of primitives specific to that topic area, and the models are provided in such a way that the students can look inside them, can modify them, and can go on to create their own models.

Yet a third option for creating models was provided by the programming language Prolog, a language more suited to qualitative models based on logical rules than to quantitative models based on numerical relationships. The rapid development of expert systems in the commercial world during the 1980s encouraged Prolog-oriented educationalists to turn their attention towards expert systems. One result of this was the creation of Knowledge Pad — a simple expert system shell that allows students to create their own qualitative models.

Groups supporting these various approaches to modelling — mathematical modelling, dynamic systems modelling with DMS/CMS, Logo and microworlds, Prolog and expert system shells — have been arguing for a place for modelling in education over the last ten years, and in the last two or three years they have started to come together in trying to create a more unified case for using modelling with students.

As modelling has begun to be taken up by teachers, a number of different emphases on aspects of modelling have appeared in classrooms. At the present time it is possible to discern at least five different emphases:

Modelling is sometimes seen as a problem solving tool — as when students are asked to determine the siting of bus stops. In this case the variables used are created in order to solve the specific problem, different students may create different variables.

Modelling is sometimes used to test the validity of the choice of variables — as when students are asked to examine the meaningfulness of measures of economic success in a model of a business.

Modelling is sometimes seen as a way of expressing logical or mathematical relationships between 'given' variables — as when a student is asked to model the path of a point on a circle as the circle rolls.

Modelling is sometimes seen as a way of expressing causal theories about relationships between 'given' variables — as when students are asked to model the behaviour of a mass constrained by a spring.

Modelling is sometimes seen as a way of describing relationships between 'given' variables that do not have a direct causal link — as when students are asked to model population growth.

These differences of emphasis are rarely made explicit, and as a result there is sometimes a degree of misunderstanding between different groups using modelling in their teaching. There is likely to be a particular problem of communication where emphases on certain aspects of modelling have become associated with specific curriculum areas.

The Future of Modelling in Education

Modelling in education is presently a very active area of research and development. The way in which modelling will be used in schools in the future is likely to be influenced by three kinds of changes presently taking place:

— those relating to our knowledge of how teachers and children can work with computational modelling tools;
— those relating to the computational tools available;
— those relating to the kinds of models it is worthwhile trying to build.

This section looks at recent work relating to these three issues.

The first group of developments likely to affect modelling in schools is the wide variety of research programs in the area presently under way. Here is not the place to examine in detail the aims of these various projects, but a list of some of them will perhaps indicate something of the directions such research is taking:

— 'Computer based modelling across the curriculum' project is looking at the use of modelling in mathematics, science, business studies and geography;
— 'Conceptual'change in science' (Driver and Scanlon, 1988) is exploring the effects of the use of tools such as Stella and the

Alternative Reality Kit (ARK) — a computer based environment for exploring physics which allows users to play with the
laws of physics;

— 'Tools for exploratory learning' (Bliss and Ogborn, 1988) is
looking at the way in which children reason with the aid of a
variety of computational tools both when children are exploring models written by others, and when they are expressing
their own ideas in models;

— the MODUS project (Hassell and Webb, 1989) is an ambitious
software development project aiming to produce an integrated
set of software tools supporting a wide range of modelling
activities in education;

— the Systems Thinking and Curriculum Innovation Project
(Mandinach, 1989) is looking at the teaching of system dynamics and the use of Stella in high schools.

The second group of developments are those in the modelling tools
themselves. In the near future we can expect to see greater use of
modelling tools incorporating graphical user interfaces, of qualitative
and 'semi-quantitative' tools, and of symbolic mathematics packages.

Figure 1 shows a model constructed using Stella, a modelling
package which incorporates a graphical user interface. Models are
created in Stella by putting symbols representing variables and arrows
representing the relationships between them onto the computer
screen. The student uses a hand controlled by the mouse in order to
pick up the symbols and the connecting arrows from the menu at the
left hand side of the screen and to put them down on the screen.
Models created in Stella are system dynamics models in which the
numerical relationships between all the variables must be spelt out
before the model can run. It is often the case, however, that when
students are trying to build a model that they know the direction of
the effect of one variable on another, but not the magnitude of
the effect. Models constructed using such ideas have been described as
'semi-quantitative' (Ogborn, 1990) and a computational tool (IQON)
for constructing such models is under development (Miller et al 1990).
IQON uses the same direct manipulation techniques as Stella but does
not require the numerical relationships to be spelled out. Figure 2
shows an example model using IQON.

Qualitative modelling involves modelling with relationships between ideas, without the use of numerical relationships. There are
essentially two forms of qualitative modelling being used — those
based on expert systems (such as Knowledge Pad) and those based on

Figure 1   a STELLA model of free-fall

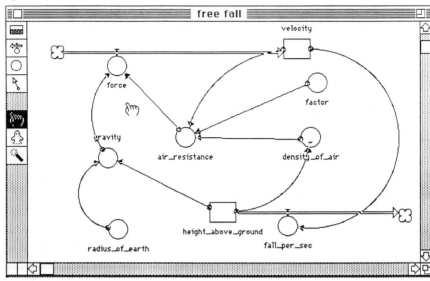

Figure 2   an example model using IQoN

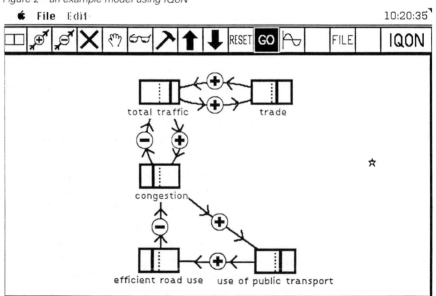

hypertext systems (such as Linx88). In expert systems the model is expressed in terms of rules such as 'the food should not be eaten IF the food is meat AND the food has been left un-refrigerated for over 24 hours AND the season is summer'. With hypertext systems the model is expressed in terms of links that take you from one item of information to another, something like the cross referencing in a card index system. Hypertext systems are good at creating the kinds of structures we associate with adventure games. There is continued experimentation and development aimed at making tools based on expert systems and hypertext systems easier for students to use as modelling tools. These developments will have importance for areas of the curriculum where quantitative modelling is not applicable, and it may also turn out to be the case that qualitative modelling provides a good entry point to modelling for areas where quantitative modelling is used.

Symbolic mathematics packages capable of working directly with algebraic and differential equations have been available for some time for microcomputers (e.g. muMath) but these packages have been rather difficult to use. This situation seems to be improving, 'Derive' is a development of muMath that is much easier to use, it is controlled through menus and can provide graphical displays of functions. Symbolic mathematics programs have already found a place in the teaching of groups such as engineering undergraduates (see for example, Barozzi and Clements, 1987). The move in school mathematics away from symbolic methods towards numerical methods over the last few years has commonly been regarded as having had positive educational side effects, and students are said to find such methods easier to understand. Ironically, symbolic mathematics packages might encourage the next generation of teachers to move away from numerical methods and back to symbolic ones!

The third group of developments likely to have effects on modelling in schools is changes in ideas about useful ways in which to model. In recent years both chaos theory and neural networks have created new varieties of model making in the worlds of physics and psychology respectively.

Chaos theory (for a popular account, see Gleick, 1988) has shown that quite simple models can have very complex behaviour. Indeed some of the simple spreadsheet models a student might write to model population growth with a limiting factor will have chaotic behaviour for large values of the growth parameter. Both mathematics and physics teachers are beginning to bring chaos into their classrooms, and as a result we may soon see students building models of much more complex phenomena than those they presently are expected to model.

Deriving their inspiration from neurology, neural networks are models which consist of a great many interacting elements, each element having some very simple processing rules and connected to many other elements. The overall behaviour of such a system depends on the weights of the connections between the elements and not on a set of rules. Neural networks are particularly well known for their use in modelling human cognition (see Rumelhart *et al.*, 1988), but they can be used for other problems. One of the interesting features of neural networks from an educational point of view is that a neural network can learn associations between input and output patterns by being shown those patterns. As an example, a neural network program has been taught to 'read' English text, that is to take digital representations of text and pronounce the words. In order to 'teach' the network to 'read' English, it was presented with an English word as input and simultaneously presented with the required output signals for the voice synthesiser. This was done many times. At the end of this training the network could not only 'read' words it had seen before, but could read most English words, in other words it contained a 'model' of English pronunciation. Despite its potential interest to educationalists there is as yet no sign of neural networks having begun to influence modelling in schools.

These three sets of developments, developments in ideas about how to use modelling with students, developments in the software available, and developments in modelling methods, are all likely to have an effect on the way in which modelling can be used in schools in the near future. If we are to be able take advantage of these changes then we need to resist any factors that might contribute to a freezing of the development of modelling ideas at their present stage.

The Value of Modelling in Education

In the process of moving modelling from the status of a developing idea within education to that of an assessed set of levels of attainment targets, the National Curriculum has restricted the value of modelling arguments on work on children's informal theories (e.g. Driver, Guesne, and Tiberghien, 1985), or on work on mental models (e.g. Gentner and Stevens, 1983). An example of this approach is Law's (1988) work in eliciting students' models of dynamics, models which had very different assumptions from those of Newton's model.

Through building and exploring such models students may come to change their understandings of the topic, and hence to construct new models. In this way of using modelling the students are using the computer to express their own computational ideas.

These various aspects of the view of modelling as a powerful aid to exploration and learning stand in strong contrast to the National Curriculum's view of modelling as a set of techniques useful to technology and commerce. Moreover, the two contrasting views have different implications for the way in which modelling is taught, for if students are to use modelling as a way of exploring their own ideas they will need to be encouraged to find ways to express their ideas, to create models and then to explore them, whereas in the National Curriculum the student must first explore someone else's models and only later are they expected to analyse situations and create their own models. If students are taught to model with a computer in the way the National Curriculum implies, that is, they begin by looking at models created by others, and go on to learn a series of techniques, each tested and assessed in turn, then these students are not likely to turn to computational modelling as a form of expressing their own ideas.

References

BAROZZI, G. and CLEMENTS, R.R., 1987, 'The potential uses of computer algebra systems in the mathematical education of engineers', *International Journal of Mathematical Education in Science and Technology*, **18**, pp. 681–3.

BERRY, J.S., BURGHES, D.N., HUNTLEY, I.D., JAMES, D.J.G. and MOSCARDINI, A.O. (Eds), 1984, *Teaching and applying mathematical modelling*, Chichester: Ellis Horwood Ltd.

BLISS, J., and OGBORN, J., 1988, 'Tools for exploratory learning', *Journal of Computer Assisted Learning*, **5**, pp. 37–50.

BOOSS-BAVNBEK, B. and PATE, G., 1989, 'Information technology and mathematical modelling, the software crisis, risk and educational consequences', *Computers & Society*, **19**, 3, pp. 4–22.

BRONSON, R., 1985, 'Computer simulation', Byte, **9**, pp. 95–105.

BURKHARDT, H., 1981, *The Real World and Mathematics*, Glasgow: Blackie and Son Ltd.

BURNS, S. and SMART, T., 1989, 'Sixth-Form Girls Using Computers to Explore Newtonian Mechanics' in C. HOYLES (Ed.), *Computers and Girls: General Issues and Case Studies of Logo in the Mathematics Classroom*, London: Kogan Page.

DES, 1987, *New Technology for Better Schools*, DES circular to Chief Education Officers, July 1987.

DES, 1989a, *Statistical Bulletin 10/89 July 1989: Survey of Information Technology in Schools*, London: DES.

DES, 1989b, *Information Technology from 5 to 16: Curriculum Matters 15, an HMI series*, London: HMSO.

DES AND WELSH OFFICE, 1989a, *Design and Technology for ages 5 to 16*, London: HMSO.

DES AND WELSH OFFICE, 1989b, *Science in the National Curriculum*, London: HMSO.

DES AND WELSH OFFICE, 1989c, *Mathematics in the National Curriculum*, London: HMSO.

DES AND WELSH OFFICE, 1990, *Technology in the National Curriculum*, London: HMSO.

DRIVER, R., GUESNE, E. and TIBERGHIEN, A., 1985, *Children's Ideas in Science*, Milton Keynes: Open University Press.

DRIVER, R. and SCANLON, E., 1988, 'Conceptual change in science', *Journal of Computer Assisted Learning*, **5**, pp. 25–36.

FORRESTER, J.W., 1968, *Principles of Systems*, Cambridge: MIT Press.

GENTNER, D. and SREVENS, A.L. (Eds), 1983, *Mental Models*, Hillsdale: Lawrence Erlbaum Associates.

GLEICK, J., 1988, *Chaos: Making a New Science*, Harmondsworth: Sphere Books Ltd, Penguin Group.

HASSELL, D.J. and WEBB, M.E., 1989, MODUS — *The Integrated Modelling System*, Paper presented at CAL 89 Conference, University of Surrey, April 1989.

HOOPER, R., 1977, *National Development Programme in Computer Assisted Learning — Final Report of the Director*, London: Council for Educational Technology.

HOUSTON, S.K., 1989, The Northern Ireland Further Mathematics Project', *Teaching Mathematics and its Applications*, **8**, pp. 115–21.

HOWE, J.A.M., 1979, *Learning through model Building*, Edinburgh University, Department of Artificial Intelligence Research Paper 120.

LAW, N., 1988, *Knowledge Structures: Where Can We Find Them?* Proceedings of the AERA Annual Meeting, New Orleans, April 1988.

LEVY, S., 1989, 'A spreadsheet way of knowledge', In FORESTER, T. (Ed.), *Computers in the Human Context: Information Technology, Productivity and People*, Oxford: Basil Blackwell.

MANDINACH, E.B., 1989, 'Model-building and the use of computer simulation of dynamic systems', *Journal of Educational Computing Research*, **5**, pp. 221–43.

MASON, J., 1988, 'Modelling: What do we really want pupils to learn?', in PIMM, D. (Ed.) *Mathematics, Teachers and Children*, Sevenoaks: Hodder & Stoughton Ltd.

MILLER, R.S., OGBORN, J., TURNER, J., BRIGGS, J.H. and BROUGH, D.R., 1990, *Towards a Tools to Support Semi-quantitative modelling*, Paper accepted for the International Conference on Advanced Research on Computers in Education, Tokyo, Japan, July 1990.

OGBORN, J., 1990, 'A future for modelling in science education', *Journal of Computer Assisted Learning*, to be published.

PIMM, D. (Ed.) 1988, Mathematics, *Teachers and Children*, Sevenoaks: Hodder & Stoughton Ltd.

RUMELHART, D.E., MCCLELLAND, J.L. and THE PDP RESEARCH GROUP, 1988, *Parallel distributed processing: explorations in the microstructure of cognition. Volume 1: foundations*, Cambridge, Massachusetts: MIT Press.

WONG, D., 1987a, 'Teaching A level physics through microcomputer dynamic modelling: I. Teaching methods', *Journal of Computer Assisted Learning*, **3**, pp. 105–12.

WONG, D., 1987b, 'Teaching A level physics through microcomputer dynamic modelling: II. Evaluation of teaching', *Journal of Computer Assisted Learning*, **3**, pp. 164–75.

Software Referred to in the Text

'Cellular Modelling System' (1986), Longmans, London.

'Derive' (1989), A Mathematical Assistant, Soft Warehouse, Inc. 3695 Harding Avenue Suite 505 Honolulu Hl 96816.

'Dynamic Modelling System' (1984), Longmans, London.

'Expert Builder' (1989), The Modus Club, The Advisory Unit for Microtechnology in Education, Endymion Road, Hatfield, Herts, AL10 8AV.

'Knowledge Pad' (1989), PEG, School of Education, University of Exeter, EX1 2LV.

'Linx88' (1989), PEG, School of Education, University of Exeter, EX1 2L'.

'muMath' (1983), Soft Warehouse, Inc. 3695 Harding Avenue Suite 505 Honolulu Hl 96816

'The Newton Microworld for Nimbus Computers' (1988), Gem Software, 58 Parklands Avenue, Lillington, Leamington Spa, Warwickshire

'Stella' (1987), High Performance Systems Inc 13 Dartmouth College Highway, Lyme, New Hampshire, 03768 USA

From Notional to National:
questions of implementation

10   From Notional to National Curriculum: the search for a mechanism

Andrew Brown

Introduction

Although much time and space is lavished on consideration of the content of the National Curriculum, relatively little attention appears to be given to the mechanisms by which the Government proposes to implement the structural changes that have been made. One possible reason for this might be the fragmentation of curriculum content into academic subject areas each with its own working party and report. Such an arrangement immediately marks out the 'subject specialist'[1] as the appropriate respondent to the proposals of the working parties. Thus, whilst questions of content and subject-related pedagogy are hotly contested, general questions of implementation of the National Curriculum are neglected.

Mathematics teachers, primary school mathematics co-ordinators, mathematics advisers, inspectors and teacher educators, and other 'mathematics educators' all have their attention focused on the content of 'Mathematics in the National Curriculum' and can legitimately voice their concerns as 'experts'. It would be a grave mistake, however, if we as mathematics educators maintain this as our sole legitimate focus. It is important that we acknowledge that being a mathematics educator is but one aspect of our identities as educators. A primary school teacher might, for instance, have a particular interest or responsibility in the area of mathematics, and thus may be identified as a mathematics educator, but will also have, as a class teacher, responsibilities to teach, and interests in, all other areas of the primary curriculum, in general pedagogic and organizational matters, in questions of pupil welfare and so on. Likewise the secondary school mathematics teacher will be involved in the pastoral work of the school, and will, as a member of the school staff, have concerns relating to the structure and organization of the school. Thus, whilst someone might be identified as a mathematics educator with particular concerns relating to this, there are other general concerns that they will share with other subject specialists, with people working in other phases of the education system and with people doing other forms of work within education. These particular and general concerns do not, obviously, stand apart from each other, rather the particular concerns of mathematics education exist within, and act to constitute, the context of general educational concerns.

In this chapter I wish to critically address a fundamental question. However, in addressing the Government's strategies for implementation of the National Curriculum and the process of change in schooling, I am not dealing with something that is particular to mathematics education but with a subject of general educational concern. As such the arguments elaborated, the evidence cited and the conclusions drawn will not be specific to the teaching and learning of mathematics. This is not to say, however, that they will not be relevant. Whilst it is obviously important to question proposed curriculum content, structures and modes of assessment from the point of view of specific curriculum areas, much of the current debate is likely to be of little value if we do not address questions of how such elements relate to classroom practice and its transformation. In the sections that follow I will consider the manner in which it is proposed to put the National Curriculum in place and from this, drawing on some of my own research in primary schools, raise a number of questions about the processes of curriculum and pedagogic change. In the conclusion to the chapter I will make both general observations and point to some of the specific implications these have for mathematics education and mathematics educators.

Proposed Mechanisms for Bringing Practice in Line with Structures

The process of producing a National Curriculum, as practised by the present Government, is relatively straightforward. The basic building blocks of the curriculum are defined (the subject areas) and their relative importance signalled (core subjects, foundation subjects and cross-curriculum themes). A universal structure for the content of each of the areas (attainment targets broken down into statements of attainment arranged hierarchically into ten levels and collected into profile components) is also defined and the relationship between this structure and a pattern of assessment is outlined. Panels of 'experts' in each of the defined areas are appointed to consider what the content of each area might be and to organize this content in such a way that it fits the structure given. The main point of reference in each case is the collective experience of good practice[2] of each of the panels, with a token and somewhat ill-defined process of consultation to give the appearance of professional and lay approval for the proposals put forward. The collected final publications of the panels (a collection of vast numbers of statements of attainment and related programmes of study) are taken to constitute a national curriculum and pass into law. All that remains is for this curriculum to be 'put in place'.

Whilst it is relatively simple, particularly given the lack of any effective opposition from within the teaching profession, to set up a mechanism that works to exclude or suspend consideration of awkward questions and leads to the production of something tangible that can be called a national curriculum,[3] ensuring implementation is somewhat more problematic.[4] For the Government's claims to have reformed education to retain any credibility some attempt must be made to show that serious moves are being made to bring classroom practice in line with the proposed curriculum,[5] that is that through translation into particular forms of practice the 'notional curriculum' becomes a National Curriculum. There is no single statement of what this mechanism might be but, drawing on a variety of sources Emerson and Goddard (1989) list three forms of Government support for implementation of the National Curriculum:

i) The provision of grants to Local Education Authorities (LEAs) for in-service training and support related to the implementation of the National Curriculum.

ii) The provision of a programme of training comprising of materials designed by the National Curriculum Council (NCC) and the School Examinations and Assessment Council (SEAC).

iii) Two additional school closure days in 1989 dedicated specifically to whole staff training in matters relating to the implementation of the National Curriculum.

Following Andy Hargreaves (1989) we might also add to this list a fourth item: the revision of guide-lines for the accreditation of initial training courses to include specific preparation for teaching the National Curriculum.

The revision of the means by which in-service training (INSET) is funded in recent years allows the Department of Education and Science (DES) a far greater degree of control in the determination of educational priorities (see, for example, Harland, 1987). Thus it is relatively easy to redirect money towards training for the National Curriculum and monitoring of its implementation. To this end the brief for the appointment of local authority advisory and other non-teaching staff to provide support in the areas of science, mathematics, technology and English under the Education Support Grant (ESG) scheme can be orientated towards the implementation of the National curriculum in those areas. The success of the bids that LEAs put in for this money is contingent upon each school in the authority drawing up a National Curriculum Development Plan outlining how the changes in curriculum, organisation and use of resources will be developed in line with the National Curriculum. Later ESG money will be allocated to support for other areas of the curriculum within a brief drawn up by the DES. In addition to this subject specific allocation of funds, grants will be available for the period 1989 to 1994 to support the appointment of additional LEA inspectors to enable effective monitoring of the implementation of the National Curriculum and of the introduction of Local Management of Schools (LMS).

The Local Education Authority Training Grants Scheme (LEATGS) provides the DES with a mechanism for defining national INSET priorities and then preferentially funding LEA schemes that meet these. The 1989/90 priorities included training for the National Curriculum in terms of content and of management and assessment. The 1990/91 priorities include 20 day courses in Mathematics and the National Curriculum for primary school teachers (and similar courses for science). The criteria for the accreditation for these courses states that there is a 'need to enhance the subject knowledge of a large proportion of the primary teaching force; a long term need which this new initiative seeks to address' (from the DES document 'Framework for INSET Courses for Primary Teachers in Mathematics and the National Curriculum' sent to LEAs and higher education institutions in July 1989). The message here is quite clear: primary school teachers need more subject knowledge in order to implement the National Curriculum.

The second strand in the Government's strategy for putting the National Curriculum 'in place' is a rolling programme of training developed by the NCC and SEAC. This hierarchically arranged programme, announced by Kenneth Baker in his speech to parliament on 4th November 1988, has run throughout 1989. Starting with a series of conferences to inform senior education officers and representatives of higher education institutions and professional associations, the programme involved one-day regional courses for LEA officers, advisers and inspectors and subsequently one-day courses for head-teachers and primary school coordinators and secondary school heads of department in the core areas of the curriculum. This process culminated in the third aspect of the strategy, two school closure days for whole school training support material for these being commissioned from the Open University by the NCC. The central concern of each of the levels of this process has been the dissemination of information with some consideration of appropriate strategies at each level and the relation of the proposals to existing practice.

The Assumptions Underlying these Mechanisms and the Implications of this Mode of Implementation

Two conclusions can be drawn from the strategies outlined above. Firstly that the Government sees it as necessary to disseminate information about the National Curriculum to successive levels of a hierarchy of education professionals, each level being challenged to consider the degree to which present practice matches with the proposals and, where there is a disparity, how the two might be brought in line. Secondly, that it is assumed that there exists a skill and knowledge deficit on the part of teachers which can be addressed through INSET and other forms of specialist support. Re-orientation of initial teacher training can also be used to ensure that such deficiencies do not manifest themselves in the future. In simple terms the Government's answer to the question of supporting the implementation of the National Curriculum is to tell people what will be expected of them, ask them what they are going to do about this and then provide courses that will make up for existing deficiencies in teachers by giving them the skills and knowledge that are seen as necessary.[6] The assumption here is that educational change is a technical problem; that once policies are formed and a motive for change established (in this case a system of assessment that can also be used to evaluate the relative performance of teachers) all that needs to be done is for practitioners to be armed with appropriate techniques and knowledge and the planned change[7] will take place.

The programme (if indeed it can be called such) outlined above can be seen as focusing on both the structural (in terms of disseminating information about policy and structural changes) and the personal (in terms of the stress on building of individual teachers' skills and knowledge) at one and the same time. The effect of this can be seen as identifying teachers as the key agents in the implementation of the National Curriculum and thus as the prime source of 'causes' (e.g. difficulty in compensating for deficiencies in the workforce) in the event of crisis in the translation of policy into practice. Failure of implementation can thus be located at the level of the individual teacher, that is at the furthest possible distance from the Government itself. This bears striking resemblance to the argument that high levels of unemployment are the result of a lack of particular skills in certain sections of the population. In this case opportunities can be offered to gain these skills thus giving the impression that the Government is making an effort to address the problem. Failure in the uptake of these opportunities or the failure of newly trained people to gain employment can then, once the level of explanation is located within the individual, be blamed on the unemployed themselves (i.e. 'They were offered every opportunity to gain employment but, through their own personal dispositions, failed to take this up or make the most of it'). Questions of why this might be so remain unasked for fear that in attempting to address the more awkward problems might come to light for which there cannot be a simple, visible, universal strategy to adopt as a supposed solution. Thus no real attempt to address problems is made, only attempts to rationalize difficulties in such a form that distance between policy and failures of implementation is maintained. Middle-order factors, such as those which effect transformations in the meanings of the policies and guidelines, and the forms of practice associated with them, remain untouched.

Approaches to change and innovation that act to pathologise teachers are not restricted to the present government. For example Skilbeck (1976) identified what he felt to be factors that may cause difficulties for school-based curriculum development. Amongst the eleven factors listed are: a sense of low esteem and inadequacy in staff and the lack of relevant skills; lack of conviction in staff, particularly in sustaining change; conflicting priorities on the part of the teacher (e.g. planning, teaching, leisure, interests, private study etc.). Skilbeck's list does, at least, also include a number of contextual factors, such as inadequacy of resourcing, institutional inertia, conflicting demands from inside and outside the school, discontinuance of new practices before they are fully established: all of these are completely ignored by the DES.

I wish to argue that it is unhelpful to adopt an approach that views teachers as obstacles to change and which posits the need for remedial action to compensate for the perceived inadequacies of the workforce in the form of the teaching of decontextualized skills and knowledge. Rather I shall suggest, on the basis of my own research, that we need to acknowledge the contingencies that act upon teachers in the formation, maintenance and transformation of their classroom practice.

Is Change at the Level of Classroom Practice as Straightforward as it is Made to Appear?

The research on which I wish to draw sets out to investigate the processes that generate differences in pedagogic practice between primary schools serving different areas of the same inner city local education authority, which, to maintain anonymity, I have called Dockton (Brown, 1985). Two groups of schools were studied: the five major feeder schools of the largest co-educational comprehensive school in West Dockton and the four major feeder schools of the equivalent secondary school in East Dockton. Of particular note was the reputation of the schools in West Dockton as being innovative and sites of frequent pedagogic and curricular change, whilst schools in East Dockton were seen as generally more conservative and static in terms of pedagogy and curriculum.

Also of note was a distinct difference in the social characteristics of the intakes of the two groups of schools. Using census material it was established that the populations of both the areas being studied could be considered to be predominantly working class (as could the population of the borough as a whole) with only slight variation in the distribution of the population between the categories used (the Registrar General's social-class classification devised for census purposes). Having ascertained the catchment area of each of the primary schools being studied from the headteacher, small area statistics were used to produce profiles of the populations in those areas. Whilst the characteristics of the areas were similar in many respects (for instance in the proportion of households without a car, overcrowded accommodation, unemployment) they were found to vary significantly in terms of the proportion of owner-occupied households (higher in the east), the proportion of council-tenanted households (higher in the west) and the proportion of heads of household from the New Commonwealth (higher in the east).[8]

Table 1

West Dockton	East Dockton
Parents seen as having a low opinion of schooling.	Parents thought to have a positive attitude to schooling.
Parents in the area seen as not being knowledgeable in ways of dealing with the school system.	Parents seen as being at ease in their dealings with school.
Regular aggressive entries into school by parents.	Few, if any, aggressive incidents involving parents.
Headteacher takes up a predominantly 'social-worker' type role as a result of 'social pressure'.	Minimal 'social pressure' felt. Headteacher takes up a largely 'educationalist' role.
Children generally seen as being difficult to teach.	Few problems, children seen as generally easy to teach.
Large proportion of children seen as uninterested and poorly motivated.	Vast majority of children considered to be well motivated.
Much of the school's time seen as being spent on behavioural and social problems.	The educational function of the school seen as being to the fore.
Constant change and innovation as a result of pressure from staff.	Little pressure for change from the staff.
Staff resistance to purely headteacher initiated innovation.	Change often engineered by the headteacher.
Informal staff relations.	Formal staff relations, especially in the acceptance of the headteacher's authority
High staff turnover.	Low staff turnover.

The schools were visited and the headteachers interviewed to confirm information about the school and its intake and to gather their perceptions of innovation and change within the school (including recent developments and the process by which these came about), of the social characteristics of the school's intake and of the effects the latter might have on the work of the school. Analysis of the data indicated that the schools fell into three groups in terms of the accounts of the headteachers, this clustering being in line with the schools' relative positions in terms of the social characteristics of the population of the catchment area. Two of the groups of schools (one consisting of three schools in the west, the other of three schools in the east) marked out extreme and clearly distinguishable positions whilst the third group consisted of three schools which seemed to share some characteristics with the schools in both the other groups. The characteristics of the two extreme groups are summarised in Table 1.

Whilst it would be inappropriate to discuss this research in great detail here, there are a number of observations that can be made that might be illuminating when considering the implementation of large scale change such as the National Curriculum. Firstly that there appears to be, across the schools studied, two distinctive orientations to change. In one group of schools, all in West Dockton, pressure for change was seen as coming from classroom teachers in response to the conditions of their everyday work. This was spoken of by the head-teachers in positive terms. For instance the head of one of the east Dockton schools said that the staff of the West Dockton school where he had previously been head were:

> ... a completely dedicated group of teachers who you were all the time restraining ... there was always something happening there ... the teachers didn't need me to inspire them educationally.

The previous deputy at this school, who at the time of a study had become the headteacher of one of the other schools in the West Dockton sample, confirmed this by saying:

> There was a certain amount of team teaching going on and it wasn't one of those things that was forced from the management, it was one of those things that came from the staff. You only had to float an idea in the staff room and someone would take it up ... given the situation that we had ... we were pretty innovative. Looking back on it I am surprised at some of the things we did.

He also stated that at his own school:

> The vast majority of curriculum innovation ... has come from the staff.

This pressure for change from the staff was matched with a resistance to take on board any changes or innovations that were initiated by the headteacher that were not seen as meeting needs as expressed by the teachers. One of the West Dockton headteachers stated that:

> Everything I've done had to be done ... there are times now when people come to me and put things to me and I have to modify my views.

Another, drawing comparisons between his present West Dockton school and a previous school in another LEA, observed:

> I'm put into a position that I used to put others in, where I
> have to give way and accept changes, sometimes, that I don't
> particularly want ... At different times when I have tried to
> change the way people work ... I've tried to influence them
> and failed.

The headteacher of a neighbouring school described how he had failed
in his attempt to introduce the Nuffield maths scheme into the school
despite having spent four years prior to coming to the school working
as a member of the team developing these materials. As one head
stated the feeling amongst the West Dockton heads seemed to be that:

> Your curriculum is, like politics, the art of the possible.

A contrasting situation seemed to prevail in three of the schools in
East Dockton. Here there appeared to be very little pressure for
change from teachers, with a greater likelihood of any changes that
did take place being initiated by the headteacher. The staff were seen
by headteachers as tending towards complacency. As one stated:

> I've still got some teachers here who'll say 'I'm not coming to
> that thing being done by the maths person because I've been
> teaching maths for 30 years and I know how to do it'.

In these circumstances the head becomes the agent of change. For
instance, one head stated that:

> I've taught the teachers ... that there is more to education
> than teaching the children how to read from a reading book
> and how to write sentences in an exercise book and adding up,
> taking away, multiplying and dividing.

Secondly there appeared to be distinctly different sets of relations
between the schools and their public. In East Dockton the relationship
between the school and the pupils and their parents was presented as
being harmonious by the headteachers. The pupils were seen as being
easy to teach and the parents as holding values that were in line with
those of the school and as having a high regard for schooling. One
East Dockton headteacher said of the parents, most of whom were
Asian:[9]

They are completely supportive, they are completely behind schools. They think schools are great, they think English schools are great, and they back us to the hilt.

He considered that the children had:

... a fantastic lot to offer this country because of their attitudes and their work ... a lot of university material here, and they're going to go to university as well.

and that the school was:

... very very fortunate to pick up highly motivated Asians who are very calm anyway ... and will accept ... things.

Another East Dockton headteacher stated that:

Generally we tend to be fairly, touch wood, lucky in our catchment. We don't get that many problem families that we can't handle, we don't get that many problem children and we don't get very much vandalism.

He also stated that on coming to the school he:

... was told by several parents, quite forcefully, that this was an excellent school.

In the west the relationship between the schools and their public appeared to be more problematic with the headteachers describing a situation fraught with tension between the school and the pupils and their parents. Parents and children were seen as having a low opinion of schooling. One headteacher claimed that:

There's no motivation, no drive even to attempt it and that's something we're fighting against all the time ... One of the problems is getting them (the children) to come (to school) at all.

Another saw poor attendance as an indicator of the low opinion held of schooling:

> ... children will have time off for no reason, really. 'Oh well, I had to go to the shops', I had to stay in to look after me mum'... It rather shows the attitude of the parents towards education. That it is something, alright, that keeps the children off their hands, but if it's necessary there are other more important things, like doing the shopping.

Adding that:

> ... you've got to keep in mind that the child is as it is because of possibly something that you have no control over which makes teaching that much more difficult.

Factors such as these lead the headteachers to see themselves not predominantly as educationalists but rather, through force of circumstance, as more like social workers. As one, interviewed just a few days before he retired, stated:

> When I came here I was an educationalist, now I'm a retiring social worker.

and another:

> I think we spend a lot of time on social problems. You sometimes wonder whether you're a social worker or a headteacher.

The relationship between educational institutions and their publics has received some attention. Boudon (1980), in a study of the lead-up to the French University crisis in 1968, explored the relationship between the students' 'situation' within the university and within wider society. He posited that the university, presented as almost static in terms of pedagogy, curriculum and ethos, was brought under pressure by a change in the social composition of its intake. Unable to cope with the transformation in the aspirations and orientations of its clientele (and the dynamics of the relations between the various groups within this) and thus make the transition from a bourgeois to a middle class institution,[10] crisis ensued. In Dockton the question is not one of a change in social composition within an institution[11] but differences in social composition between groups of schools. Although, as schools within the same authority they are similarly resourced and subject to the same forms of teacher support and INSET, and to the same overall policies and initiatives, there are distinct differences in the relationship between the implicit and explicit demands of the schools and the aspirations and orientations of their publics.

In West Dockton the tensions manifest in this critical state[12] can be seen as pressuring the headteacher into focusing primarily on social issues that are highly visible in the perceived problematic relationship between home and school, addressing the establishment of the conditions necessary for the teachers to carry out the educational work of the school. The teachers themselves are also in the position of having to cope with a range of contingencies. Their attempts to resolve the need to 'survive'[13] the events generated by the tensions between the implicit and explicit demands of the school and the attitudes, motivations and orientations of the children with their own educational concerns give rise to pressure for curricular and pedagogic change within the school. With this pressure for 'classroom-up' change comes a resistance to 'top-down' change that is seen as being irrelevant or impractical given prevailing conditions. Often this form of change and development is viewed negatively as being 'merely reactive' (Alexander, 1984, makes this accusation of primary school practice in general) rather than being based on the technical-rationalist ideal of planned change informed by theory and research. In Dockton this did not seem to be the case. Developments from within West Dockton appeared to spread and staff from these schools seemed to move on to take up senior positions both within the borough and elsewhere.

The form of innovation taking place here has no place within the strategy for the implementation of the National Curriculum. This programme ignores middle order factors such as the school's relation to its public, the sets of contingencies that act upon teachers in their everyday practice and the factors that create, maintain and transform practices. The demands being made will manifest themselves as another set of pressures acting upon the school and its teachers. The effects of this are impossible to judge given the importance of the relation of the form of change being proposed and other contextual factors. It may be that teachers in schools such as those in West Dockton might resist elements of the National Curriculum in ways similar to the resistance shown to centralized curriculum development projects and materials in the past. Aspects of the National Curriculum might on the other hand be appropriated and transformed by the schools to meet perceived needs. What is important here, however, is that a source of change and development is neglected. Rather than attempt to create structures or develop strategies to foster worthwhile innovation and encourage the growth of reflexive practice which could be informed by research, a token mechanism is adopted.

The futility of the search for a universal mechanism or technique for the implementation of the National Curriculum is demonstrated by the differences in the orientation to change between the schools in East and West Dockton. In contrast to the situation outlined above there appeared to be little pressure for change from teachers in East Dockton who appeared, from the headteachers' accounts, to view their practices as adequate even in the face of educational arguments to the contrary. In these schools the headteachers felt they could take up an 'educationalist' role which placed them in the position of forcing through planned changes by drawing on their structural (and personal) authority. Questions regarding the appropriateness of the strategies employed by the Government for the implementation of the National Curriculum can also be raised in this context. Whilst information about the structure, content and demands of the National Curriculum, poured onto the classroom teacher via a cascade, can be seen to be important, this does not necessarily effect change in practice. Teachers in these schools can be presumed to have been informed of curricular and pedagogic developments in primary education in the past but their practice has remained static. The static nature of the practices can be linked to the perceived match between the implicit and explicit demands of the school and the aspirations and orientations of its public. The children are viewed by the headteachers as being compliant and easy to teach whilst their parents are seen as being generally supportive of schooling. The non-problematic nature of the relationship between schooling and the intakes of these schools does not lead to the same array of immediate classroom problems found in West Dockton and thus the same demand for change. The motivation for development must come from elsewhere. The provision of skills and knowledge orientated INSET seems unlikely to provide this nor does 'consciousness raising' style material. It seems more likely, paradoxically, that it is solely the 'authority' of the National Curriculum, acting through the authority of the headteacher and the LEA, that will facilitate its implementation. The effects of this, however, are once again difficult to predict.

Conclusion

Often presumptions are made about the degree of fit between policies and practice and between intended outcomes and actual effects. The present government presumes a high degree of fit:[14] policies are formulated on the basis of a set of professed outcomes, this being achieved through rational argument, calculation and political expedience. Achievement of these outcomes once policies are in place is seen as a technical matter: suitable methods of implementation have to be designed that overcome the barriers to transformation. The failure to bring practice into line with policies focuses attention on the adequacy of the techniques for implementation adopted and on the inadequacies or intransigence of the practitioners. The feasibility of the form of the project of 'top-down', planned, rational change does not itself come under scrutiny, however. The methods chosen by the Government for supporting the implementation of the National Curriculum can be seen as shifting any explanation of difficulties in implementation in the direction of the practitioner: already we are being told that mathematics teachers do not have the skills or knowledge necessary.

It is not only within the domain of the Government's attempts to implement the National Curriculum that unshakable faith in this form of change is evident. In attempts to counter social inequalities, for example, stress is often placed on the formulation of policies, for instance anti-sexist policies, with the translation of these into practice seen as being a matter of development of appropriate methods. The existence of the policy enables statements to be made about how every possible effort is being made to address social inequality, a public display has been made which can be lauded as a first step or foundation for later action. The failure to effectively transform practices leads in two directions: the search for more effective methods for bringing practice in line with policies and the pathologising of the practitioner. The latter might involve focusing on the attitudes and feelings of the practitioner as a source of explanation and the adoption of forms of consciousness raising as solutions. Once again we have the dual focus on the structural and the individual. The factors, particularly day-to-day contingencies, that act to both maintain and transform practices remain untouched.

Similarly in the domain of mathematics teaching prescriptions for practice, such as those made by HMI, the Mathematics Working Party of the National Curriculum Council, by other curriculum development projects and authors of schemes, may be highly specific in both form and content but are decontextualized. The presumption is that either new forms of practice can be overlaid on existing practices in a non-problematic manner or that techniques can be developed that act to translate prescriptions into practices without transformation of the form and content of the prescriptions themselves. Being a teacher of mathematics becomes an engagement with a set of technical problems, a question of translation of prescriptions into practices via mechanisms, the effectiveness of which can be judged by way of comparison of outcomes. The form and content of the prescriptions and the framework and methods used to assess effectiveness become unquestionable. The mathematics educator, whatever phase or level of the education system s/he is engaged in, becomes a technician charged with the effective delivery of a curriculum formed elsewhere. Failure to deliver is explained away at the level of the individual teacher; inadequate mathematics qualifications, insufficient mathematical knowledge or insecurity about mathematics, being out of touch with contemporary practices and so on. Whilst these might be important factors, concentration exclusively on them leads us away from consideration of the middle order, local and contextual factors outlined above.

The development of an alternative view of change and innovation is not just a matter of proposing greater complexity. Change does take place in schooling and changes in practice arise from the active engagement of teachers and other educational workers with the conditions of their everyday work. This also acts as a basis for the generation of resistance to change. Structural, resourcing, policy, assessment and other forms of change enter the work of the teacher as various orders of contingent factors, the effects of which are unpredictable without consideration of the context which they both act to constitute and are a part. If serious attempts are to be made to implement large scale pedagogic or curricular change then it becomes essential to examine the forces that give rise to and maintain new practices and develop means of implementation that chain on to these in some way (see articles by Dowling and Noss, in this volume). It would also be important to be aware that there are forces that act to maintain existing practices and forces that act to maintain resistance. For instance, the study outlined above draws attention to the differing orientations towards change of two groups of schools. This introduces the nature of the receiving institution as a factor in change and makes clear that different strategies for change would be appropriate in different conditions.

Questions are also raised regarding the relationship between forms of practice and the social characteristics of the intake of the school, a factor often treated in very simplistic terms, or not at all, when considering changes in pedagogy[15] and curriculum. The study indicates that the relationship between the implicit and explicit demands of the school and the aspirations and orientations of its public have to be taken into account when considering the nature of the institution. Care has to be taken in making assumptions about the unitary nature of social classes when doing this. The working class, for instance, in this level of analysis cannot be considered a homogeneous group but rather as an aggregate of occupational and cultural communities (see Roberts *et al.*, 1977, for elaboration of this) each with its own distinctive set of values and attitudes and each inter-cut with other social divisions. This indicates a possible difficulty in making general statements about the effects of the National Curriculum on the educational experience of working class children.[16]

It is not enough, however, to simply introduce contextual sensitivity to a technical-rational model of change. One also has to acknowledge that meanings of practices may differ from context to context as the sets of relations in which they are positioned change. This moves us away from being able to assert that particular practices have particular effects and that practices that are possible in one context are possible in all others. This in turn casts doubt on the project of large scale change that is mechanically tied to particular practices, or contents, with predictable outcomes or consequences, and points in the direction of providing support for critical reflexive practice. As mathematics educators we have to take care not to reinforce the former view of practice. The apparent long-standing opposition to theoretical and critical work in the study of mathematics education and the predominance of narrowly focused empiricist research helps us little in this respect. Limited, and unfortunately often patronising, views of what is useful for the classroom teacher also lead to forms of in-service training that act to reinforce a technical view of mathematics teaching and contribute little towards the development of reflexive practice.

In conclusion, by adopting a particular type of educational reform the Government has generated a particular set of problems. It has effected a structural change that has implications at the level of practice. What these implications are is, however, difficult to divine. The purpose of the reforming and restructuring of curriculum content, and the transformation of the structures, mechanisms and means of assessment, is, it would be reasonable to assume, to bring about certain changes in classroom practice and thus the educational experiences of children. The fit between these structural changes and changes at the level of classroom practice is conceived of by the Government, on the evidence provided by their chosen means of implementation, in terms of a set of technical problems. There has been an attempt to transform one technical problem (how can the Government translate the National Curriculum into a set of practices) into another (how can teachers find the most effective means of teaching the National Curriculum). The effect of this is to transform one unanswerable question into another but in doing so effecting a change in the subject of the question. Thus by presuming an oversimplified model of change and development (i.e. 'if we tell people what we want and give them the skills that they will need to do this then the desired change will take place') and adopting strategies to address the problems identified (a 'cascade' of information-orientated meetings and courses aimed at development of the skills and knowledge of individual teachers) the Government effectively moves responsibility for the implementation of the National Curriculum (and thus blame for perceived difficulties in its implementation) from itself to the classroom teacher.

Given the complex of factors that form, maintain and develop classroom practice, some of which have been elaborated in this article, it now seems pointless to talk of the 'success' or 'failure' of the implementation of the National Curriculum. It is here with us as a policy and will have a multiplicity of effects. I hope to have demonstrated that we cannot assume that these effects will be universal, easily predicted or have any direct link to intention.

Notes

1   Andy Hargreaves (1989) has thoroughly explored the effects of subject divisions and specialism on the work of the teacher.

2   There is, of course, no systematic research on what might constitute 'good practice' in mathematics education. What emerges, from reports such as those produced by HMI (DES, 1987; 1989), might more sensibly be called the ideology of mathematics education, that is what can be said at the level of rhetoric about forms of practice (proposed or existing) which can be presumed to meet with general professional approval. Outlining what constitutes good practice has the effect of marking out an ideal to which both the visible and invisible aspects of a teacher's practice have to be related in order to be evaluated in terms of quality of provision. This also has the effect of creating the illusion of consensus, or at least defining the area in which debate can occur, which in turn has the effect of excluding, without debate, particular practices and positions. There is no need, because of the status of good practice, to have to produce any evidence of the extent of existence or the conditions of such practice, hence the unsupported assertions of the mathematics working party in the consultation document (DES, 1988). See also Dowling, in this volume, on the notion of 'collective experience' of working parties.

3   Whether or not these collected lists of statements of attainment can

reasonably be considered a curriculum in any sense is of course another question.

4   Kenneth Baker obviously appreciates this, having moved from the DES at a time when he can claim the kudos of having transformed structures without having to face up to the ultimate assessment of the success of the reforms, in the Tories' own terms, through the transformation of educational practice and, beyond that, outcomes.

5   Assuming, that is, that practice is not already in line with the proposed curriculum. If it were this would cast the tories claims to have reformed education in somewhat pale light.

6   Again no evidence is cited to indicate the basis on which it is assumed that teachers do not have these skills and knowledge or that they do indeed need them to be effective teachers.

7   It is tempting to consider this as, in Schon's (1983) terms, a form of technical-rational change. This would, however, not be appropriate. Technical-rational change involves an attempt to engineer change on the basis of social-scientific research. In the case of the National Curriculum there is no evidence of reference to appropriate research. Instead there is frequent reference to the knowledge of good practice of the working party members; what this is, how it is gained and any rational basis for the assertions made remain unclear. Even less clear is the rational basis for changes that take place as a result of the comments of the Secretary of State for Education, for instance the disappearance of the 'applications' profile component from the proposals of the mathematics working party.

8   An average of 9.6 per cent of the householders were owner occupiers across the catchment areas of the schools studied in the west compared with 56.9 per cent in the east; 83.3 per cent in the west were council tenants compared with 27.2 per cent in the east; 10.7 per cent of heads of household were from the New Commonwealth in the west compared with 33 per cent in the east.

9   The interview material contains a number of references to the perceived orientation of particular groups identified by the headteachers. For instance one headteacher stated that 'Asian parents want a straight, traditional, formal education for their children'. It must be remembered that these typifications are no more than the perceptions of the headteacher with no guarantee of accuracy. It must also be remembered that such typifications have concrete effects.

10 Boudon argues that prior to the 1950s the French university was a 'bourgeois' institution recruiting its students predominantly from the upper-classes. The 1950s and 1960s saw a sharp rise in middle class recruitment and a decline in bourgeois intake and thus a rapid change in the social composition of the student population. Throughout this period of change in the background, aspirations and expectations of the student intake, the university system, through institutional inertia, remained static in terms of organisation, structure, curriculum and pedagogy. Unable to adopt reforms that would have enabled it to fulfil the new functions being demanded by the transformation from a bourgeois

to a middle class institution subsequently led to student alienation and crisis.

11　There had, however, been an apparent change in the social characteristics of the intakes of the schools in East Dockton in the ten years prior to the study. In this time what was considered to be an aspirant white working class had been replaced, according to the headteachers, by Asian families. Both groups were, however, seen as having a similar orientation to schooling.

12　Bourdieu and Passeron (1977) have identified two limiting states of the relationship between schooling and its public: the organic and the critical. In the former state the school system deals with a public that perfectly matches its implicit demands whereas in the latter, because of the social characteristics of the clientele, a state of intolerable misunderstanding and tension is reached. The schools in West Dockton can be seen as tending towards a critical state whereas those in the east tend towards an organic state.

13　There is a substantial body of ethnographic work based around the study of teacher, and pupil, survival strategies. See for instance Woods (1979).

14　It is, admittedly, difficult to see how they could not be committed to such a view. The very structures within which state education takes place are predicated on such assumptions.

15　The often repeated claim that the National Curriculum only constrains teachers in respect of content but not the means by which this content is 'delivered', and thus pedagogy, neglects the necessary relationship between curriculum and pedagogy (and assessment). The manner in which curriculum contents are structured and the principles on which items are selected and excluded carry with them implications for, and assumptions about, what may or may not be appropriate ways of teaching.

16　At a later stage, however, it might become possible to make statements about the systematic social distribution of educational performances within the framework provided by the National Curriculum and its assessment mechanisms.

References

ALEXANDER, R., 1984, *Primary Teaching*, London: Holt, Rinehart and Winston.

BROWN, A.J., 1985, 'Primary School Variation in an Urban Education Authority', unpublished MSc dissertation, Polytechnic of the South Bank, London.

BOUDON, R., 1980, *The Crisis in Sociology*, London: Macmillan.

BOURDIEU, P. and PASSERON, J-C., 1977, *Reproduction in Education, Society and Culture*, London: Sage.

DES, 1987, *Mathematics from 5 to 16 (second edn)*, London: HMSO.

DES, 1988, *Mathematics for ages 5 to 16: Proposals of the Secretary of State for Education and Science and the Secretary of State for Wales*, London: HMSO.

DES, 1989, *The Teaching and Learning of Mathematics*, London: HMSO.

EMERSON, C. and GODDARD, I., 1989, *All About the National Curriculum*, London: Heinemann.

HARGREAVES, A., 1989, *Curriculum and Assessment Reform*, Milton Keynes: Open University Press.

HARLAND, J., 1987, 'The new INSET: A transformation scene', *Journal of Education Policy*, **2**, 3, pp. 235–44.

ROBERTS, K., COOK, F.G., CLARK, S.C. and SEMEONOFF, E., 1977, *The Fragmentary Class Structure*, London: Heinemann.

SCHON, D.A., 1983, *The Reflective Practitioner: How Professionals Think in Action*, New York: Basic Books.

SKILBECK, M., 1976, 'School-based curriculum development' in WALTON, J. and WELTON, J. (Ed.), *Rational Curriculum Planning*, London: Ward Lock.

WOODS, P., 1979, *The Divided School*, London: Routledge and Kegan Paul.

11 Training Teachers in Crisis: a case study of a part-time Postgraduate Certificate in Education

Pat Drake

Introduction

The latter half of the 1980s have seen radical changes in the control of education in England and Wales. The Education Reform Act which established a National Curriculum in schools was moved through parliament with astonishing speed. This feat was accomplished by the Thatcher government at least in part because a case had been created to cause alarm at the so-called poor quality of education meted out to children in schools. There were two main thrusts to the mounting attack. Firstly the curriculum was deemed to be incoherent and irrelevant, in that what pupils learned was not what the country needed, i.e. a skilled workforce. The second theme was what came to be known as 'teacher bashing'. A long and exhausting period of teacher action against imposed conditions of service left schools undefended against accusations of not implementing the curriculum effectively.

However teachers could not be blamed for failing to deliver the curriculum in subjects for which teachers did not exist. The Government priority for a scientific and numerate workforce meant recruiting teachers for the shortage areas of Mathematics, Physics and CDT. This was easier said than done. Existing routes to qualified teacher status were full-time BEd and PGCE courses, and new teachers were simply not coming through in sufficient numbers to fill the vacancies in schools (DES, 1986). In mathematics, this situation resulted in two specific aspects of teacher shortage. Even before mathematics became a core subject in the statutory National Curriculum, it was studied compulsorily by all pupils in Primary and Secondary schools. So actual shortages became hidden shortages as teachers of other (sometimes) related subjects covered the mathematics timetable.

Thus there was scope for action on teacher supply on these two counts, that is finding alternative ways of recruiting and training more well-qualified mathematicians, and retraining teachers of other subjects to make their diversion into mathematics effective. Two courses were developed at the Institute of Education — A Course of Retraining in Secondary Mathematics and what came to be known as the Part-time PGCE in Secondary Mathematics. The course of retraining has been documented elsewhere (Drake, 1989). This chapter explains developments leading up to the establishment of the Part-time PGCE, and describes, by considering influences and constraints on the initiative, its planning and implementation.

Reflecting on the circumstances which generated the course leads us to wonder how far this small project, developed as it was in the shadow of the National Curriculum, illustrates general issues relating to innovation at this time.

Firstly there is the context of the National Curriculum. Emphasis on delivery of the Curriculum so far has been in terms of content, determined by Attainment Targets. Yet delivery of the curriculum, national or not, requires well-qualified teachers, and this in turn necessitates quality training programmes.

Drives to recruit more teachers have led the government to initiate alternative teacher-training patterns, notably Articled and Licensed teacher schemes. As will be described, the development of the Part-time PGCE began to move towards school-based training, and lessons learned from this experience are surely germane to both Articled and Licensed teacher schemes, which also aim to train teachers whilst they work actively in schools.

Secondly, there are issues which are exemplified by the case presented emerging as the implementation of a curriculum idea becomes a reality.

> The rhetoric of curriculum development ... is based on an unexamined assumption: that all of us concerned with the education of pupils — teachers, administrators, advisers, researchers, theorists — basically share the same educational values and have overlapping visions of curriculum excellence. (Macdonald and Walker, 1976: 44)

Development of the course began with extensive discussions with representatives from different groups with an interest in training mathematics teachers, and distance learning, i.e. the Department of Education and Science, Institute administration, staff in the Department of Mathematics, Statistics and Computing both established and newly appointed to the project, the Open University, LEAs, teachers and the students themselves. These discussions backed up our hunch that a common set of educational values did not exist. I should say first that was no suggestion of opposition to the project by any group, more a desire to reconcile different positions. Recognition of these positions certainly helped devise strategies for implementation, and there may be no more significance to them than that. However the development of a 'curriculum rhetoric' was an issue in itself, and potentially problematic areas in the course development emerged through these discussions. It was through the 'curriculum rhetoric' that different positions were reconciled.

The processes of building a curriculum are the nuts and bolts of putting the course together. This included deciding fairly early on at whom the course should aim as different groups have different needs in terms of the time they can allocate to study. For example women with families want day sessions, whereas redundant industrialists prefer evenings and weekends, and people from a long way away opt for block residential courses. During this planning, various factors arose which greatly affected the innovation.

The first is the tension between what is done and what is said to be done. This is particularly illuminated in the use of the term 'distance learning'. We found that 'distance learning' conjures up images of students far away working in isolation on piles of printed material arriving through the post. This was not a sympathetic image of a trainee teacher. We realized that even though distance learning in this sense would be part of the course students would also be attending the Institute from time to time, and thus were similar to other part-time students. No-one calls part-time students distance learners, yet this PGCE was known as the distance-learning PGCE. We changed the name of the course to the Part-time PGCE in Secondary Mathematics and thus it was possible to allow teacher training to encompass the concept of distance learning without implying that there was no communication with and between students, tutors and schools. It seems strange now to those working on the course to hear outsiders referring to the 'correspondence course', and we always correct it. It seems that part of the process of implementing this innovation has been a struggle to reach acceptable meanings and interpretations of our brief, within the context of our profession.

A further development was that once a within-house rationale for the course had (apparently) been accepted, and that the planning process had been seen to be within the spirit of the department, then changing circumstances expedited quite rapid decision-making and adaptations, without a lengthy justificatory rationale. I was alerted to this by a drop in full-time PGCE applications. This resulted in speedy negotiations to combine resources where possible. From the point of view of the part-time course this could not have been better, as it knitted the innovation more closely to the department. However it certainly was not planned in advance.

Lastly comes the question of support in school, where a substantial part of the course was to take place. The concept of distance learning was also expanding to include the idea that a substantial part of the course should be based in schools local to the students. (Quite apart from the value of this experience, it also enlarged the potential catchment area for students). This necessitated choosing suitable schools, and finding ways of supporting the students once they were there. Schools were nominated by LEA Mathematics Advisers, as was a teacher-tutor within each school. This person was identified not only on the strength and quality of their mathematics teaching, but also on their personal qualities as a potential mentor. Here was another issue, that of the need for support for the teacher-tutors. It transpired that the Institute may yet again alter its traditional role with regard to the supervision of students in school, offering in addition to normal activities some Inservice training to teacher tutors, in other words, becoming a 'trainer of trainers'. Again this was not anticipated at the beginning. I wonder if it is too much to infer that this innovation will help instigate shifts in practice resulting from practical needs which arose during its implementation.

The Initiative

During the academic year 1986–87 the Manpower Services Commission offered funds to support initiatives to increase the supply of teachers in Mathematics, Physics and Technology. Research funding was secured by means of a proposal (Hoyles, 1986) for a pilot study to look at the potential for a Post Graduate Certificate in Education by distance learning. This was an ambitious idea, explored by a Research Officer during three intense months in Spring 1987.

Advertisements in the press invited potential students to a meeting at the Institute. Approximately 15 people attended this meeting, and many more made enquiries and asked to be kept informed. These people declared their interest in training to teach Mathematics by some alternative to a full-time PGCE. Some were unemployed, some facing redundancy, some wanted a change in career, and some were in the midst of a career break, with young children. Most of them completed a questionnaire which enquired into qualifications, occupation, domestic circumstances, age and preferred modes of study. These questionnaires were kept on file and used later in determining the structure of the course. All respondents were circulated when the course was set up and given the opportunity to apply.

During the pilot study, the possibilities for distance learning were tentatively investigated, with a view to how such materials might be generated — whether through collaboration with another institution, or by being produced at the Institute.

During 1987 the government became sufficiently concerned about the shortage of teachers to support larger initiatives to help combat the situation. Universities through the University Grants Committee, and polytechnics through the National Advisory Board, were invited to bid for grants to support schemes designed to attract people into teaching mathematics. A bid was submitted for work on two further initiatives at the Institute. These were A Course of Retraining in Secondary Mathematics (mentioned earlier) and a feasibility study into PGCE in Secondary Mathematics through distance learning. £75 000 was granted for three years, enough for 2.5 extra academic staff to work on both initiatives, and 0.5 secretary. Appointments were made for work to begin in September 1987.

Influences, Constraints and Resistance

The DES were concerned about the shortage of mathematics teachers, and had committed themselves to resourcing training — in the provision of extra courses, in the bursary of, at the time, £1250 payable to student mathematics teachers, and in the 'taster' courses aimed at encouraging people from other walks of life into teaching. The DES, through its Council for Accreditation of Teacher Education (CATE), has oversight of PGCE courses in England and Wales. The new PGCE had to meet CATE criteria established by the DES in a series of circulars issued between 1983 and 1986. Furthermore, Local Education Authorities[1] take advice from the DES on the awards of grants to students. The grant system is complicated; particularly relevant is the working definition of 'part-time', which states that such courses have to comprise a certain proportion of the equivalent full-time tuition before awards are payable to the students. For instance in our case, we proposed that students should spend one day a week in school. This was questioned by the DES as to whether it formed a necessary part of the compulsory tuition. We had to argue quite hard for it to be so counted; had our arguments fallen on deaf ears the course structure simply could not have been sustained, as students would not have been awarded grants.[2] The point I am making is that whilst the DES are keen to train more mathematics teachers, it is not axiomatic that the recommendations of experienced teacher trainers be adopted, and that ultimately the DES control the situation by controlling both the accreditation system and student grants.

The second group, teacher trainers, particularly those inside the Institute are nearer home. The notion of a 'distance learning PGCE' evokes the idea of a correspondence course, and the provision of the course a matter of writing distance learning materials. Neither of these seem particularly appealing prospects to busy people, even if feasible. The polite response of academic colleagues is to avoid getting involved, especially if they suspect they may turn out to be fundamentally opposed to what is proposed. This was a time when teachers and teacher-training by implication were being heavily criticised, and it has been suggested that colleagues suspected this project to be an attempt at training teachers 'on the cheap', thus devaluing further existing PGCE provision. On the other hand substantial financial benefit accrues to the department through this and other outside-funded projects. Increasingly prolific, these projects bring in new ideas. INSET provision for teachers was increasing within the department too; changes in the way the department functioned were bound to be in the air. The cooperation of the department was essential for the success of this project; fortunately goodwill prevailed amongst the staff, who took the opportunities offered to contribute to the development of a rationale for the new course.

The Open University is committed to distance learning. Having itself been funded by the DES to write a course Frameworks for Teaching (1988), it is anxious to form links with institutions and for these institutions to adopt the distance learning mode in the new PGCEs which are springing up in response to teacher shortages. On the other hand the Open University was unwilling to relinquish its renowned expertise in the field of distance learning, and so was keen to maintain control over how the course was used. For instance, it insisted on appointing its own tutor for Frameworks. We were keen to adopt Frameworks, but were also anxious, not unreasonably, that it be tutored by one of the Institute course developers to maintain continuity across the course. This was allowed, but not until after the person concerned had submitted a formal application to the Open University, been interviewed and had a testimonial from the Chair of the department of Mathematics, Statistics and Computing at the Institute.

LEA Mathematics Advisers have to deal with untrained people teaching mathematics in schools in their region. This hidden shortage of teachers is a mixed blessing: there are at least people in classrooms with the pupils, but people who need a great deal of help and advice. Thus experienced mathematics teachers in school are already 'training' their colleagues. So even though a partially school-based PGCE course does get mathematics graduates into schools, and is clearly a sensible way to train teachers on the job, it actually puts a lot of pressure on already stretched experienced teachers of mathematics. So LEA Mathematics Advisers were understandably anxious about commiting their experienced teachers to supporting students because the teachers could not afford the time, nor could the advisers find replacement cover. At the planning stage the concern of LEAs in the London area was the immediate shortage of mathematics teachers, juxtaposed against local surplus of secondary teachers owing to cuts. Further away from London, shortages of mathematics teachers are not so urgent, either absolutely or relative to shortages of teachers in other subjects. Thus it was clear that support for the course would vary according to local conditions.

The possibility was that teachers themselves would be potentially more antipathetic, for yet a different reason. Suspicion was that it is an insulting anachronism to propose to train people to teach through distance learning, a proposition which devalues the skills and experience of teachers and fails to recognize the essential communicative nature of the profession. This, allied with hesitancy within the department, suggested a possible conflict with the advocates of distance learning.

Finally the students: the course had to attract the target group and we knew that if it were not attractive enough, people simply would not apply. In short we are witnessing, in the creation and implementation of this course by a university, what Halsey (1987) calls 'channels of consumer sovereignty over what is offered by these businesses (i.e. the business of cultural products).' The other side of this coin is that demand for this course had been deliberately created, in that sectors of the community were to be persuaded to enter mathematics teaching. The significance of this development is that there was then a triangular relationship in which the Institution had been persuaded, through funding, to cater to a national need; groups in the public were to be persuaded that a teaching career is a possibility, and then that this public exerts the pressure of a market force on the Institute to provide the course it wants.

Under the terms of the contract with the University Grants Committee, a Steering Group was constituted, and individuals who represent different groups interested in such a course invited to join, e.g. from industry, LEA Mathematics Advisers, teachers, and the Open University, as well as Institute staff. The purpose of the group was to maintain the progress of the project, and to make suggestions as to the direction it might take. The Steering group influenced the structure and content of the curriculum, including the Mathematics curriculum, both directly and indirectly. This is in contrast to the full-time PGCE, the mathematics component of which is planned entirely by the department.[3] For example, it was suggested through the Steering group that the term 'Anti-racist maths' as a topic heading should be made less significant in the part-time course brochure. This particular topic is an overt element of the full-time PGCE and appears in its literature. However, the part-time course literature is disseminated more widely in advance of student enrolment, as part of the drive to create a demand for the course. Because of this, and because the course is a result of a government initiative, it was felt by the steering group to be more politically expedient to relegate this particular topic to, if not quite the 'hidden curriculum' (Hargreaves, 1982), then at least the small print. Although only a small example, this shows an external influence directly affecting the curriculum at university level.

Planning — A Course Evolves

It seemed to us that the keys to devising a workable course were collaboration with and negotiation between the people concerned. Reconciling different viewpoints was clearly in the interest of the development. Hitherto, the project had assumed a classic Research, Development and Diffusion model in that there had been an initial feasibility survey, and we were granted a development year, with a view to running the course from the end of this time. As House observes

> ... an R, D & D approach assumes passive consumers at the end of the R, D & D chain who will adopt the innovation ...

such a scheme for innovation might work if the various actors in it — researchers, developers, diffusers, teachers — shared a common value system and worked towards a common end. But they do not. (House, 1979: 139)

The primary strategy then was to seek areas of common ground, to find ways of legitimating a process which is acceptable to all the interested parties. The one common value held by all is that at the time there was believed to be a serious shortage of mathematics teachers. Secondly, not only was it strategic to take and be seen to act upon advice from members of the profession, both teachers and teacher-trainers, this advice was also invaluable. Thirdly, it was decided to devote time to convincing those with influence outside the immediate teaching profession that the decisions being made were in their interests. Finally, I should be honest and state that we intended the resulting course structure and choice of student teachers on the course to be in line with our ideas of 'good practice', and our perceptions of what would constitute a satisfactory approach to the question of training mathematics teachers.

The course, to run at all, had to recruit students and so it was that decisions began to be made in order to produce some course literature. (The production of publicity material was a driving force in the decision-making process). It was decided by the course developers and agreed by the Steering Group to target mainly mature women mathematics (or related subject) graduates, and to attempt also to attract one or two individuals who were currently teaching mathematics without qualifications, or who were unemployed, or who wanted to transfer from Industry. This choice of target group arose partly because enquiries came from women with children looking to enter mathematics teaching: this group appear nowhere else in the system, as they are out of the workforce and so we knew least about them. The course developers believed that here was an untapped resource of well-qualified potential teachers. Apparent enthusiasm from the DES for retraining people from Industry, yielded little support from our industrial contacts. In fact the research officer spent hours in making contacts trying to establish secondments and/or sponsorship, but in the end we had to accept that Industry wanted to keep its 'good people', and were reluctant to sponsor the others. Conflict over the course structure was thus avoided and the course became deliberately designed to accommodate the particular needs of this main group of mature women.

We decided that the course should be two years part-time, and depend on a combination of face-to-face with distance learning. After a week in a Primary school, and a week's Induction course, students were to attend the Institute one day per week to study a Mathematics curriculum course, a course very similar to that followed by full-time students. They were also to attend a school local to them one day per week for practical school experience, together with two periods of continuous teaching practice, one in each year of the course. The Open University were to provide a third component, Frameworks for Teaching, for home study via distance learning materials, and a fourth component, Independent Professional Studies, was geared towards students' own professional work encouraging them to make links between each course element, and to draw upon their previous work and life experience. In this structure, distance learning takes place in different ways, working on the premise that most of the students' experience takes place other than at the Institute. There is study of materials, organized by the students at a time, place and to a degree pace to suit themselves. There is also practical teaching organized by the teacher-tutor, and there are the students' independent study projects, the choice of which, although guided and advised by Institute tutor and teacher-tutor, is very much determined by the students' location and circumstances as well as their interests. Students on the course were to be supported by an Institute tutor and a seminar group, a school-based teacher-tutor, an Open University tutor, and a self-help study group.

Publicity material was produced in early 1988, and a more detailed document which outlined the proposed structure and its rationale. On the basis of these documents alongside the discussions and negotiations taking place, the proposed PGCE was sanctioned by the University Senate and temporary approval was granted by the DES to run a trial cohort of 16 students from 1988–90.

Recruitment

Spring 1988 saw the beginning of the recruitment drive. At this stage, the course structure was determined, but detailed planning was yet to be done. This planning continued, informed by suggestions and advice from those interested parties already discussed. As potential students began to come forward, their concerns influenced yet further the contents of the course and its supporting framework.

Approximately 400 people in total were sent a brochure. All the respondents to the original questionnaire from the pilot study were circulated, as was a database of names supplied by the Engineering Council of qualified engineers who might be interested in teaching. Advertisements were placed in *The* Guardian as well as local London papers, and some of the ethnic minority press. Enquirers from these advertisements were sent details and an application form. The benefits of collaboration with the Open University began to pay off in so far as the OU advertised the course to all its higher level mathematics students, and published a short article about it in the magazine Sesame circulated to all students and recent graduates. Several enquiries came through this route.

The nationwide campaign to attract more teachers in shortage subjects was coordinated by the Teaching as a Career unit, TASC.[4] TASC organised exhibitions around the Home Counties at which providing institutions were strongly urged to display material; these exhibitions were quite 'high profile', for example being attended by Ministers, and were given press and television coverage. TASC also provided 'taster' courses in various places, and our PGCE was advertised through both of these initiatives.

In the event we received applications from 32 people with suitable mathematics qualifications. These people were invited for interview at the Institute from March to July 1988. At interview it became clear that it was the part-time nature of the course that attracted the applications, together with the element of distance learning. Several of the applicants were Open University graduates who knew and had benefited through study at a distance, and several lived quite a long way away from London. Some were unemployed having been made redundant, a few were teaching in the private sector without qualifications, some were teaching in colleges of Further Education and one or two in state schools. But by far the majority were women currently out of the workforce because of their families, whose previous careers had not been in education at all. The ages of the applicants ranged from early thirties to late fifties.

Interviewing the applicants made us confront our assumptions about what we were looking for in a potential teacher. Some people in the department were used to interviewing full-time PGCE students, but no-one had experience of part-timers. Furthermore there were changes in the PGCE staff that year which meant that new members of staff were interviewing for the first time. We enlisted the help of two very experienced mathematics teachers one of whom was on the Steering group, and more experienced PGCE tutors. The applicants were subjected to a three stage procedure: they were invited in groups and given an activity to do as a group on their own, the aim of which was to focus their thoughts on mathematics education, and to begin discussion. Then there were short (20–30 minute) individual interviews with a teacher and a member of staff together. Finally the Research Officer spoke individually with each applicant to alert those who did not already know to some of the implications of distance learning and to forewarn them as to the likely upheaval to their lives that undertaking a course for two years was liable to provoke.

We looked for evidence that the applicants were adaptable, imaginative, had qualities of empathy, and were good listeners. We enquired whether people had actually been inside a secondary school recently, and we insisted that those who had not should visit one before we offered them a place. The applicants themselves expressed their concerns. Some were actually qualified to teach mathematics, having graduated before 1974, and some were already teaching privately. Many had attended a mathematics taster course, and some, living in Hertfordshire, were eligible for the HATS[5] scheme which offered a more speedy route into teaching than either a full or part-time PGCE. It became clear that these applicants, despite their entitlement to teach, did not feel competent to do so without some extended training. Several observed that schools nowadays are so different from their own experience, and expressed similar fears regarding mathematics content. It was clear too that some of the women were anxious about rejoining the workforce after some time out of it, and preferred the gradual induction that a part-time course could offer. The day-a-week in school concerned some people, notably those already teaching, who enquired whether they might continue this at their own establishment. We had already decided that each such request be judged individually, depending on how far the school was prepared to support the student, and the opinion of the LEA Mathematics Adviser as to the quality of experience the student would receive. In the event, no students actually began the course under this arrangement, and in fact neither of the two male students took up the places offered them because of this difficulty.

After interview we offered 26 places, and 22 students accepted the offers. Thus, at the end of the Summer term 1988, there was, on paper at least, a course and we were oversubscribed with students to begin it. When the course began the following September, exactly 16 students turned up. The reasons why six dropped out are in themselves interesting and have implications for alternative routes into teaching in general. The two men already mentioned were teaching in schools, and failed to obtain support for their day-a-week as a student. Neither were prepared to lose salary for this day. One person decided to train full-time nearer her home: another joined the Civil Service instead. These two lay at opposing ends of the same spectrum, the first having been turned on to teaching by our publicity and procedure, and the other having been turned off. Two were unable to obtain full grants, without which they could not manage financially, owing to domestic circumstances which deviated from the assumed societal norms upon which the DES regulations are based. I shall return to this particular point later.

The sixteen students who began the course were all women with children. All were graduates of mathematics or related subjects, and four had gained their degrees through the Open University. All bar two had spouses who were working. Geographically they clustered around London and the Home Counties, mainly to the North and West, with the extremities being Colchester in the East and Oxford in the West. We failed to recruit anyone from industry. Despite interviewing a few people who had been made redundant we were not able to offer them places as they did not meet the criteria we imposed. As mentioned earlier, neither did we recruit anyone already teaching in a school. No-one applied as a result of the advertisements in the ethnic minority press, and all the students who began the course in that first year were white.

Articled and Licensed Teacher Schemes

During the 1980s the 'teacher bashing' indulged in by a relentless Tory campaign had fostered a view that teaching is a simple matter, and that unfortunately the only people who cannot do it properly are teachers themselves. Under this reasoning, the PGCE is a necessary but useless impediment to the provision of teachers in shortage subjects, yet in 1987, the beginning of the project, it was the case that teachers needed to be qualified.

During 1988 Secretary of State for Education and Science Kenneth Baker circulated a Green Paper which raised for the first time the likelihood of an alternative pattern of teacher training, through what was then called a Licensed Teacher Scheme. This paper was heavily attacked by teachers and teacher trainers; what finally emerged from the DES in 1989 were proposals for two distinct schemes. One retained the name Licensed Teachers, and was geared towards employing teachers whose qualifications were either thin, or were not recognised for some reason (e.g. qualifications obtained overseas). The other was called the Articled Teacher Scheme, and aimed at recruiting graduates into teaching. Both schemes emphasised the desirability of training teachers in schools. Detailed discussion of these schemes is beyond the scope of this paper, but the emergence of the Green Paper signalled a trend towards school-based teacher training. The part-time PGCE was obviously a step in that direction.

Because there is very limited experience anywhere of alternatives to full-time college-based teacher training, it is worth commenting briefly on these schemes, given the issues raised during our selection procedure. Firstly, many potential teachers do want training and support before entering a classroom, especially those returning to work after a career break. Without such training, they will not teach. To many of these people, a recognized professional qualification like the PGCE is most appealing. Secondly, we did not offer places to all those who applied and who had suitable academic qualifications. Right or wrong as these individual decisions were, they do point to institutions of teacher training as filters which can weed out 'unsuitable' people before they reach schools. Thirdly it is problematic for schools employing unqualified teachers because of teacher shortage, to then facilitate the extra help and training that those teachers need.

Some Preliminary Evaluation of the Course

The first cohort of students is at the time of writing in the second year of the course, and a second group began in September 1989. It is therefore too early to evaluate fully, but it is possible to flag four issues which are emerging as fundamental.

The first of these is the time commitment of the students. Although carefully designed to be a part-time equivalent to a full-time PGCE in terms of content, the students claim to spend more time on their training than they had bargained for. It is a feature of our notion of distance learning as evolved during the planning that students do not stop being on the course just because they are not physically present — indeed this is true of most forms of study. But we could consider this declared very heavy workload alongside the consistently high standard of work submitted by the students, and the fact that they are all mature women most of whom have had a career break, most of whom are returning to study after a gap, and all of whom are changing direction careerwise. It is interesting too in the context of teacher training in general, to consider whether in fact a part-time course offers more time to students for reflection hence facilitating more self-generated work by the student. If so, do part-time courses need to match exactly their full-time partners in terms of content and contact time?[6] Either way, as one of the students said on a Woman's Hour feature made about the course:[7] 'The course does definitely take more than two-and-a-half days of one's week'.

The second major issue is that of financial support for students. This is a knotty question which will take time as well as widened perception on the part of the authorities to resolve. As I described earlier, four people did not begin the course for financial reasons. There are now thirteen students remaining, another three having dropped out during the first year. Of these three, two did not have domestic partners who were working. This is no coincidence. One was a single parent, and the other had a partner who was chronically sick; the part-time grant plus bursary shared between two years simply does not cover child-care costs and living expenses, and it can be argued that the living expenses of mature people are higher than those of young graduates.

The part-time grant is currently means tested against spouse's income. This practice discriminates against women (and men) whose partners for one reason or another will not support them. It is wickedly tempting to suggest to applicants who are separated from their spouses that they should get a divorce before coming on the course.

> I get a grant of £95 per term which doesn't go very far towards paying for child care, travel, books, even photocopying which we have to get done. It's actually costing us money — we've actually had to buy a second old banger for me to Box and Cox around picking up children and the like for me to do this course. (Student on Woman's Hour)

The women remaining on the course frankly admit to subsidising the true cost of the course from their established life style and partner's income, as well as doing part-time paid work. All own their own houses, bought several years ago before upwardly spiralling prices meant high rents and mortgage repayments. It seems unlikely that initiatives to increase the supply of teachers will succeed if students have to live with unreasonable financial hardship in order to train. It is clear from our experience in setting up this part-time PGCE that the grant system favours (if that is an appropriate word under the circumstances) people who live in 'normal' married relationships. If students are married women, the inbuilt assumption is that their husbands will support them. If they are unmarried and without independent means, then it is more or less impossible to train part-time to teach unless they are also childless.

The third and fourth issues arise out of the teacher-tutor meetings which have been taking place twice a year since July 1988. These meetings provide the forum through which experience of teacher-tutors is disseminated. The two years which have elapsed since the beginning of the scheme have seen some changes in staffing at schools where students are placed. Replacement teacher-tutors, and new teacher-tutors of students in our second cohort are inducted through these meetings, which are used for information, discussion and planning. Clearly they perform a useful In-service function, yet teacher-tutors find it difficult to attend them. Schools cannot find cover for their release, and travel expenses are found on an ad hoc basis depending on the creative accounting of the LEA Adviser. This problem will certainly have repercussions in any Articled and Licensed Teacher schemes; it remains a fact that school-based teacher training is expensive.

The final point which has emerged through the teacher-tutor meetings is that in the experience of teacher-tutors in schools, the part-time women students are different from full-time students, and that extra support does indeed have to be given to aid the transition from a career break to being at work. This can create a tension with the demands of the school day, extended as it is in reality for teacher-tutors to before and after school to allow time for preparation, discussion and reflection. On the other hand, the benefits brought by mature students with a previous career are legion, and teacher-tutors are enthusiastic about the ideas which such students bring to their classrooms, and the way that they quickly form successful working relationships with not only the pupils but also colleagues.

Conclusions

I have only highlighted some of what seem to me to be key features of the work in building up the new part-time PGCE in Mathematics. This is a personal account; others involved may perceive things differently. I hope that it is clear that this venture is a new approach to teacher training, which was instigated at a time of crisis. In this case, the apparent crisis of the shortage of mathematics teachers motivated a partnership and accommodation between different groups involved — government agencies, LEAs, teachers and teacher-trainers, universities, distance learning specialists and researchers — negotiated to arrive at an acceptable alternative teacher training pattern.

This innovation has succeeded insofar as a small cohort of well-qualified mathematics teachers graduate from the Institute in July

1990. Were it not for the existence of this particular part-time route, it is unlikely that these teachers would have trained. There is success too in the high regard in which these neophytes are held in school and at college. It would seem sensible to suggest that there be scope for initiatives of this kind to continue to develop. Teacher-trainers at the Institute and elsewhere have experienced some of the very positive benefits that school-based training can bring to both schools and students, provided that the student is carefully inducted into the school system, and would hope that Articled and Licensed Teacher schemes may take account of this experience.

As I hope to have made explicit, short cuts to the classroom do not come cheaply. The degree of planning required and potential pitfalls in alternative modes of teacher-training cost; they cost in terms of time, research, resource and support. It would be a great pity, and doomed to failure too, were schemes addressing the urgent need for teachers in schools to be too hastily drawn up and implemented in order for the government to be seen to complete its juggernaut over-haul of the education system.

The crisis continues; as other authors in this volume have pointed out, the Thatcher government's radical Education Reform Act and National Curriculum are built on questionable assumptions about learning practices. It remains as obvious at the end of this chapter as it was at the beginning that for the National Curriculum to enhance and extend the learning experiences of children there must be a supply of well-qualified teachers. Nonetheless, as many of the other contributions have made clear, the commitment of the government to the curricular content of the National curriculum is in doubt. Unless continued consideration is given to the question of qualified teacher supply, and how this may best be achieved, this doubt can only be reinforced.

Acknowledgements

I am indebted to suggestions from Richard Noss and the other authors in this book in preparing this chapter.

Notes

1 The relationship between the DES and Local Education Authorities (LEAs) is complex. LEAs are responsible for providing education in a particular area, and are funded for this partially through direct taxation and partially from central governement.

2 This argument is interesting in retrospect, given current DES interests in school based teacher training through Articled and Licensed teacher schemes.
3 Outside consultation being organised on a less formal basis.
4 The TASC unit was set up in 1985 by the DES to spearhead a campaign to recruit more teachers in shortage subjects; at the time these subjects were Maths, Physics and Technology.
5 Hertfordshire Action on Teacher Supply: trainee teachers are paid a salary during a short course which combines blocks of time in college with time in school and at the end of which they are qualified to teach in Hertford-shire.
6 Of course full-time students are also expected to put in time over and above five days per week!
7 Woman's Hour, 31 May 1989: 'Women training to teach mathematics', A report by Marya Burgess, broadcast on Radio 4.

References

BRUNER, J., 1966, *Towards a Theory of Instruction* Cambridge, Mass.:Harvard University Press.
DES, 1983–86, *CATE Circular 3/84 and Cate Notes 1,2,3,4 and Summary*, London: DES.
DES, 1986, *Action on Teacher Supply in Mathematics, Physics and Technology: A consultative document*, London: DES.
DES, 1987, *National Curriculum: Task Group on Assessment and Testing*, London: DES.
DES, 1988, *Qualified Teacher Status: Consultation Document*, London: DES.
DES, 1988, *Teachers in Service and Teacher Vacancies 1986–87*, Statistical Bulletin 9/88 July 1988.
DES, 1989, *Circular 24/89 Initial Teacher Training: Approval of Courses*, London: DES.
DRAKE, P., 1989, *The Development and Nature of Retraining*. Unpublished MA dissertation, Institute of Education, University of London.
FERGUSSON, R. *et al.*, 1988, *Frameworks for Teaching*. Open University Course EP228, Milton Keynes: Open University Press.
HALSEY, A.H., 1987, 'Who owns the curriculum of higher education?', *Journal of Education Policy* **2**, 4, 343.
HARGREAVES, D., 1982, *The Challenge for the Comprehensive School*, London: Routledge and Kegan Paul.
HOUSE, E.R., 1979, 'Technology versus craft: A ten year perspective on innovation' in TAYLOR, P.H. (Ed.) *New Directions in Curriculum Studies*, Lewes: Falmer Press.
MACDONALD, B. and WALKER, R.,1976, *Changing the Curriculum*, London: Open Books.
STENHOUSE, L., 1975, *An Introduction to Curriculum Research and Development*, London: Heinemann.
STENHOUSE, L., 1975, Humanities Curriculum Project, London: Schools Council.

Afterword: Multiplying by Zero

Paul Dowling and Richard Noss

Most of the chapters in this volume focus on general or particular shortcomings of the National Curriculum with more or less specific reference to mathematics education. Whilst the papers in Theme 3 offer positive alternatives, is there a sense in which they are laments for what might have been; if their opportunities are indeed lost then can they do more than tease? Is there a sense in which we really have little alternative but to make the best of what we have been given, to implement as thoughtfully as possible the curriculum which has been imposed upon us? In this concluding chapter we wish to oppose such shortsighted pragmatism by offering a direct challenge to teachers and educationalists to deny the government's affront to their professional and creative abilities. We are advocating that rather than succumb to the very real pressures to spend all of their time and energy in the torturing of existing practice (good and bad) with the instruments of the Attainment Targets, those directly involved in education direct themselves to precisely the sort of innovative work that is illustrated in Theme 3 — and that good teachers have always been involved in — and that they broadcast the results, not as illustrations of what can be done within, or even despite, the National Curriculum, but as direct critiques: 'if a curriculum dominated by assessment objectives is allowed to take hold, then this good practice will not be possible'.

We must be clear, however, that we are offering a challenge, not a worksheet. Our own school teaching experience notwithstanding, this book is produced in a context which is distinct from the diverse conditions within which teachers, pupils and parents will confront the National Curriculum; our 'theorising' is no more unfettered than are teachers' actions in the classroom. But our 'theorising' is, nevertheless, a practice, for all that, a practice which is no less relevant to the classroom than is a demonstration lesson (which also has its own distinctive context): it is offered, not as a prescription but as an exemplar, an invitation.[1]

As we hinted in the foreword, we locate the question of subject specialism as a crucial theme — all the more crucial because of the apparently central role envisaged for mathematics within the curriculum. The effect of much of the discourse in this volume is to empty subject specialisms — in particular, school mathematics — of their content by criticising that which is on offer from the DES; Theme 3 can only partially replace this loss. What is still needed is some understanding of what we might mean by a subject specialism, what value we place on it, and how we might recognize, or at least where we might look for, good practice.

Firstly, we reject as simplistic, any notion that mathematics (or any subject specialism) has an intrinsic value independent of the culture within which it is embedded. Mathematics as we know it is a feature of specific cultures and is attributed value by those cultures.[2] We need, therefore, to consider the value of subject specialisms within a broader context than that of the specialisms themselves. For the purposes of this paper, we will consider the context of the curriculum as a whole: we are therefore dealing with the longstanding tension between subject specialisms and cross-curricular work. Secondly, a major thrust of the arguments (made with respect to mathematics) in this volume — especially in the papers by Dowling, Küchemann and Hoyles — is that a subject specialism which is defined in terms of assessment objectives has, essentially, no value as educational content;[3] nothing will be achieved by organizing the curriculum in such a way even within subject specialisms. There is a sense in which there has long been a tendency for mathematics curricula — at least in the secondary phase — to be defined in terms of assessment objectives in the form of a high degree of explicitness in examination syllabuses; however, the extension of this form of content determination throughout the compulsory school age range finally completes the devaluing of mathematics.

Considering the cross-curricular dimension: it seems to be the case that mathematics, as a subject specialism generally defined in terms of assessment objectives, tends to assert its own priority in the face of attempts to broaden the context outside of the strictly mathematical. Most of us who teach, or studied mathematics at school, will remember the contrived nature of most of the 'everyday problems' used in school mathematics, and even where there would appear to be a genuine attempt to study something which is important and non-mathematical, the assessment objectives always seem to dictate the

courses and, not least, in the classrooms of good teachers. We are not suggesting that such examples somehow be crystallised as rules for good practice, nor that we must all agree on which are the best examples (or even which are 'good' and which are 'bad'); as with our own multidisciplinary work described above, it is the very diversity which is generative of good practice. We are suggesting that all teachers should broadcast whatever of their work they are proud of, and that as wide a range of media as possible is used for the purpose.[7] As the chapters in Theme 3 of this book have illustrated, good practice, in these terms, should be contrasted with the National Curriculum to highlight the impoverishment of the latter. In their actual working, it may be that teachers will have to pay some attention to the National Curriculum if they are to stay within the law. However, we contend that, unless teachers spend all of their time trying to convert their existing practice into the language of assessment objectives, they should be able to avoid getting arrested and still direct most of their energies to the more creative working suggested here.

It should also be asserted that, if there really are such things as 'basics', they will necessarily emerge naturally in teachers' celebration of their subject specialisms (it is suspected, however, that there really are no such things). On the other hand, it is not being suggested here that all of current practice, complete with its hierarchical ordering of the curriculum implicit and explicit in textbooks and other published schemes, be thrown out: one clearly has to start from somewhere and where you are at the time is generally a good place provided, of course, that current practice is understood as a starting point for critical development and not a template for all future action.

The celebration of the subject specialism must, however, be only a part of the curriculum, which must also involve objects of study which are serious and important themes, and which are approached in the sort of dialogical way suggested above. The aim should be the development of understanding of the theme, and not the sacrifice of the latter on the altar of the subject specialism (which is worshipped elsewhere). The role of the subject specialist is not that of curricular jackal, but participant in the common study. Finally, both teachers and students must be active learners, that is, active participants in the dialogue. Again, as with subject-based work, teachers should be encouraged to broadcast their good cross-curricular practice as critiques of the reductionism of the National Curriculum.[8]

We have suggested an approach which celebrates both subject specialisms[9] and cross-curricular teaching and learning in a dialogical curriculum involving teachers and students as active participants.

However, the public nature of this celebration and its critical contrasting with the National Curriculum is essential. We have already cautioned against allowing the National Curriculum to become dominant in educational practice, but we should also beware of simply ignoring it in our public discussions. Sooner or later we may expect the appearance of a government that is willing to listen to teachers and educationalists (or listen to anybody for that matter); if, by that time, the National Curriculum has become an unquestioned ritual (along with school uniform and the interdiction against chewing-gum) then it will be very hard to shift; it will form part of the general 'common-sense' of educational rhetoric, and its potential reappearance will remain very much alive. Devoting ourselves to what may be naïvely perceived as the positive aspects of the National Curriculum will be like multiplying by zero; whilst zero has its place, it is of no value in counting what we can do in education. Ignoring the National Curriculum may render it temporarily dormant, but it will not make it go away: whilst there's a zero on the number line there's always the possibility that some damn fool is going to include it in the times tables.

Notes

1 The question of didactic effectivity and 'invitation' was introduced by Dowling in a paper presented at the First International Conference of 'Political Dimensions in Mathematics Education', London, April 1990; proceedings available from the Department of Mathematics, Statistics and Computing, Institute of Education, University of London.
2 There have been attempts to construct mathematics or mathematical thinking as a pancultural activity (Bishop, 1988; D'Ambrosio, 1985; Gerdes, 1986, 1988a, 1988b; Maier, 1980) but these end up devaluing cultural practices including mathematics — see Dowling (1989) and Brown and Dowling (1989).
3 See also Dowling, in press.
4 Secondary Mathematics Individual Learning Experience, Inner London Education Authority (ILEA).
5 There would seem to be no evidence at all of collaborative working between National Curriculum Working Parties.
6 It is clearly the case that some members of the department have additional 'objects of study' outside of this domain, but this does not detract from the case that is being made.
7 In addition to journals, teachers' centres, parents' meetings, governors' meetings, inviting politicians into classrooms, etc.
8 This may be rather more difficult at first, since there are fewer mass

medium outlets for such initiatives and perhaps this is a gap in the market that needs filling.
9   Although there is no hard and fast rule as to which subject specialisms.

References

Bishop, A.J., 1988, *Mathematical Enculturation: A Cultural Perspective on Mathematics Education*, Dordrecht: Kluwer.

Brown, A. and Dowling, P.C., 1989, *Towards a Critical Alternative to Internationalism and Monoculturalism in Mathematics Education, working paper number 10*, London: Centre for Multicultural Education, Institute of Education, University of London.

D'Ambrosio, U., 1985, 'Ethnomathematics and its place in the history and pedagogy of mathematics' in *For the Learning of Mathematics*, **5**, 1

Dowling, P.C., 1989, 'The contextualising of mathematics: Towards a theoretical map' in *Collected Original Resources in Education*, **13**, 2.

Gerdes, P., 1986, 'How to recognize hidden geometrical thinking: A contribution to the development of anthropological mathematics' in *For the Learning of Mathematics*, **6**, 2.

Gerdes, P., 1988a, 'On possible uses of traditional angolan sand drawings in the mathematics classroom', in *Educational Studies in Mathematics*, **19**, 1.

Gerdes, P., 1988b, 'On culture, geometrical thinking and mathematics education' in *Educational Studies in Mathematics*, **19**, 2.

Maier, E., 1980, 'Folk mathematics' in *Mathematics Teaching*, **93**.

National Curriculum Council, 1989, *Mathematics Non-statutory Guidance*, York: NCC.

Index

ability, 51–2, 54, 236
achievement: variable of, 51–2
A Course of Retraining in
    Secondary Mathematics, 217, 220
active learners: in curriculum, 238
age: assessment variable, 51–2, 54
algebra: in attainment targets,
    154–5
  and computers, 155, 163–72, 173
  definition of, 155–6
  delay in teaching, 169
  equation solving, 163
  formulae, manipulation of, 155,
    169
  and generalities, 160, 170
  as hidden curriculum, 162
  and meaningless manipulation,
    156–7
  meaning, search for, 162, 173
  and notation, 155, 170
  structures, 157
  and symbolism, 162, 164–5,
    169–71, 173
  teaching of, 155–62
  use of, 160, 162
  and use of letters, 159
algorithms, 20, 50, 59, 83, 93, 118,
    137
  and attainment targets, 44–5
Alternative Reality Kit (ARK), 185
APU survey: of mathematics, 122
  of science, 128
arithmetic: four rules of, 156
  structure, 159

Articled Teacher Schemes, 217,
    228–9, 232
artificial intelligence, 4
assessment, 1, 7, 67–75
  assessing, 5
  criterion referenced, 67, 68–9,
    100, 101
  fetishisation of, 9
  'game', 72–3
  techniques, 4
  see also SATs
attainment targets, 2, 5, 14,
    17–18, 28, 38, 115, 217, 234
  ambiguities in, 117
  and arithmetic quality of targets,
    16
  and curriculum content, 101
  empiricism of, 43–6, 59
  levels of, 100, 103–10
  logic in, 42
  rigid structuring, 42–3
attribution theory, 126
authority: and nature of
    mathematics, 38–41
  and nature of the student, 50–4
  voice of, 34–7

basics: importance of, 238
Blin-Stoyle, Professor R., FRS, 99

calculator skills: in problem
    solving, 122–5
Cellular Modelling System (CMS),
    182

Centre for Policy Studies, 26
change: in National Curriculum,
    38, 133
  orientation to, 210
  pressure for, 202, 207
  in schools, 203, 210
  structural, 211
chaotic behaviour, 187–8
  in algebra, 172
Chelsea Diagnostic Mathematics
  Tests, 88
children: and mathematics learning,
  95
classroom practice: transformation
  of, 196, 211
coaching: for tests, 131
Cockcroft Report 'Mathematics
  Counts' (1982), 35, 49, 131,
  137–8
comprehensive system: destruction
  of, 27
computer-based education, 4
computers: and algebra, 6
  personal, and spreadsheets, 181
  role in learning process, 6
  as a tool, 122–5
  see also modelling: computer
concepts: entity, 125
  incremental, 125
  mathematical, 18, 105, 118
    and teaching sequence, 116
  and tools, 124
  and truth, 48
Concepts in Secondary
  Mathematics and Science Study
  (CSMS), 5–6, 42, 77–95, 124
  and algebra, 159
  lack of controls in, 84–5
  and levels of attainment, 106–7
  samples
    children, 81
    schools, 81
content, of mathematics, 128
  artificiality, 19
  and attainment targets, 101, 102
  as high priority, 29
  of National Curriculum, 21
  to be 'used', 19

contexts, 116, 119–22, 132
  and CSMS research, 90–1
contextualization, 67, 69
  of skills, 58
cooperation, 23
Council for Accreditation of
  Teacher Education (CATE), 220
coursework; applied, 148
  centre set, 150–1
  disadvantages of, 49
  and grade scripts, 151
  marking, 151–2
creativity: in mathematics, 38, 58,
  133, 238
criterion-referenced assessment, 67,
  68–9, 100, 101, 117
critique: and nature of mathematics,
  41–50
  voice of, 37–8
cross-curricular approaches, 2, 67,
  235–8
curriculum: 'canonical', 94
  'hidden', 223
  rhetoric, 218
  uniformity, world-wide, 94
  see also National Curriculum

databases: and modelling, 177
deduction: lack of use, in school
  mathematics, 45–6
Department of Mathematics,
  Statistics and Computing,
  Institute of Education, London
  University, 3
  and multidisciplinary approach,
  237–8
Derive package, 187
deskilling: of labour force, 24–5
development: individualism of, 80
discussion, 23
distance learning: as 'insulting
  anachronism', 222
  and part-time PGCE, 218
Dynamic Modelling System
  (DMS), 182

education: form of, 21
  and social behaviour, 21–2

Education Reform Act, 1988
(ERA), 2, 7, 216
consequences of, 75
criticism of, 9
Education Support Grant (ESG),
198
educational shortcomings: and
National Curriculum, 8
Educational Testing Service (ETS):
and ethnic group differences, 74
empiricism: of attainment targets,
43–6, 59
epistemological pluralism, 129
equal opportunities: and
marginalisation, 128, 133
and National Curriculum,
116–17, 128–9
ethnic bias, 133
and assessment, 67, 73–4, 116
examination results: and schools'
effectiveness, 71–2
extrinsic: constraints, and
motivation, 126
rewards, 126, 127

Foucault, Michel, 33
foundation list, 25,
of Mathematical Topics, 35
fraction notation: and CSMS
research, 82–5
and hierarchical ordering, 46–8
fragmentation, 58
in mathematical curriculum, 42,
99–103, 132, 159, 195
Frameworks for Teaching (OU),
221, 235
function/graph plotting, on
computers, 168–9, 187
French University crisis, 206

GCSE mathematics, 6
gender: bias, 129, 133 and
assessment, 67, 73, 116–17
and CSMS research, 84–5
stereotyping, 56
grading: as function of tests, 116,
128
Graham, Duncan, 99

grants: to LEAs, for
implementation, 197
for part-time PGCE, 220, 221,
230
graphical: displays of function, 187
user interface, 85
group work: decrease in, 131–2
Guttman Scalogram Analysis, 87

headteachers: as agent of change,
204
innovations, and staff, 203–4
as social workers, 206
hierarchies, and mathematical
concepts, 4, 18, 105, 117–18
and algebraic notation, 170
of attainment, 23
of concepts, 115
constraints of, 130
formulation, 86
learning, 67, 118
sequence 80
levels, 86–9, 99
logic sequence, 80
in mathematics, 38, 41, 46–8,
77–95, 105, 132
multiple, 129
outdated, 84
scalability, 87
stages, 89–90
and topic levels, 89–90
of understanding, 89, 91, 99
variables, 88

implementation, of National
Curriculum, 195–212, 216
failure of, 200, 210
Government support for, 197,
208, 209
mechanisms of, 196–201, 210
monitoring of, 198
responsibility for, 212
techniques for, 208
independence of thought, 20
Independent Professional Studies,
225
individualism: and National
Curriculum, 131–2

industry: views of, and National
  Curriculum, 22–3
information: dissemination of, 199
innovative work, 234
  see also creativity
inquiry: curiosity of, 115
in-service: courses, 7
  training (INSET), 197, 198, 199,
    208, 219, 221
intake achievement: and school
  results, 71, 72
intuition, 118–19, 121, 124, 132
investigations: and ability, 141
  examples, 143–6, 147
  in GCSE mathematics, 137–52
  grading, 147
  and practical tasks, 148
  and SMP 11–16, 141, 142
IQ: in CSMS samples, 81, 83
IQON models, 185, 186
IT: and computer modelling, 177,
  178
  from 5–16, 177

Knowledge Pad system, 185

LEA: exam results, 71
  Mathematics Advisers, 222
learning: deep approach, 126–7
  model, 122
  order, 104
  orientation to, 128
  surface approach, 126–7
  way of, 115
levels: and dissemination of
  information, 199
  hierarchical view of, 105, 117
  and 'stoats', 99, 103–10
Licensed Teacher Scheme, 217, 228,
  232
Linx88 system, 187
Local Education Authority
  Training Grants Scheme
  (LEATGS), 198
Local Management of Schools
  (LMS), 198
Logo: and algebra, 163–7
  environments, 3
  functions in, 165

and modelling, 182–3
and symbols, 165
variability in, 159

mathematical: coherence, 87
  proof, 171–2
  relationships, 168
  structure of problems, 138
  thought, importance of, 30
mathematics: activity, 118, 130
  application to work place, 4, 49
  applying, 16, 33–4, 50, 137–40,
    148, 149, 160
  artificiality in, 19
  as 'content', to be 'used', 19
  and culture, 235
  day courses in, 198
  devaluation of, 235
  essence of, 118
  ethnocentrism, 34
  instruction, purpose of, 15–16
  and intuition, 118
  nature of, 18, 118
  'new', 157, 158, 160
  and new technology, 24–5
  as set of tools, 16, 33
  and social function, 23
  social and political dimensions, 4,
    23
  structuring, 42
  utilitarian view, 16, 19, 40–1, 59
maturity: as assessment variable, 54
  and class, 55–6
metaphorical relationships, 47
metonymy, 47
modelling, computer, 176–89
  aspects of, 183–4
  boundedness, 181
  building one's own, 182
  curriculum, 178–9
  examples, 178
  future, in education, 184–8
  manipulation, 181
  as means of expression, 179–80,
    189
  purpose, 181
  qualitative, 185
  research programs, 184–5
  semi-quantitative, 185

as series of techniques, 179
as structure, 180–1
tools, 185
value, in education, 188–9
models: positivist, 6
MODUS project, 185
motivation, 20, 25–8, 133, 134
orientation of, 126
social-psychological theories of, 126
type of, 127
multicultural mathematics, 57
muMath package, 187

National Curriculum: and algebra, 162
alternative views, 4–5
'authority' of, 208
changes in, 38, 133
changing teacher attitudes to, 28–9
and computer modelling, 176–89
Consultation Report 1988, 20
construction, and research, 36
content, 21
contradictions in, 14, 20, 22
control of, 95
criticism of, 8–9
Development Plan, 198
fluidity of, 38
and grading, 28
intentions of, 13
and lack of government concern, 21
Mathematics Working Party, 2, 35
and 'new' mathematics, 158
Non-Statutory Guidance for, 131, 137, 140, 236
planning diagram, 38, 39
positive alternatives to, 234–9
as unquestioned ritual, 239
National Curriculum Council (NCC), 99
National Development Programme in Computer Assisted Learning, 182
neural networks, 187, 188

objects of study: in curriculum, 238
Open University: and distance learning, 221
and PGCE, 226

Part-time PGCE in Secondary Mathematics, 217–32
evaluation of, 229–31
finance for, 228, 230
interviewing students, 226–7
planning, 223–5
recruitment, 225–8
and support in school, 219, 222, 225, 231
time commitment, 229–30
PGCE, Postgraduate Certificate in Education, 216–32
pedagogic differentiation, 55–7
perserverance, 20
phi coefficient, 86
photography: and computer modelling, 179
Piaget: stages in, 79, 159
politics, party: and voice of authority, 35
practical applications, 6
pre-service course, 7
problem solving: and algebra, 157
child methods, 94
and computer skills, 122–5
and mathematical skills, 17, 19, 48, 125, 137, 139, 142
hierarchies of, 92
and modelling, 183
and motivation, 126
problems: mathematical structure of, 138
processes: and attainment targets, 102
profile components, 15, 16
programmes of study, 38
and attainment targets, 17, 102, 106
programming languages: and modelling, 177
Prolog modelling system, 183
proportion, 119
pupil: behaviour, individual, 115, 122, 125

conceptions, 122
performance, 51
progress, 10 point scale, 105

quotidian mathematics, 58

Radical Right proposals, 26
ratio, 6, 119
  and pupil variations, 110
  settings of, 109
  and 'stoats', 98–110
    order of, 107–10
  unitary, 108
research, 4
  and curriculum construction, 36
results: reporting of, 67

SATs, Standard Assessment Tasks,
  1, 27, 28, 67, 69
  design of, 74
  and GCSE investigations, 137,
    141, 152
school closure days: for staff
  training, 197
schooling: as social, not training,
  function, 21
  and system, 22
schools: change in, 210
  comparisons between, 70–3
  'extreme', 72
  measure of effectiveness, 71–2
  and relations with public, 204–5
  social characteristics of, 201, 202
  and social composition of intake,
    206–7, 210
Schools Examination and
  Assessment Council (SEAC), 67
self-criticism: by teachers and
  students, 37
skills: contextualized, 58
  mathematical, 18, 102, 134, 177
    marks for, 142
SMILE (ILEA) programme, 42, 236
SMP (School Mathematics Project),
  11–16, 42, 47, 140–1, 150
  and algebra, 157
  and class and ability, 54–6
  Training Package, 138

social function: and control, 24
  of mathematical learning, 4, 23
  of schooling, 21
societies: different, and CSMS
  research, 92–4
socio-economic class: and
  implementation of National
  Curriculum, 201, 202, 209
  and LEA exam results, 71
  and SMP, 55–6
special needs: stereotyping of, 56
spreadsheets: and algebra, 165–7
  and behaviour, 172
  and modelling, 177
  and personal computers, 181
  rules in, 166–7
standards: national, 69–70
  raising of, 15, 75
statements of attainments, 1, 5
  child friendly, 7
  and computer modelling, 177
  'stoats', 39–40
    order of, 107–10
    number of, 101
    and ratios, 98–110
    relationship between, 40
    vagueness in, 40
statistical software: and modelling,
  177
Stella model, 185, 186
stereotyping: and age, 56
  and gender, 56
  and race, 56–7
'stoats': *see* statements of attainment
subject specialisms, 235, 238
  as live disciplines, 237
  value of, 235
symbolic mathematics computer
  packages, 187
symbolism: computer-based, in
  algebra, 162, 164–5, 169–71
system: priority of, 22
Systems Thinking and Curriculum
  Innovation Project, 185
systems: expert, 185, 187
  hypertext, 187
synecdoche relationship, 47–8, 49,
  59

Taiwan: and CSMS research, 92–4
teachers: assessments, 5, 26, 67,
    69–70 and GCSE mathematics,
    137, 150–2
  role of, 70
  'bashing', 216, 228
  as key agents in implementation,
    200, 212
  as obstacles to change, 200–1
  pressure on, 103
  pressure for change from, 202,
    207
  proletarianization of, 24
  qualified, 216
  recruitment, 217
  restrictions on, 28
  retraining, from industry, 224
  shortages, 8, 216–17, 222, 224
  supply, 7, 232
  training, 197, 221, 224, 231
    costs, 232
    and part-time PGCE, 216–32
    school-based, 229
  -tutors, and PGCE, 218, 222,
    225, 231
Teaching as a Career (TASC), 226
teaching: algebra, 155–62
  effects of test on, 130–1
  methods, 94
    technical view, 211
  modelling, 180
  schemes, 84
  sequence, and National
    Curriculum, 129
  to the test, 130

technology, new: and deskilling
    labour force, 24–5
  employment in, 24–5
  and hierarchies, 78
TGAT, Task Group on Assessment
    and Testing, 14, 25–6, 51, 67
  Report, 100, 103–4
tools: for exploratory learning, 85
  modelling, 185
  for teaching, 122–5
training: programme of, for
    teachers, 197, 198–9
transfer: notion of, 4

understanding: children's, 79
  hierarchies of, 89, 91, 99
  levels of, 90
unity: principle of, 53
USA: national standards in, 130–1
use-values, 59
utilitarian perspective: in
    mathematics, 25
  and pedagogic differentiation, 57
  and unity, 53
  see also under mathematics

variables: and modelling, 183–4

working group, 99
Working Party Report for
    Mathematics: Maths 5–16, 14,
    138
workplace: application of
    mathematics, 4, 49
  see also under mathematics: applying